Writing Skills for Public Relations

5th edition

Writing Skills for Public Relations

Style and technique for mainstream and social media

KoganPage

LONDON PHILADELPHIA NEW DELHI

PR in Practice

John Foster

First published as *Effective Writing Skills for Public Relations* in 1998
Second edition 2001
Third edition 2005
Fourth edition 2008
Fifth edition published as *Writing Skills for Public Relations* 2012

120 Pentonville Road	1518 Walnut Street, Suite 1100	4737/23 Ansari Road
London N1 9JN	Philadelphia, PA 19102	Daryaganj
United Kingdom	USA	New Delhi 110002
www.koganpage.com		India

© John Foster 1998, 2001, 2005, 2008, 2012

The right of John Foster to be identified as the author of this work has been asserted by him in accordance with the Copyright, Designs and Patents Act 1988.

ISBN   978 0 7494 6543 8
E-ISBN   978 0 7494 6544 5

British Library Cataloguing in Publication Data

A CIP record for this book is available from the British Library

Library of Congress Cataloging-in-Publication Data

Foster, John, 1926-
  Writing skills for public relations : style and technique for mainstream and social media / John Foster. – 5th ed.
       p. cm.
  Rev. ed. of: Effective writing skills for public relations. 4th ed. c2008.
  Includes index.
  ISBN 978-0-7494-6543-8 – ISBN 978-0-7494-6544-5   1. Business writing–Handbooks, manuals, etc.   2. Public relations–Handbooks, manuals, etc.   I. Foster, John, 1926- Effective writing skills for public relations.   II. Title.
  HF5718.3.F67 2012
  808.06'6659–dc23
                                                                                    2012020102

Typeset by Graphicraft Limited, Hong Kong

CONTENTS

PR in Practice Series

Published in association with the Chartered Institute of Public Relations
Series Editor: Anne Gregory

Kogan Page has joined forces with the Chartered Institute of Public Relations to publish this unique series, which is designed specifically to meet the needs of the increasing numbers of people seeking to enter the public relations profession and the large band of existing PR professionals. Taking a practical, action-oriented approach, the books in the series concentrate on the day-to-day issues of public relations practice and management rather than academic history. They provide ideal primers for all those on CIPR, CAM and CIM courses or those taking NVQs in PR. For PR practitioners, they provide useful refreshers and ensure that their knowledge and skills are kept up to date.

Professor Anne Gregory PhD is Director of the Centre for Public Relations Studies at Leeds Metropolitan University, UK. She has authored over 70 publications, as well as being editor of the Kogan Page/CIPR series of books which she initiated, she is Editor-in-Chief of the Journal of Communication Management. Anne also leads specialist commercial research and consultancy projects from the Centre working with prestigious public and private sector clients. She is a non-executive director of Airedale NHS Foundation Trust. Originally a broadcast journalist, Anne spent 12 years as a senior practitioner before moving on to academia. She was President of the Chartered Institute of Public Relations (CIPR) in 2004, leading it to Chartered status and was awarded the CIPRs Sir Stephen Tallents Medal for her outstanding contribution to public relations in 2010. In May 2011 she was voted Chair-Elect of the Global Alliance of Public Relations and Communications Management, the umbrella organisation of over 60 public relations institutes from around the world.

Other titles in the series:

Creativity in Public Relations by Andy Green
Effective Internal Communication by Lyn Smith and Pamela Mounter
Effective Media Relations by Michael Bland, Alison Theaker and David Wragg
Effective Personal Communication Skills for Public Relations by Andy Green
Evaluating Public Relations by Tom Watson and Paul Noble
Managing Activism by Denise Deegan
Online Public Relations by David Phillips
Planning and Managing Public Relations Campaigns by Anne Gregory
Public Affairs in Practice by Stuart Thompson and Steve John
Public Relations: A practical guide to the basics by Philip Henslowe
Public Relations in Practice edited by Anne Gregory
Public Relations Strategy by Sandra Oliver
Risk Issues and Crisis Management in Public Relations by Michael Regester and
    Judy Larkin
Running a Public Relations Department by Mike Beard

The above titles are available from all good bookshops. To obtain further information, please go to the CIPR website (**www.cipr.co.uk/books**) or contact the publishers at the address below:

Kogan Page Ltd
120 Pentonville Road
London N1 9JN
Tel: 020 7278 0433   Fax: 020 7837 6348
www.koganpage.com

ABOUT THE AUTHOR

John Foster spent several years in journalism with weekly trade papers, finally as assistant editor of a leading printing industry magazine and as editor of a quarterly journal on print production.

He subsequently held public relations posts with Pira International, the technology centre for the printing, paper, packaging and publishing industries, and with the Institute of Practitioners in Advertising (IPA), the industry body for UK advertising, media and marketing communications agencies.

He has written, edited and produced a variety of printwork, from house journals and books to posters, brochures and leaflets plus writing news releases, speeches, film scripts, slide presentations and exhibition panels. As a specialist freelance journalist, he has written on management and technical issues in the printing industry. He has also undertaken public relations projects in the field of healthcare.

A keen advocate of good, consistent style in the written and spoken word, John Foster contributed to the 'Last Word' column in the CIPR magazine *Profile* and later in their digital newsletter *The Conversation*. He is a Fellow of the CIPR and holds the CAM Diploma in Public Relations. A member of the Institute since 1954, he has served on the Council, Board of Management and Membership Committee, and was Programme Director 1979–81. He is an honorary member of the IPA, a member of the CAM Education Foundation, a Fellow of the Royal Society of Arts and a Senior Associate member of the Foreign Press Association.

In July 2003, John Foster was awarded the Stephen Tallents Medal by the then President of the CIPR, John Aspery, for 'his contribution and commitment to the effective use of the written word'. The Tallents Medal, presented annually, recognises exceptional achievement in, and contribution to, the development of public relations practice by a member of the Institute.

John Foster welcomes comments on matters of style and communication, particularly those relating to the written and spoken word. He may be contacted by email on **jonf@dircon.co.uk**.

FOREWORD

Writing good English must be one of the most difficult jobs in the world. The tracking of a developing language that is rich, diverse and constantly evolving in use and meaning is not an easy task. Today's rules and uses quickly become outdated, but this book captures English as it should be used now.

There have been many books on grammar and most of us, if we are honest, have to sneak the occasional look to check whether an apostrophe is in the right place or where a quote mark goes.

This book by John Foster gives invaluable advice, not only on the rules of English grammar, but on how to make the language come alive. How do you make people excited by your writing style and keep them reading on? How do you delight and surprise them, even if the topic is essentially dull?

Of course there's writing and there's writing. Writing for social media is very different from writing for the press. John takes us through the basics of style for all occasions, right down to pronunciation.

Also included in this fifth edition are three useful appendices: similar pairs of words that are often confused, a glossary and jargon buster of terms in IT, publishing and investor relations and some tips for when you are lost for words. There is also an excellent reading list at the end of the book. Particular attention has been given in this edition to social media and to internet-related subjects, for example what makes a good website and the writing skills needed in a digital age.

The book is written in a lively, imaginative style and is suited not only for the new practitioner who is eager to improve his or her mastery of the English language, but for the more experienced practitioner who needs a quick checklist of the essentials of grammar and some hints on how to pep up their writing style.

Writing Skills for Public Relations is intended to be a no-nonsense guide for busy practitioners. It avoids the traps of being so comprehensive and detailed that it confuses, or so superficial as to be of no use at all. It covers all the major grammatical constructions that we use day-to-day with the one objective in mind: writing good, readable English. Every PR practitioner should have one. Its potential readership extends to the wider reaches of the communications industry – in fact to anyone interested in words and their usage.

Professor Anne Gregory
Series Editor

ACKNOWLEDGEMENTS

I wish to thank the many friends and colleagues who have helped in the preparation of this and earlier editions, including Pat Bowman, former head of PR at Lloyds Bank; Philip Spink, head of information services at the Advertising Association; Roy Topp, former creative services consultant; and Feona McEwan, communications director at WPP Group plc.

I would particularly like to thank Philip Circus, Legal Affairs Director of the Institute of Promotional Marketing and a partner in Lawmark, the specialist legal consultancy, and Chairman of the Sales Promotion and Direct Response Panel of the Committee of Advertising Practice for his guidance and help on all matters legal.

My special thanks go to Keren Haynes, joint managing director of Shout! Communications, for her invaluable contributions to the social media chapter and to Robin Corry, a former Fleet Street editor and now owner of a news and features agency, for his advice and help on editing matters. My gratitude also goes to Peter Prowse, of Waylines Consulting and Michael Mitchell, general manager of the Investor Relations Society, for their input on annual reports and to Judi Goodwin for her comments and advice on press releases.

Special thanks must go to Robert Harland, former vice-president and director, International Public Affairs, the Coca-Cola Company; to Steve Sawyer, commercial director and web integration specialist at Iris Software Group Integra; to Diana Thompson of PlusPoint PR; and to Catherine 'Cat' Ham, business analyst, for their help with the chapter on writing for the web.

I also wish to thank Catherine Park of the Institute of Internal Communications for help with obtaining winning entries in the IoIC 2011 awards. The *Mail Made Easy* leaflet in Chapter 6 is copyright © Royal Mail Group plc 2004. Reproduced by kind permission of Royal Mail. All rights reserved. Internet usage statistics were provided by Computer Industry Almanac (**www.c-i-a.com/pr0904.htm**) and the International Advertising Bureau (**www.iabuk**). Design of the front cover of the Royal Commonwealth Society's quarterly magazine, *RCS Exchange* (May–August 2011) in Figure 6.4 by **www.fabrikbrands.com/**. Front Cover Image: © M. Hallahan/ Sumitomo Chemical – Olyset net.

Grateful acknowledgement must go to Professor Anne Gregory, Director, Centre for Public Relations Studies, Leeds Metropolitan University, a former President of the CIPR and editor of this series of textbooks for the Institute, for her constant support and encouragement.

I also wish to thank most sincerely Amanda Foran, former editor of *Profile* and series co-editor, and Nicola de Jong, assistant editor at Kogan

Page, who has dealt so efficiently with my constant stream of enquiries throughout the production of this edition.

Several reference books published by the Oxford University Press are mentioned, including *Fowler's Modern English Usage*, the *Oxford A–Z of English Usage*, the *Oxford Style Manual* and the *Oxford Dictionary of Grammar*, and I would particularly like to thank Kate Farquhar-Thomson and Kirsty Doole for their help in checking details and providing illustrations. Acknowledgement is also given to Headline Book Publishing for permission to quote examples from *Debrett's Correct Form*.

Introduction

Style is the crucial ingredient for everything we say and do: in writing, it is the way sentences are structured, the choice of words and the way they are used, plus punctuation. If the style is outmoded and all over the place, the reader will soon lose interest and might not even get beyond the first few lines. Style calls for clarity, brevity coupled with the use of plain language, and the avoidance of clichés and jargon. It means making sure spellings are correct and that words are not misused. Above all it means consistency.

This book has been designed for students and others entering the communications industry, in particular for those intending to follow a career in public relations. It will also be helpful for those already employed in the public relations profession either in consultancies or as in-house practitioners – in fact for all those earning their living by their writing skills.

The advice in these pages is based on the authority of established style guides, in particular the *Oxford A–Z of English Usage* and the *Oxford Style Manual*, which embraces the *Oxford Dictionary for Writers and Editors* and the *Oxford Guide to Style*, itself replacing the classic reference source, *Hart's Rules for Compositors and Readers* (now published by OUP as *New Hart's Rules*), and also on personal experience. This has covered many years of close involvement in writing, editing and producing publications of several kinds; from technical and scientific material to professional and trade journals, news releases, and general printwork including booklets, brochures, manuals and leaflets. I must also include *The Oxford Dictionary of English*, 3rd edition, an essential reference source for much of this work.

Writing Skills for Public Relations deals not only with the printed but also the spoken word: for messages to be properly communicated and understood, clarity of speech is essential and a chapter is included for those giving audio-visual presentations and taking on public-speaking assignments.

While readers will benefit from reading this book from cover to cover, some will doubtless wish to dip into individual chapters as needs dictate. If some sections, such as the positioning of apostrophes, appear to be elementary, there will always be someone not far away who is getting it wrong!

This is not a book of grammar, but does serve as a reminder of some of the basic principles. The emphasis throughout is on those style points which are frequent causes of argument and disagreement: for example when and where to put capitals, how to deal with figures and abbreviations, plus the skills of hyphenating, punctuating and paragraphing. A chapter on editing skills discusses what editors and subeditors look for and why they change your hard-crafted copy. The fewer corrections they make, the better for you, the writer.

The range of subjects to help writers communicate effectively has been broadened to include tone of voice, the essential ingredient for every message, annual reports, Americanisms and the legal issues facing all writers. The reader will find help on designing and writing websites as well as other internet-related topics including developments in social media and the language of information technology.

The skills needed for successful presentations are outlined, but the technicalities of presentations, and the equipment needed, are not covered since these are beyond the scope of this book. The essential requirements for handling headlines and captions are covered in detail as are the basics of news releases, and the need for concise language coupled with the readability of the printed word.

I cannot stress too strongly the need for good readability. We do not all have the eyes of a teenager: few things are more frustrating than a page so full of grey type, unrelieved by headings or illustrations, that it is virtually unreadable. I have no hesitation to repeat my mantra that there is no point in writing it if you can't read it. Chapter 6 details the prime requirements for text that is an easy read. That must be your first objective from the word go.

In all, the book provides practitioners with a useful reference source for their day-to-day work. Most chapters in the earlier editions have been updated and expanded, with new material added where appropriate.

Every organisation should have a house style, and that very often calls for a 'style police officer' to make sure that the rules are followed by everyone, from director and manager to all support staff. If that is achieved, and if as a result there is closer interest in and awareness of style, then this book will have met its objective.

For this and the previous edition, a number of style changes have been agreed with the publishers. Chief among these are the adoption of lower case for internet, web and website as one word, and no hyphen in email and online. Readers in North America may notice that words with -ize in them have been changed to -ise since this is the style generally favoured in the UK both in style guides and in the media. I hope that those readers will appreciate the reasons for adopting this style.

There are four appendices online, giving information on English grammar definitions, confusions between similar words, a glossary and jargon buster and what to do when lost for words. You can find these at **www.koganpage.com/editions/writing-skills-for-public-relations/9780749465438**.

01
The importance of style: an overview

Effective communication demands clear, consistent style. Everyone in public relations – whether in-house or a consultancy practitioner – should put style at the top of their priority list. This book is about the various characteristics of the written and spoken word, or the manner of writing and speaking; in other words the style, the ultimate hallmark of professionalism. It is not about English grammar, although it touches upon some of the hotly argued rules that tend to be the territory of the pedant. The basic terminology of grammar is explained in online Appendix 1 to enable the reader to check upon the technicalities and to provide a refresher if needed.

The following chapters enlarge upon the topics discussed in my regular column in the *IPR Journal* since 1993 and in the CIPR's *Profile* magazine from November 1999 to March 2010, and subsequently in the CIPR's digital newsletter, *The Conversation*. The interest generated by these articles led me to embark upon this work which, it is hoped, will lead to a greater awareness of the importance of style. First, pay close attention to what newspapers and magazines do, and also to developments in book publishing. As soon as a new book comes out on style and usage, get a copy and start a collection. This will be invaluable when you want to establish a set of house rules, to update an existing one, or just for day-to-day reference. Set up a library of books on English style and usage that is accessible to everyone – not just to your own department but to everyone in the organisation – from managers to office juniors. A list of such books will be found in the Further Reading section at the end. Some newspaper style guides, for example those issued by the *Guardian*, *The Economist* and *The Times*, can be viewed online.

Style on the move

Style changes fast. Compare, for instance, a magazine or newspaper of today with one printed only a few decades ago: overuse of capitals, stilted phraseology and solid slabs of type unrelieved by subheadings were all commonplace in the 1950s and 1960s. Even now, it is not hard to find press releases ridden with banalities, boring headlines, 'label' headings devoid of verb and verve, poorly punctuated reports and letters; and, probably worst of all, inconsistencies in spelling (let alone howlers like 'one *foul* swoop' and 'rekkernise' from BBC newscasters).

The ignorance which surrounds modern style trends emanates through lack of interest in the subject. For young people entering the competitive world of communications it is essential to have a grasp of the basics: to know, for instance, that *media* and *data* are plural nouns, to understand the difference between a colon and a semi-colon, to appreciate that a dash and a hyphen are not the same thing. (It was this last point, incidentally, which led to my first 'Verbals' column in the *IPR Journal*, later titled *Profile*.)

Some will no doubt wonder what all the fuss is about. But the hyphen masquerading as a dash is symptomatic of the lax attitude towards style; few keyboard operators bother whether style is consistent, or even know what it means. So it is up to the public relations practitioner – in fact all professional communicators – to get the message across that consistent style matters in everything an organisation does.

The way we all write has changed dramatically over the last few years, often without our even noticing it. Information technology has brought scores of new words. Newspapers and magazines have led style changes: hyphens are dropped to make one word, two-word phrases become one. All this reduces clutter, speeds up the copy and helps the reader. Unless we keep up with style trends we soon become outdated, out of step with everyone else. And a reminder: make sure you edit your copy, follow house style and watch out for inconsistencies as you go along. They are just as important as getting facts and figures right.

Appreciating style

Acquiring a grounding in grammar is not enough: the finer points of style and presentation will often make all the difference between a good and a mediocre publication – between a stodgy leaflet or complex, wordy brochure and one which is lively and appealing. This means printwork or digital copy that promotes a product or service and turns a glancer into a reader; that tells a story succinctly and in plain language; and is consistent in every respect. If this is achieved then the style has worked, communication has done its job and the public relations effort has paid off.

It is essential for everyone in PR and communications to have an appreciation of style so that the reader, or receiver of the message, is on the side of the sender from the outset. Just as important is visual presentation style: well-crafted slides where the logo is always the same size and colour, and text mirroring the typeface, are but two essential requirements for a corporate identity – the hallmark of a successful and profitable company or organisation.

Packs and display panels with a recognisable visual style are instantly identified with the company and product. If that happens, the PR effort has worked and produced tangible results. Clear, unambiguous, concise copy written like a front-page news story is usually the best means of getting your message across and making it work for you, your company or your client. There are other times, however, when a more measured style is appropriate – much depends on the target audience and the marketing objectives.

It is important when looking at your style that you take tone of voice into account. As discussed more fully in Chapter 20, the tone you adopt for print and on-screen publications, correspondence and all other communications must be warm, friendly, easily understood and free of jargon and technospeak. How you go about this is, of course, a matter for management decision, but once agreed it should be followed rigorously and should be included as a major item in your rules for house style.

Your organisation's style

Style extends beyond the confines of publications and the printed word in packaging. It applies to the livery for your delivery van or lorry; to news releases; to film; to audio-visuals; to print and online news releases; to radio and TV broadcasts; to how your story is put over in speeches at conferences and seminars; the platform arrangements; product labelling and design; office stationery; the layout and wording of the website; and even to the way your receptionist answers the telephone. Stick to the style you have adopted in absolutely everything concerning your company or your client's products and services. Think about it in all the tasks you perform. Is it consistent? Is it doing justice to your endeavours? Is it, in fact, good PR?

There are a number of style guides to assist you and some of the best known are mentioned in later chapters. They deal mainly with the printed word, for that is where style is most important and where guidance is often needed. Journalists are inculcated with a sense of style from the moment they join a newspaper or magazine, and it is helpful to see how the print and online media treat the printed word. Most newspapers produce style guides for their editorial staff and it is worthwhile asking for copies.

There is, for instance, wide variation between one newspaper or magazine and another in the use of titles, the way dates are set out, and how abbreviations are handled. When writing articles for the press you should preferably key the copy in the publication's style, so check on the way figures are set; how names are written; when and where capitals are used; how quotes are dealt with; whether copy is set ragged right or justified with both edges aligned; whether *-ise* or *-ize* endings are used. A public relations executive who writes material specifically for a target medium and follows its style has a far better chance of getting material published than one who ignores it.

Press releases should follow the general style adopted by newspapers for the treatment of quotations, for example double quote marks rather than single, with short sentences and paragraphs. If points like these are all followed then the subeditor will be on the writer's side, and your copy is less likely to be changed. This is certainly a bonus for the public relations executive if the chairman's favourite phrase remains unaltered!

PR practitioners must also keep abreast of style trends in broadcasting and in social media platforms: radio and TV stations usually have their own rules for scripts. The BBC has its own style guide for presenters and contributors; to take a recent example, they are told that it is memorandums not memoranda, an argument with listeners that was settled in a flash on Radio Four's *Broadcasting House*.

Keep it consistent

There is nothing sacrosanct about style: it is constantly changing, with spellings, 'vogue' words and phrases falling into disuse, to be replaced smartly by new ones. Favourite sayings become clichés, and myths that infinitives must not be split, that sentences must never end with a preposition or start with 'but' or 'and', that job titles must always be capitalised and never put a comma before 'and', are now mainly discarded.

On the other hand, some style rules like never starting a sentence with a figure, or numbers up to and including ten always being spelt out unless they are part of a table or figure, are still firmly established in style books. But whatever you decide on, keep it consistent throughout the whole piece.

Points to watch

Be on your guard against repetition, or using the wrong word and putting your reader off for good. Perhaps it won't be noticed, but mostly it will. *Imply* is not the same as *infer*; there are no degrees of uniqueness (something is either unique or it isn't); *fewer than* is often used for *less than* and vice versa (*fewer* is not interchangeable with *less*); and so on. Keep it simple and understandable: use short rather than long words, write snappy sentences, cut out jargon and over-worked words, and leave foreign words to the specialist journal. But don't hesitate, occasionally, to launch into 'Franglais' (*le Weekend*) or German-English (*Die Teenagers*) or even *ein steadyseller* (for the bookshop) to provide a breather and a spot of humour.

Usage differs enormously: English is spoken as a first language by up to 400 million people throughout the world (257 million in the United States alone, 60 million in the UK), while almost as many speak it as a second language. As a percentage of the world's population, 7.2 per cent use English as their mother tongue, second only to Chinese. English is the official language of over 70 countries.

Writers have at their command more than half a million words (there are some 600,000 words and phrases in the latest edition of the *Oxford Dictionary of English*), yet it has been estimated that most people go through life with only some 2000 words at their command. This limit on the average person's vocabulary shows there is good reason for avoiding long or little-used words: not only do they fail to communicate, but the writer is felt to 'talk down' to the reader.

A number of rules for style and usage have been proposed by journalists, lexicographers and others, but few are set in stone; the advice and examples given in this book are based on current best practice, although allowance must be made for individual taste. English is a living language always on the move: today's style will soon be yesterday's.

When you are thinking about your company's style and following the rules that have been established, it is crucial not to be pedantic and over-zealous with your corrections. But what is the difference between being pedantic and being correct? Pedantic is being over-fussy, like never ending a sentence with a preposition; on the other hand, there are shades of correct-ness depending on constantly changing style tenets.

However, there are some points of grammar like verb agreeing with subject on which there can be no argument: they are either correct or they are not. The overriding rule is, follow trends but keep the grammar right.

Language must never get in the way of the message. It is therefore import-ant to be aware of the significant style differences existing between American English and ours, particularly now that so many websites and press releases are targeted to the United States. For instance, while it is acceptable to write 'shop' for 'store' on both sides of the Atlantic it is wrong for a motoring journalist over there to talk about a 'bonnet' when he should say 'hood', or put 'boot' for 'trunk'.

The question of whether or not to adopt Americanisms such as in spelling or vocabulary for communications to US and global markets is discussed in a later chapter.

The guidance in these pages will help public relations practitioners and other communicators to lay down effective style rules for their own companies and organisations. Once these have been established, they should be rigorously followed. If they are not, then style becomes inconsistent and that is almost as bad as not having any rules at all. All the work that has gone into establishing house style will be wasted. But not for long: it will be revision time again before you know it.

Good style is good manners

Good style means good work. It also means good manners: letters and emails, as well as tweets and Facebook messages being answered promptly, returning telephone calls, sincerity in everything you say and do. If you cannot do something, say so – don't just leave it and hope that the problem will go away. When Christmas comes, don't send out unsigned cards, even if your company's name and address is printed inside.

And when something goes seriously wrong, don't be afraid to apologise for it, preferably in writing. If you make a mistake in someone's name or get a figure wrong, a telephoned apology will usually be sufficient. An apology costs nothing, but can mean so much to the other person. After all, that is what good manners is all about.

Style is just as important with the spoken word. Few speakers at a conference would think of muttering and mumbling their way through a talk. Carefully enunciated speech without clichés or jargon is essential for avoiding slipshod presentation and ensuring effective communication.

Some hints and tips on pronunciation style will be found in Chapter 17. And as Sir Trevor McDonald, the TV presenter and newscaster, confirms, well-articulated speech can raise someone from humble origins to the very top. McDonald advises young people aiming for wider horizons to speak their language well. Diction and grammar really do matter. This is particularly true when most people entering the PR profession soon find themselves making presentations – sometimes to packed conferences – and frequently appearing in broadcast interviews and in company videos.

Appreciate the need for style – be aware of style trends – and follow it through relentlessly and consistently. This book will help you to do that.

At a glance

- Make good, consistent style your priority.
- Follow style trends. Don't be old-fashioned.
- Good style means clear, plain, lively, concise language.
- An instantly recognisable style helps to get your message across.
- Build a library of style guides accessible to all.
- Adopt the right tone of voice for your audience.
- Distinguish between being pedantic and correct.
- Never let language get in the way of the message.
- Good style, good manners mean good work – and good PR.

02
Trouble with plurals and possessives

How many times have you seen attempts to make words ending in -y into plurals just by adding an 's' and ending up with *daisys*? Or even worse – *tomato's*, a familiar notice in the high street? Errors like these would be immediately spotted by professional communicators, and staff in PR departments making them would not last for long. But there are plenty of difficult plurals and it is not always easy to tell from the office dictionary how to deal with them. Similarly, there is often confusion about how to handle possessives: not just to know whether an apostrophe should be there, but where to place it. Again, how frequently have you seen the possessive *its* with an apostrophe shouting at you, pretending that *it's* is OK?

Plural matters

Common problems

Most nouns require an 's' to make them plural. Because of the needs of pronunciation, with some words it is necessary to put in an 'e' to give an extra vowel (branches), with different rules for changing vowel sounds (stomachs). Particular difficulty is encountered with words ending in -o: embargoes but mementos. A useful rule here is that -e is never inserted when another vowel comes before -o: an instant answer to any thought of putting an 'e' in ratios. Note that there are roofs, not rooves; wharves but dwarfs; scarves but turfs. The preferred plural of hoof is hoofs, but hooves is allowable.

Compound words made up of a noun and adjective, or two nouns connected by a preposition, form plurals by a change in the main word as in courts martial, heirs presumptive, poets laureate and in sons-in-law, hangers-on, runners-up, passers-by and men-of-war. Note, however, that there are brigadier-generals and sergeant-majors. And there are runthroughs, set-ups and forget-me-nots, handfuls, stand-bys and spoonfuls.

Care is needed with plurals for words of foreign origin and it must be noted here that media/data are plural nouns and take a plural verb. However, the new edition of *Fowler's Modern English Usage* says 'we are "still at the debating table" on the question of the media is/are', but nevertheless recommends the use of the plural when in doubt. (In informal writing, or speech, only the purist will object to the media is/data is.) Misuse of criteria and phenomena is common as they are mistaken for being collective, singular nouns: the singular forms are criterion and phenomenon. It should be noted that graffiti is the plural of graffito, termini of terminus, viruses of virus and bacteria of bacterium.

Some other plurals: analyses, appendices, basis/es, bureaux (but often Anglicised to bureaus), indexes (but indices in mathematics), memorandums (but memoranda in a collective sense), moratoriums, referendums, quorums (but addenda, curricula), stadiums (try saying stadia/syllabi and you are in danger of being pedantic and bowing to the purist); also synopses, syllabuses, theses. An extensive list of foreign words in their singular and plural forms will be found in the *Oxford Style Manual* and in *New Hart's Rules,* also OUP.

Singular or plural for collective nouns?

There is a problem for the writer using a collective noun: should it take a singular or plural verb? The choice will depend on whether the noun is considered as a single entity or as a group of people or things. Thus, whether to write the committee is or are, agrees or agree can be answered simply by saying to yourself does it refer to the committee as a whole or to the views of separate members? Similarly, the mass noun audience can take either the singular or plural as in 'the audience was seated, ready for the speaker' or as in 'the audience were all clapping madly'. The same applies to other mass nouns like board, cast (of actors), committee, company, family, group, government, staff.

It is important to decide if the emphasis lies on the individual or the group with a word like *board*, to take one example. If it lies on the individual members of the board, then write the board 'who broke off for lunch' but if the sense is collective, the construction would be 'the board which made a decision'. When we use the singular word majority we write 'the majority of people are'. That is because it is people being talked about, thus the noun takes the plural. But if it's the majority itself that is being discussed then it needs a singular verb (the majority is smaller). Again, if number is the subject then it takes the singular, but plural if 'of people' is added. The singular always follows if the noun has a qualifier like this, that, every as in 'every manager has a part to play'.

As a general rule, it is better to have a singular verb with a collective noun, and to treat names of companies and organisations as singular entities. The plural form tends to smack of informality: 'XYZ company are announcing' is a relaxed and friendly style, but loses crispness. Avoid a mixed style of singular verb and plural pronoun as in 'the committee *has* made *their* decision' ('the committee *has* made *its* decision' is preferable). In the end, however, house style will decide – another reason for every company to have a set of rules for basic style points such as this.

Whether to write *is* or *are* for companies with more than one name, such as Legal & General, is somewhat of a conundrum, and one faced sooner or later by everyone. While it is largely a matter of house style, Marks & Spencer and the multi-name styles for PR consultancies and advertising agencies mostly take the singular verb, thus adhering to the general rule of 'keep it singular'.

Watch out for company or brand names ending in 's'. They will invariably be singular as in Boots is, Harrods sells – again a matter of house style. The same applies to organisations, such as the United Nations and US Congress, which always take the singular, and this is so even in the case of the United States.

Note, however, that a pair and a couple take the plural, as do two singular nouns linked by *and* unless the conjoined words form a single idea as in wining and dining. Conversely, note that the number *is*, public relations *is*. Other nouns taking a singular verb include advice, equipment, furniture, knowledge, machinery, stationery, traffic. There are a number of nouns which only take the plural: people, police, clergy and some others recognisable by their -s endings, notably briefs, clothes, congratulations, glasses, goggles, outskirts, pants, pliers, remains, riches, scissors, thanks, tights. Nouns with a plural form which do take a singular verb are billiards, measles, news. Trousers, on the other hand, have not always been a plural. Gone are the days when the assistant in a menswear shop might have declared 'A good *trouser*, Sir'.

The crucial point in any singular/plural dispute is to maintain consistency throughout the piece as a whole, through each sentence and each paragraph. If that consistency is lost, news releases may be rubbished, and printed documents and contact reports will mostly fail to command the reader's respect.

Communication or communications?

Difficulty also arises in distinguishing between the terms communication and communications. Even public relations practitioners have a problem with this and argument rages: both refer to the act of communicating, the latter relating to the technicalities or the hardware of communicating – email, blogs, tweets, telephones and so on. Confusion is compounded by the fact that there are courses in communication management, and that communications can be managed. In reality, there is little difference in meaning. So, take your pick.

It is relevant to note that the titles communications director/manager/ consultant have largely replaced the title public relations officer, which has now become somewhat outdated. But whatever the title – whether for undertaking the mechanics of communications or for advising how a company communicates with its public – the context will usually clarify job descriptions. Again, consistency is the watchword.

Apostrophe problems

Trouble with possessives

The missing or misplaced apostrophe was once dubbed by a newspaper columnist 'that errant tadpole'. True enough. It seems that knowing where to put the apostrophe in possessives – indicating possession or ownership – causes as much difficulty as any other mark. Kingsley Amis in *The King's English* says that if it hasn't been mastered by the age of 14 then the chances are that there will always be the possibility of error. There is often confusion between *its* (in the possessive) and *it's*, the shortened form of *it is*. And the apostrophe is further misused when denoting the plural – the so-called greengrocer's apostrophe as in *potato's* (or perhaps even *potatoe's*!) – or when letter(s) have been omitted.

First, take the basic rules for positioning the apostrophe for a possessive. When the thing or person is in the singular then the apostrophe goes before the 's' as in the *boy's* tie. If, however, there is more than one boy, the apostrophe goes after the 's' as in the *boys'* ties. Another example: in *the cat's paws* there is one cat and as the paws belong to the cat it is the cat that is in the possessive, and since it is one cat the apostrophe goes before the 's'. You talk about the *campaign's objective* (where there is one campaign and one or more objectives); *John's* brother (or brothers, it doesn't matter) there is one John and the name is in the singular. When there are several journalists, you talk about *journalists'* needs.

For singular words ending in 's', just add 's as in *the boss's* office. To form the plural possessive, add 'es' apostrophe after the 's' as in *the bosses'* bonus, *the Joneses'* dog. With plural words that end with an 's', simply add the apostrophe as in the *ladies'* room, the *Smiths'* house. For nouns that are already plural as in children, men, women add an apostrophe 's' in the same way: *children's, men's, women's, people's*. For goodness' sake never write childrens', mens', womens' or peoples' or leave out the apostrophe altogether, even though you might be tempted to do so.

It is quite common to see *four weeks* holiday wrongly written without an apostrophe as a matter of course. While the clumsy holiday *of* four weeks would be pedantic in the extreme, it is far better to write *four weeks'* holiday with the apostrophe correctly positioned than not having one at all and risk offending the reader. And, of course, you go on a *fortnight's* cruise.

In distinguishing the difference between *its* and *it's*, two examples will help: *its* in the possessive – the dog wagged *its* tail; *it's* as the shortened version of *it is* – the client said '*it's* a good presentation'.

Many other purposes, but don't put one if not needed

The apostrophe is a multi-purpose mark: it can signify omitted characters as in isn't, doesn't, and the verbal elisions I'm, I'll, you'll, we'll. It indicates the plural of single letters: *A's* and *B's*, *p's* and *q's*. Note that the apostrophe is omitted in the plurals of groups of letters and numbers as in *MPs*, *1990s* and in whys and wherefores. It would, however, be used to show an omission as in the '90s.

There is, of course, no apostrophe in hers, ours, yours or theirs (an apostrophe is needed in *one's*), but care is needed in distinguishing between the relative pronoun whose and *who's*, the shortened version of *who is*.

Leaving it out when it should be there is bad enough, but putting one in when it is not needed is worse still: not only is there the illiterate use of the apostrophe for plurals as in the greengrocers' signs for *carrot's* and *pea's* – there are now 'garage' apostrophes in advertisements for *Fiesta's* and *Mondeo's* and there are headlines for *Suzuki's* but, curiously, they advertise at the same time Range Rovers and Cavaliers, while cafés have notices for *tea's* and *coffee's*, and roadside restaurants displaying signs for *lunch's* and *dinner's*. Ouch! It happens more often than you might think.

Much of the problem comes from designers who either don't know or don't care whether there should be an apostrophe: Grannys (a shop), Henrys Table (a restaurant); but it is gratifying to see that *Sainsbury's* has stuck with tradition. And the apostrophe is often at the mercy of the designer who readily turns it into a dagger, pen or heart without a qualm, diminishing its importance and contributing if not to its demise, to uncertainty about positioning.

It is quite common in emails to drop the apostrophe, along with capitals where they are normally needed. Such disdain for the rules of grammar practice can mean trouble: an important yet pedantic client could deliver a sharp rebuke in return for a sloppy message.

Missing apostrophes can perhaps be excused in text or Twitter messages where space is limited, but for websites, blogs and other media platforms such as Facebook and YouTube you cannot afford to be lax: put them where you need them. If you don't it seems you don't care. That attitude runs against your reputation and that of your company. And that's not good PR is it?

Inconsistencies to watch for

Organisations discard their apostrophes without hesitation, perhaps in an attempt at making them user- and customer-friendly. Thus we see *Chambers English Dictionary*, Debenhams and Barclays Bank; or Queens' College

(Cambridge) but Queen's College and All Souls (Oxford), which all add to the inconsistencies. Some of the above can easily be checked in telephone directories, but where writers struggle is in knowing where to put the apostrophe in words ending in -s or in names like Charles. The *Oxford Style Manual* says: 'Use 's for the possessive case whenever possible.'

The guidance here is that the 's should appear in all monosyllables and in longer words accented on the next to last syllable as in *Jones's*, *Thomas's*, *St James's Square*. Another striking inconsistency is Earls Court which does not have an apostrophe according to style books. Yet it is given one by London Transport for the Tube station and by the exhibition centre. And in addition there is a long tradition of the possessive apostrophe being dropped from some proper names, Boots, Harrods and Horlicks.

There was fierce reaction from the Apostrophe Protection Society when the chairman of stationer and bookseller Waterstones, announced in January 2012 that the apostrophe would be dropped before the possessive 's' from the company name. 'Grammatically incorrect' declared the Society's chairman and reported on the Radio Four *Today* programme. However Professor David Crystal, the respected linguist and author, said in a *Front Row* BBC interview that the usual rules of punctuation could not be applied to place names, personal names or shops. 'They are there to express identity, not meaning. It's your democratic right to decide how your name is spelt, and it's the same with other names.'

So it seems that apostrophe enthusiasts should restrict their efforts to traditional rules of grammar and punctuation. This will result, no doubt, in more examples of Selfridges and Thorntons despite the inconsistencies with other well-known trading names including Sainsbury's and McDonald's.

And, of course, there are retailers which don't use the possessive 's', Homebase, Tesco, Waitrose to name a few. So, when it comes to spelling and punctuating names, do as you want to.

In general usage and apart from naming names, I would prefer to keep this 'aerial comma' or 'errant tadpole', call it what you will, if only for reasons of consistency. But as in everything else, there's a contrary view, and that says the mark just causes clutter. There's even the opinion that the apostrophe in Earl's Court should go after the 's' simply because there were a number of earls who were part of the original courthouse. So you could be right (or wrong) whatever you do.

In multi-syllable words like Nicholas, it is equally acceptable to put the apostrophe alone as in *Nicholas'* or *Nicholas's*, but if in doubt always add the 's. Where two possessive nouns are joined by 'and' the apostrophe falls only on the second, as in members and guests' rooms and Bill and Mary's wedding.

It would be unwise to put *public relations* in the possessive. Try it, and the result is awful if not a tongue-twister: public relations' or public relations's are equally ugly; a better way would be to treat public relations as an adjective and so achieve, for example, the public relations objective, or the wordier objective of public relations.

FIGURE 2.1 OUP reference books on English style and usage, essential writing tools for public relations practitioners. The *Oxford Style Manual* is a comprehensive guide while the other three titles are handbooks, two of which are in A-Z format for quick look-ups

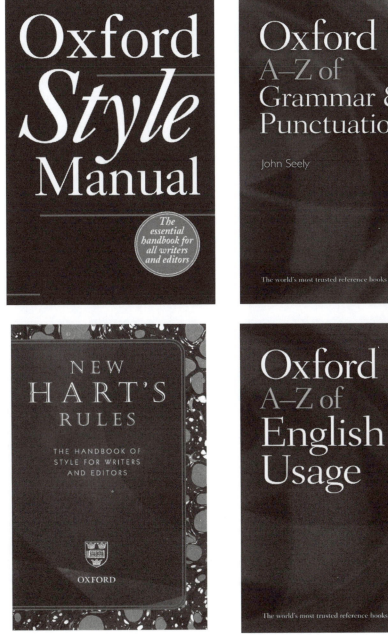

While no apostrophe is needed when writing 'He will be taken to the cleaners', it should appear in such constructions as 'He is going to the butcher's' when there is ellipsis of the word 'shop'. However, to say (or write) 'I am going to the doctor's' without the word 'surgery' would offend many an ear or eye. In these and similar examples, it would be better to omit the possessive 's' altogether.

There are, shown above, a number of inconsistencies in the use of the apostrophe, and it seems that incorrect usage is increasing both where the apostrophe is omitted or where it is included when it shouldn't be. The *Oxford A–Z of English Usage*, as well as *Fowler's* and other style guides should be consulted whenever in doubt. Dictionaries do not help much for dealing with these matters although some of the lengthier ones, including the *Oxford Dictionary of English*, provide usage guides.

Responding to an appeal for its abolition by *Guardian* columnist Matthew Engel, the Queen's English Society points out that the apostrophe aids clarity. 'If we had no apostrophes someone reading Mr Engel's article would not know if he was Engel or Engels,' says Dr Bernard Lamb of the QES. Linguists agree that the apostrophe does have a purpose and should be retained so long as we have possessives.

Further help on whether and where to place an apostrophe will be found in the excellent and intellectually vigorous handbook *Eats, Shoots and Leaves* by journalist Lynne Truss. Of all the points she makes, it is the unnecessary apostrophe in *it's* when in the possessive that disturbs her most.

At a glance

- Watch the spelling when adding 's' for plurals.
- Plural noun/adjective compounds need special care.
- Misuse of Latin plurals easily occurs.
- Collective nouns take singular or plural verbs but singular is usually best.
- Some nouns only take the plural.
- The apostrophe goes after the 's' for plural possessives, before the 's' when singular.
- Don't confuse the possessive *its* (no apostrophe) with *it's* for it is.
- The apostrophe can signify omitted characters.
- Look out for inconsistencies: Sainsbury's but Harrods.

03
Making your mark

Taking care over punctuation shows that the writer has the reader in mind. Putting the correct marks – and making sure there are no unnecessary ones – aids understanding and avoids ambiguity. The comma, stop, colon and interrogation mark are not there just to satisfy the rules of construction or even the whims of the grammarian. They have a real and active purpose: to give the reader a breather, to give a pause and, at intervals, to provide a change of pace or thought.

They are like traffic signs to take and guide the reader along a piece of written work. The full stop, if you like, is the red light to stop you moving forward and to bring the sentence to an end, the comma an amber to provide a pause.

Take the analogy a stage further: proper punctuation is a skill, it controls the speed at which the reader reads and it dictates *how* text should be read. It is an art to be mastered. If your punctuation is not up to the mark, you fail to communicate effectively.

Too many people think that punctuation is just another chore: get on with the words, never mind the irritations of having to bother with brackets, dashes or hyphens, let alone using quote marks properly or typed the right way round. On the other hand, it is easy to over-punctuate and end up with complicated, obscure sentences and a 'spotty' page. Look now at the various marks and how they should be used and presented.

Basic punctuation

'Style is the template of the times, not an irrevocable rule', declares *The Times Style and Usage Guide*. Nevertheless, there are some basic rules of punctuation to help the reader understand and follow the words: they are there not to show how clever you are at placing commas and dashes, but to provide a structure for whatever you have written whether in print or in websites, blogs or emails. Correct and properly placed punctuation gives style and presence to any news story or feature article, brochure or report. And if it is misused it can spoil the message, even give it the opposite meaning.

Let's now look at the marks one by one.

The full stop

This is the writer's best aid to crisp, clear copy. That, after all, is what the public relations practitioner should aim for when writing for the press, and indeed for all forms of written communication. But that does not mean that a piece of copy should be littered with stops like currants in a pudding. A full stop (or full point to the printer) brings a sentence to an abrupt halt, ready for the next one and an expansion of thought. No stop is needed when ending a sentence with a question mark, exclamation mark or if ending a sentence with a quotation which itself ends with a full stop.

But there are other uses: for instance, a set of three is used to show an omission (use three and only three, but if they come at the end of a sentence insert a concluding one). It will soon be noticed when the incorrect number has been used – there are plenty of examples of the writer not having the faintest idea of how many stops to put and sometimes finishing up with a line of them. Full stops are rarely seen these days in sets of initials for organisations (put them between the initials CIPR – or for any other organisation you can think of – and it will immediately look old-fashioned).

Stops are fast disappearing from initials of company names, but they can be used with great effect and impact in advertisement display heads. They should not appear in headings for press release stories for the simple reason that they are hardly ever seen in newspaper or magazine headlines. Do not put them after abbreviations like Mr, Mrs, Ms, or in lb or ft, unless of course they come at the end of a sentence.

A full stop goes after abbreviations that are part of a word, Dec. Sat., and in email and website addresses, blogs and tweets. Omit them at your peril.

The comma

This is one of the most common marks, but often misused: either it is put in when not needed or it is in the wrong place. Typically, the comma is used to encase a job title or descriptive phrase after a name. But a very usual mistake is just to put an opening comma, leaving the rest of the description dangling and yelling out for a companion comma.

The comma separates adjectives qualifying a noun as in 'a small, profitable consultancy', but there is no comma when one adjective qualifies another, for example 'a bright red tie'. They are useful for breaking up a long sentence, but take care not to put in too many and cause greater confusion than having none at all.

Some do's and don'ts. A comma would only go before *and/or* in a list of three or more items if one of them includes another *and*. The extra comma is called a serial, or so-called Oxford comma as in 'I had egg, tomato and bacon, and corn flakes for breakfast'. Do not put commas in dates or round adverbs and adverbial phrases unless special emphasis is required. They do not normally go before or after *therefore* and *accordingly*, but they always encase *however* when there is a change of thought. And do not, at least in copy for press or printwork, put a comma before a direct quote – a colon should be used here.

It is easy to go mad with commas and put them where they're not needed, or leave one out and completely change the meaning. This is illustrated well by the title chosen for Lynne Truss's book. Remove the comma in *Eats, Shoots and Leaves* and it's saying something else entirely: it thus makes the point in a striking way that commas and their placing are critical elements in any writing.

It is worth noting that commas should be kept inside quote marks when you insert 'he said' in a passage, as in 'The figures are good,' he said, 'but the year ahead will be difficult.' The *Times* guide advises that the comma should be omitted before *if, unless, before, since, when* unless sense demands it. Journalists are also advised that the Oxford comma before *and* should be avoided in, for example, 'he ate bread, butter, and jam.' The reader will find further help on positioning of quotes in relation to punctuation later in this chapter.

But for me, my firm rule is that if there are three commas in a sentence there's probably one too many. Just look at any newspaper front page and you will see what I mean. Unless it's an unedited quote, there'll be only one or two in most sentences.

The colon

The colon is used to amplify or explain something. This is a useful mark for the writer of news releases, and copy for articles and house journals. It is normal journalistic practice to use a colon to introduce a quote, as in Joe Bloggs said: 'This is the best way of doing it.' (Teachers and college instructors, who seldom have any knowledge of, or interest in typography, usually insist upon a comma before the quote – perhaps this is why this style is seen so often.) The colon is useful for starting a list, but do not put a dash after it as in :– where the dash is superfluous. It is also handy for leading the reader to fresh fact or thought or to follow these expressions: such as, for example, namely, the following.

The semicolon

This little-used mark deserves greater awareness of its attributes. While in no sense a substitute for the comma, the semicolon provides a far stronger break and a longer pause, and it can perform some of the comma's functions. It can separate two or more clauses of equal importance and is useful for listing words and phrases that cannot neatly be separated by commas. In a lengthy sentence, it can bring a thought to a halt, enabling a new one to be started, so aiding clarity. Some writers will prefer to use a full stop instead; perhaps this is why the semicolon is falling into disuse. Certainly, journalists hardly ever use them. It is rare these days for front-page news stories to carry a single semicolon. They are far more likely to be seen in feature articles. Semicolons slow down the copy and simply mean more words per sentence.

Exclamation and interrogation marks

These marks normally count as a concluding full stop and take a capital letter afterwards. But they are sometimes seen after a supporting clause in brackets within a sentence. Exclamation marks express surprise or dismay: don't use them for emphasising simple statements. Don't use an exclamation mark in a release unless it is a quote, and even then edit it out if you can. It is a perfectly valid rule to say never use one: it is hardly ever needed. They are out of place in printed and online publications and formal documents; the only time for them is for emails and for the occasional headline in feature articles. And never, never put more than one.

The interrogation (question) mark never follows indirect speech, or statements that pose a question; only direct questions – as used in quotes.

Brackets, round and square

When using round brackets to enclose a complete sentence, put the full stop *inside* the closing bracket as in (This is the way to do it.). It goes *outside* only if the last part of the sentence is in brackets. The square bracket is used to denote comments or explanations added to the original text, usually by the editor or someone other than the author.

The dash

This is used to add an afterthought or, if used as a pair, to replace commas if there are already too many in the sentence. Some writers are getting into the habit of using a hyphen instead of a dash. This on the face of it seems to matter little, but there is a distinct difference between the two marks: the dash (known to the printer as the en-dash) is twice as long as the hyphen and when they are both used in the same piece – as very often happens – something is clearly amiss. The hyphen masquerading as the dash is a common fault, but seldom seen in newspapers and magazines and in well-designed publications.

Today's keyboards do not always have a dash key and that is how the trouble starts. To print a dash with some computers two keys are usually needed, and reference should be made to the operating manual or to the software supplier for advice on achieving a proper en-dash. Don't take the easy way out and type, or even double-type, a hyphen when a little effort will show how to produce a dash. It's the sign of professionally produced work if your dashes are right.

Journalists are usually advised to avoid dashes, which can indicate that a sentence is badly constructed and needs rewriting. Too many, says Robert Thomson, former editor of *The Times*, can be 'ugly and disruptive'.

The hyphen

Hyphens indicate when two or more words should be read together and taken as one. A check with the dictionary will quickly tell whether a word is hyphenated or not. They will enable the reader to distinguish between, for example, *recover* (from an illness) and re-cover (with material). Modern style soon overturns established practice, and words that were once hyphenated are now seen as one: payphone, feedback, multi-nationals, wildlife for instance. Few in PR would think of writing lay-out or hand-out.

Once a hyphenated word assumes everyday usage, it is not long before the hyphen disappears. The closed up form usually looks and 'feels' better; a hyphen in the middle looks a touch pedantic and ugly to some eyes.

Hyphens are happiest when used in numbers (twenty-one) or as fractions (two-thirds). And they are useful for separating similar vowel sounds (co-ordinate/co-operate for instance). The main purpose of a hyphen is to avoid ambiguity as in five-year-old children. But always ensure that if you do use a hyphen it has a job to do. A consultancy once asked me whether its client should say 'state-of-the-art facility', followed by 'easy-to-use products' and even a further hyphenation 'to-the-point solutions'. Avoid such abominations: sets of compounds in the same sentence should be re-written. Do it once and once only.

Whether or not to hyphenate is hardly a subject of breathtaking importance. Study current style and decide for yourself.

If you adopt a rule which leans towards avoiding the hyphen whenever possible, that would have my vote. But for certain compounds, such as adjective/noun combinations, then the hyphen must be retained for sense and to make the meaning clear.

The apostrophe

The main use of the apostrophe is to denote the possessive case, a subject discussed at length in the previous chapter (see pages 12–16). It is also used as a mark of omission: it can signify omitted characters as in *isn't*, *doesn't*,

I'm; it distinguishes between *its* and *it's*; it indicates the plural of single letters, A's and B's.

When you are quoting...

Quotation marks often give trouble. The writer who knows that a word or phrase – for example a cliché – is not the right one gets over the problem by enclosing it in quotes; at other times, there may not be a need for quote marks at all. Further, there is often uncertainty about whether to use single or double quotes, and on the placing of punctuation within them. Consider now some of the pitfalls.

Try not to use them for facetious, technical or slang words. Their proper, and most usual place, is for direct speech quotations: hence the term quotes or quote marks. (The phrase 'inverted commas' is old-fashioned and not the way most journalists would describe them.) They should be used for words or phrases not yet in everyday use – but only sparingly. Include them for titles of articles in magazines or chapters of books, but again avoid over-use. Do not use them for household names as there is no logic or merit in doing so.

Single or double?

Most publishers nowadays use the single quote mark for direct quotations, inserting the double mark for quotes within a quote. This does not, however, apply to newspapers whose editors will favour double quotes for quoted speech and the single mark for quotes within. Consequently, the double quote style should be used for press releases and news-style publications and for social media platforms. For example, the chairman's address to an AGM might contain a quote from the marketing director; in which case the release would be typed with double quotes for the main statement and with single quotes for the marketing director's comments inside it.

Misuse occurs when there are several paragraphs of quoted speech. Quotes get closed at the end of each paragraph and opened again at the next paragraph. But the opening quote marks should go at the beginning of each paragraph and only appear at the *end* of the quote. If the text reverts to reported speech at any point the quote should be closed, and only opened again when direct speech restarts.

Punctuation marks go *inside* the quote marks (single or double as style dictates) when they refer to the words quoted, as in the managing director said: 'When will dividends be sent out?' but *outside* if they are part of a longer sentence carrying the quotation: the chairman commented on the company's 'excellent year'. If the complete sentence is a quotation the final point goes *inside*, as follows: 'The marketing director wants greater effort by the sales staff.'

Guidance on the relative placing of punctuation and quotation marks will be found in most style books, with the *Oxford Style Manual* giving detailed advice and a variety of examples. And take a look to see how newspapers deal with this point; they provide an excellent guide to the treatment of quotations, and they are at your elbow every day.

Unless the piece contains a number of direct quotes, general guidance gives that quotation marks be used sparingly. You can often avoid them altogether by indenting the paragraph (or paragraphs) and putting the type in a smaller size. Take special care when using direct quotes: make sure they are verbatim. The last thing you want is the person to whom the quote was attributed later denying the words were ever said. And it goes without saying that the writer must be sure the quoted words were not in any way defamatory.

Finally, when checking copy, ensure that the quote marks are the right way round. They are easy to spot and you will surprise yourself when you see how many word processor operators get them wrong. They can be corrected easily by typing the key twice and then deleting the unwanted one. The pity is that so many office staff cannot be bothered to do that. But they usually remember that a capital letter follows all punctuation marks except a comma, colon, semicolon and quote marks within a sentence. When and when not to use capitals will be the subject of the next chapter.

Quotes in news releases

Journalists like to use quotes whenever possible. Aim for one or two in a news story to follow the first or second paragraph. Quotes can be inserted in feature articles to good effect – perhaps a series of them throughout the piece. These would give it pace and energy.

Speeches can give significant and newsworthy quotes. In a release, you can usually include a significant quote in the intro. But don't open with a quote: it will be written out by the subeditor or placed lower down where impact will be lost.

Above all, ensure accuracy. Unless you have a tape-recording, check the source every time. Once a release has gone out and you spot a mistake, there's little you can do. Except pray.

At a glance

- The full stop is your best friend. Use it liberally.

- Don't put stops in sets of initials, they look old-fashioned.

- Only three stops to show something left out, one more as a terminator.

- If you have more than three commas in a sentence you usually have one too many.

- The colon introduces a quote. Don't use a comma instead.

- Avoid semicolons in news stories.

- Exclamation marks are hardly ever needed.

- Don't use a hyphen or even two together for a dash.

- Drop hyphens when possible. The closed-up form often looks and 'feels' better.

- Double quotes are for direct quotations, single for quoted passages inside.

- Journalists love quotes. Include at least one in main news stories.

04
Down with capitalism!

Only journalists and those committed to style principles appear to know or care where or when initial capital letters should be used. Whether to capitalise a word or not is one of the most hotly argued points in any office, particularly when preparing copy for publication. The only rule that most people can remember is: capital letter for the particular, small for the general. That is all right as far as it goes, but where is the dividing line? Is there too much capitalisation anyway? What, if any, are the guidelines?

Consistency is the essence

Dictionaries are helpful when you are uncertain whether to capitalise, and they should be consulted before reaching for the style guide or entering into a heated discussion. Uncertainty exists over words that have dual meanings. For example, a few years ago it was fashionable to give the word 'press', when referring to the media, a capital 'P'. Current style now demands a small 'p', which is logical since context will always make the meaning clear.

Similarly, new technology has bred new terms and expressions. The word 'internet' began with a capital. Nowadays most newspapers and trade papers (including *PRWeek*) give it a small 'i' simply to follow the trend for lower-case whenever possible. A cleaner and less cluttered look results. See also Chapter 19 on writing for the web.

Consistency is of paramount importance. Nothing looks worse than a publication displaying irregular capitalisation; this appears haphazard to the reader. If the name of a firm's department is used first with a capital letter and soon after with a small initial letter, the reader is immediately confused. On top of that it looks as though an amateur has been at work. If you are unsure whether to use a capital, it is better to retain consistency rather than risk style absurdities with some words of similar meaning given a capital and others not.

Always aim to restrict capitals to a minimum. Too many spoil the appearance of the page, look old-fashioned and fail to follow modern style. Imagine a line of type with the 'up and down' look; the eye is quickly distracted, making reading difficult. Such was the style of many of the books and magazines published up to the 1950s and even the 1960s. Compare today's style, and the difference is staggering: a continuous flow of small characters is easy on the eye and modern-looking.

Problem words, particularly when it comes to keying-in copy, are those which sometimes take an initial capital and other times do not. It is important for every organisation to have firm rules for the capitalisation of commonly used words. The fewer the capitals, the easier it is to be consistent and the better looking the printed page. In short, down with the capitalists!

Why lower case, upper case?

Another way to describe capitals is to call them 'upper case' and small letters 'lower case'. These terms are now universally accepted and derive from the time when printers' compositors kept their small type characters in low cases, close to hand, while those characters in less frequent use were stored in a higher (upper) case. Thus, if a line of type is set with a mixture of small and capital letters it is said by the printer to be in 'upper and lower case' and marked u&lc, as opposed to text set completely in capitals, or very rarely in lower case only (a style for just a few words for display purposes for example).

When to use capitals

A capital is used for the first word in every sentence. It follows full stops, question and interrogation marks, is used at the opening of a quote if it begins a sentence, and also for months and days of the week. Capitals should be used for proper nouns or names (words referring to a particular person or place), for formal titles, names of companies and organisations, political parties, titles of newspapers and magazines, titles of newspaper and periodical articles, books, films, trade names, names of ships and aircraft types. They are usually used for abbreviations, although some organisations adopt a lower-case style in order to reflect advertising or product branding.

Don't be influenced by the dictum that says a word must have an initial capital letter because there is only one of it. There's only one world – and it always has a lower case 'w'.

Where difficulties occur

Job titles

This is where a lot of difficulty arises. The advice here is to follow news-paper style which generally uses lower case where the title is descriptive as in managing director, marketing director or communications manager. Some will no doubt find it hard to accept a lower-case style for job titles, but once used to it the small letters look right and objections diminish. It is seen often enough in the press.

To follow each and every rule exactly is not always possible. But there are some instances where apparent inconsistencies must be observed. For example, you can talk about Miss Jones, the head teacher, but if the title is put before the name it is usually capitalised, as in Head Teacher Miss Jones.

When referring back after first mention, it is usual practice to revert to lower case, as in Oriel College, your college. When writing about government ministers and officials, it is always best to see how they are styled in the press. No two papers follow an identical style in this respect, so it is very much your choice.

For titles that are both formal and descriptive, such as President, use capitals for a full reference, as in John Smith, President, of XYZ Association. Subsequent mentions could just be John Smith, the president. The same applies to royalty: Prince Charles becomes 'the prince' and the Princess Royal 'the princess' in subsequent references. A following reference to Her Majesty the Queen should be written as either Her Majesty or the Queen. Check with *Debrett's Correct Form* and *Who's Who* when naming members of the royal family, the peerage and principal personages.

Capitals for a company?

Stockbrokers, thankfully, no longer refer to their partnerships as 'the Firm'. Nevertheless, many executives insist upon using a capital initial letter for 'company' in the mistaken belief that the capital somehow bestows importance. The only time for a capital is when the name of the firm or company is spelt out in full.

The Government

When you refer to the Government keep the capital to make it clear that you are referring to the Government of the country. However, Acts of Parliament only carry upper case when their full titles are used; the same applies to bills and white papers. Use lower case for the ministry and minister, but capitals when putting the title in full. Note that if office holders are referred to only by their office, the titles prime minister, chancellor of the exchequer, foreign secretary and so on are in lower case in some national newspapers. Most will use capitals when the complete name and formal title are given. You will never be criticised if you always put such titles in capitals. But you will soon be in trouble with the purists if you don't.

As for the word 'government' itself, styles differ. *The Times*, for instance, uses capitals for specific governments, lower case in all adjectival contexts (eg, 'a government minister') whereas the *Guardian* specifies lower case for the phrase in all contexts and for all countries. So, again, take your pick. My choice would be to follow the *Guardian* style.

Use upper and lower case for the House of Commons, House of Lords, Department of Culture, Media and Sport; but the department or DCMs in subsequent references. Put left/right (wing), the speaker, the opposition, the cabinet.

When referring to political parties, the name of the party should be in upper case as in 'the Labour Party', while retaining the capital for general references when the word 'party' is not used. However, when used as a normal adjective, write lower case as in conservative outlook, socialist objectives. Members of Parliament are capitalised to MPs, not MP's, and certainly not MsP.

The seasons

Some writers feel that somehow the seasons are so important that they must be capitalised. This is nonsense and is not supported by style guides. But note that religious festivals such as Easter take capitals. So does Christmas, but new year or new year's day need not.

Geographical regions

Recognisable regions such as Northern Ireland carry capitals, but are lower case if referring to northern England for example. Capitals are well established for the North-East, the North and the West Country, but here again it would scarcely cause offence if these regions lost their capital letters.

Derivatives

Adjectives derived from proper names carry capitals, for example Christian, Catholic. But note that you wear wellingtons (hence *wellies*) and a jersey; and that we have amperes and volts. Use lower case when connection with the proper name is remote, as in arabic (letters), french (chalk, polish, windows), italic (script), roman (numerals). Use lower case for gargantuan and herculean, but with less familiar words use a capital.

Events and periods

Names of events and periods of time should be capitalised: the First World War, Second World War (or World War I or II), but for general references use the 1914–18 war or the last war.

Trade names

All registered trade names must carry a capital letter. A frequent error is to give lower case 's' to Sellotape, an 'h' for Hoover, a 'k' for Kodak. Note capitals for Biro, Filofax, Marmite, Pyrex, Stilton, Vaseline, Xerox. To find out whether a word is, in fact, a trade name and needs a capital, check with the *Kompass Register of Industrial Trade Names*, available in public reference libraries, or with the Register of Trade Names held at the Patent Office in London, Newport and Manchester.

Committees

Names of committees, particularly those of an official nature, should be in capitals. Style will vary from one organisation to another, but so long as the writer is consistent and follows house rules, there can be little argument.

Headings in print and online publications

As a rule, use upper *and* lower case letters for headings in print and social media formats. A line in full caps is not so easy to read as one in lower case. All-cap headings are hardly ever seen in newspapers these days, and less frequently in magazines and newsletters. Feel free, however, to use underlined, bold and capitalised headings in printed and emailed news releases – they stand out much better.

The trend is to knock it down

The above examples are included to show the narrow divide between choice of capital or small letter. Style is constantly changing and words that were once always capitalised are soon lower-cased. Even if you don't follow the 'knock it down' trend, and still want to use capitals when no one else does, use lower case until to do so would look stupid and out of place. The general rule is to capitalise names of organisations, not job titles.

Do not use capitals for words one after the other in a line. This is often done in the belief that a fully capitalised line will have added emphasis and the reader will take more notice of it. While a few capitalised words might stand out, too many or a line-full will be self-defeating: they will offend the eye and not be read.

At a glance

- Check dictionaries, style guides if doubtful whether to capitalise.

- Go for lower case when you can. Too many capitals are hard on the eye.

- Follow the 'knock it down' trend: it helps the reader and looks modern.

- Use capitals for proper nouns, names of companies and formal titles.

- Newspaper style for capitals and lower case varies – but is a useful guide.

- Maintain consistency throughout.

- Don't use line after line of caps in a vain attempt at emphasis.

- Use lower case for headings where you can. Capitals are harder to read.

- Consult *Debrett's* or *Who's Who* when naming royalty and other personages.

05
Clichés, jargon and other worn words

Originality of expression is the keynote to good writing. It is the stale, worn-out phrase – the cliché – that can spoil otherwise well-written, crisp copy. Likewise, jargon words which are meaningless and unintelligible fail to communicate. Avoiding clichés and jargon is not always easy. In fact there are occasions when they can be used to good effect, so long as the reader knows they are deliberate. At other times they present the only way of getting over a specific point or idea.

The word cliché (French for a duplicate printing plate, stereotype or electrotype), means a hackneyed, overworked phrase or a saying that has lost vigour and originality. In fact the word 'stereotype' is itself a cliché as it is now taken to mean a role model (also a cliché). The difficulty for the writer is to identify such expressions and then to find others to take their places which won't turn out to be yet more clichés. Effort to express new ideas in a different way will be well rewarded. The writer will be refreshed, as will the reader.

It is important to cultivate sensitivity to the hackneyed phrase; if you can see that you have just written a cliché, this is a good sign for you can now replace it with a fresh thought. If a cliché is deliberate, or cannot be avoided, then one solution is to let the reader know you are aware of it: say so by putting the word or phrase in quotes, as I have shown in some of the examples below.

Catchphrases and metaphors, many of which have become firmly embedded in the English language, soon become stale if overused. Yet there can still be room for the idiomatic expression to liven up otherwise dull text – if used sparingly.

Recognising clichés

To help you recognise tired phrases, here are a few in current use: put on the back burner, bottom line, low/high profile, having said that, passed its sell-by date; stock similes like 'as hard as nails'; pompous phrases including wind of change, or a sea-change development should all get 'the blue pencil' treatment. Some sayings demand instant excision: address a problem, conventional wisdom, take on board, a wide range of issues, put on hold, a whole new ball game, lifestyle, in this day and age, when it comes to the crunch, quantum leap, up front money. These examples – they slip off the tongue 'as easy as wink' – are only just 'the tip of the iceberg'.

We have had Cool Britannia, a wake-up call, all over bar the shouting, level playing field, the great and the good, back to the drawing board, mind management, learning curve, ballpark figure, up to our ears. More recently there have been these horrors repeated with boring monotony: to be honest, behaviour pattern, with all due/great respect, I hear what you are saying/ where you are coming from, blue sky thinking, let's touch base, winning hearts and minds, the rest is history, 'cool', quality time, any time soon – the list is unending.

One of the more common expressions is 'at this point in time'; this is not only a tired phrase, but tedious when a perfectly good word for the same thing is *now*. Here, it should be noted that 'moment in time' is not so much a cliché as tautology since moment already means *point in time*. Other stock phrases to come from tongue or pen with ease are at the end of the day, no Brownie points, career girl, between a rock and a hard place, now for the good/bad news, not to mention some that have 'stood the test of time' and make us 'as sick as a parrot'. It's as simple as that, yer know what I mean? Ah right! Guard against what Sir Ernest Gowers in his *The Complete Plain Words* calls the 'Siamese twins' of part and parcel, to all intents and purposes, or swing of the pendulum.

But Gowers points out that writers would be 'needlessly handicapped' if they were never allowed to use such phrases as strictly speaking, rears its ugly head or even essentially – the new basically. Context coupled with judgement will indicate whether it is necessary to rewrite the sentence. But what is new is not necessarily better; the old saying that 'there's many a good tune played on an old fiddle' still holds true today. Be on constant guard against writing clichés: when you think you are 'radiantly happy' by 'leaps and bounds' or want to 'rule the roost', check with Eric Partridge's *A Dictionary of Clichés* or with Julia Cresswell's Penguin volume of the same title, for you will find these overused phrases listed among hundreds of other worn and tired expressions.

Business clichés are used extensively: some, like please find enclosed, are outmoded and, thankfully, disappearing. In public relations, a client presentation, new business pitch, account win, corporate hospitality, target audience, focus group, spin doctor, methodology (why not just method?), on/off message, soundbite, and overkill are stock expressions and hard to avoid. The dividing line between commonly used phrases and jargon is a fine one: both kinds are so frequently used that it is impossible to do without them.

Once you have heard a saying that strikes you as being clever, that's the danger signal: forget it. If you're tempted to use a slogan or catchphrase you've heard before, like the full Monty, to lay down the law, banging your head against a brick wall, stick with it, to ring a bell, like oil and water, I'm not getting any younger, think again. Start with a dictionary of synonyms and antonyms, or better still the *Oxford Thesaurus*. Hit the delete key and find alternatives for those grindingly boring words issue and key.

The Plain English Campaign's website (**www.plainenglish.co.uk**) directs viewers to an A to Z guide to alternative words and to several other free guides for download to your computer. These include *How to write in plain English*, A–Z glossaries of financial, legal and pension terms and special subjects from websites and reports to writing emails and CVs.

If you want to use any of these free guides in publications or on your website you must get permission from the Plain English Campaign. If they are for your company intranet, there is a fee of £200 plus VAT.

Tony Maher, PEC manager, plans to publish apps in late 2012 to give similar information on free guides such as the *A–Z of alternative words* and *How to write in plain English* in popular form aimed at the next generation. Look out for them, also for podcasts from the Campaign.

Check for clichés

As a last check for clichés go to **www.clichesite.com** where you'll find hundreds of stale words and phrases. There's a cliché of the day, an A–Z list of everyday sayings and phrases, and a search box. A Google search will reveal many more such sites. But that doesn't mean you must never use a cliché. Sometimes Hobson's choice can be useful.

Nightmare thoughts

Martin Cutts, author of *The Plain English Guide* (OUP) and research director of the Plain English Commission, sent me his thoughts on clichés when I contacted the Commission: 'It was hard not to be gleeful when a newspaper's leader column criticising "fundamentally flawed" as a hideous cliché appeared next to an article condemning a government policy as, er, fundamentally flawed.

'Journalists regularly trot out clichés like "grinding poverty", "mass exodus", "innocent victims", and "he didn't suffer fools gladly" (a staple in obituaries of irascible civil servants and military leaders). Yet there's one, above all, that brings a shudder. (No, not "They've got a yen for..." in articles about Japan, though that's grim enough.) It emerges whenever a good meal's the focus of the story.

'Unfailingly, the authors will say it was "washed down" with some fabulous bottle of wine. Washed down, as if they were hosing their Fiat Puntos. Washed down, as all those millions of food particles were sluiced through the oesophagus. Disgusting. Or, as cliché mongers would say: "It's a nightmare".'

Jargon: help or hindrance?

The word jargon was used in the late fourteenth century to mean 'the twittering of the birds' or *Fowler's Modern English Usage* puts it: 'a term of contempt for something (including a foreign language) that the reader does not understand... any mode of speech abounding in unfamiliar terms... eg the specialised vocabulary of bureaucrats, scientists, or sociologists'.

FIGURE 5.1 Here, you will find over 350 simple, short alternative words for ponderous, pompous expressions from 'buy/get' for 'acquire' to 'if' for 'in case of'. Download from www.plainenglish.co.uk

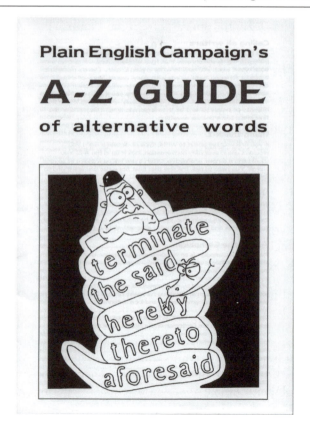

Jargon is jargon when words are so technical or obscure that they defy comprehension. They contribute nothing to sense or meaning and might just as well not be written at all. Public relations and advertising jargon soon slide into the vernacular, as opposed to formal or literary English, and is used without hesitation just because everyone else speaks or writes it. That is all very well, but if it fails to communicate to those outside 'media village-speak', then there is a case for reducing it as much as possible.

There is little to choose between public relations jargon (networking, publics, press kit/pack, coverage, perception) and marketing idiom (positioning, conceptual, target, focus, strategic planning). It does not take long for jargon like this to drift into cliché and for readers quickly to tire of it: upmarket, downsizing, downshifting, niche marketing, layered management, interface/interact, state-of-the-art are all firmly in the language of communications. Phrases and words like in-depth, on-going, user-friendly, cutting edge, parameters, definitive and conceptual should be used sparingly or preferably avoided altogether.

Jargon is often embedded in public relations terminology. Take this example from a trade directory entry: 'Well researched communication messages, disseminated through appropriate influence channels to target professional audiences are the hallmark of an approach which...' Quite what the writer expected the reader to glean from that defies imagination.

A recent example of jargon getting out of hand is the use of upskilling to mean improving performance through training. Although understandable, this is jargon that is unlikely to last or ever find a place in a dictionary along with can-do, core business and eye contact. But some jargon words can provide an element of fun and are likely to last longer, for example: yuppie, dinkies (double income, no kids), woolfie (well-off older person), wrinklie, along with bimbos, foodies and toyboys, all of which have earned a place in the English language. Soon we are to have mouse potatoes (computer addicts), netizens and cybernauts (regular internet surfers) as firm entries in the *OED*.

Apart from the specialised jargon of the legal fraternity, it is in the area of information technology where technical words are used freely in the belief that they will always be understood. For example, news releases on computer technology are notorious for being packed tight with jargon. That is acceptable for journalists from computer publications who know and understand the technical terms used, but those writing for the popular press or broadcasting will have difficulty in putting over the information and giving clear and unambiguous explanations.

Two contrasting examples of typical jargon illustrate the point: 'the stylistic expressiveness of vector based brush strokes with the speed and resolution independence of an advanced drawing application', and 'automatically generated site map using HotSauce MCF (Meta Content Format Files)'. The first assumes the reader knows exactly what is meant, but leaves room for mistake and misinterpretation, while the second makes an attempt at explanation within the body of the text, while also giving full details of the technical terms used as a footnote. If there is no alternative to a jargon word or phrase, then explain the terms in straightforward language, perhaps inserting a word or two of explanation in brackets.

Foreign words are also jargon to most readers; steer clear of them unless context demands their inclusion. The occasional foreign expression gives a lift to articles and speeches, but they should not, repeat not, go in releases. Examples are *schadenfreude* (malicious enjoyment of other people's misfortunes), from the German *schade* (harm) and *freude* (delight), and *zeitgeist* (spirit of the time). More familiar, perhaps, are *bête noire* (disliked person or thing) and *de rigueur* (required by custom). Words and phrases like these soon find their way into volumes of clichés. Use sparingly.

Jargon baffles the reader and specialist writers should never use it for audiences outside their own field. Unless the audience is steeped in the jargon of commerce, little sense can be made of ROI (return on investment), PBR (payment by results), CSR (corporate social responsibility) or AVE (advertising value equivalent). Ideally, such abbreviations should be explained at first reference.

Catchphrases quickly become stale...

Like clichés, catchphrases quickly lose originality: the source of catchphrases is mostly the entertainment industry (films, radio and TV shows in particular), but some also come from advertising and public relations campaigns such as It's good to talk (BT), a diamond is forever (De Beers Consolidated Mines), one of the longest-running advertising campaigns last century, ... refreshes the parts that other ... cannot reach from the Heineken beer slogan, Because I'm worth it (L'Oreal).

These have only a limited life, but others like *virtual reality* are more likely to find a permanent place in the language. Popular catchphrases such as mindset, nice little earner, or have a nice day, and catchwords like loadsamoney and other permutations of loadsa should be avoided since any originality has long since vanished.

It is advisable, particularly with press releases and articles, to watch out for the catchphrase that might be used unwittingly and lead to editorial deletion. If catchphrases are overdone, predictability takes over and the writer is not able to take the reader by surprise and attract attention.

... So can metaphors and similes

A metaphor is a figure of speech, a way of describing an object or action imaginatively and without being directly related to it (a *glaring* error), enabling the writer to convey thoughts briefly and without having to resort to lengthy explanation. But they can easily be overdone. As Sir Ernest Gowers points out, 'sometimes they are so absurdly overworked that they become a laughing stock and die of ridicule'.

Avoid mixed or inappropriate metaphors, where incongruous and incompatible terms are used for the same object: 'We have the key to the 21st Century', as quoted in the *Oxford A–Z of Grammar & Punctuation*. Gowers gives further explanation and examples.

A simile, also a figure of speech, compares one thing with another of a different kind and is usually identified by insertion of *as* or *like* (cold as charity, deaf as a post, blush like a schoolgirl, look like grim death). As with metaphors, guard against overuse.

Make room for the idiom

Readers soon become bored by dull, continuous text; there is always room for idiomatic expressions. Attempting to find a suitable idiomatic expression to fit the flow of thought is not easy and dictionaries are not much help. Useful collections will be found in the *Oxford Dictionary of English Idioms*, which contains 7,000 idioms and their variant forms plus examples in modern writing. Or there is the *Wordsworth Dictionary of Idioms*, which also has several thousand examples with meanings cross-referenced by head words and first words, in three distinct categories – formal, informal and slang. Lastly there is *Chambers Idioms*, which contains several thousand entries.

In the region of (formal), hit the headlines (informal) and pack it in (slang), offer a few examples. Often defying grammatical and logical rules, idioms can give colour and vitality to a piece of writing without risking faded and overused phrases. The English language is particularly rich in idiom, but use it sparingly – slang expressions are fine in speech but should be avoided in writing.

Beware of slang

Slang can, however, offend. Most of it comes from cant, the jargon of a trade or business. If you say something is awesome when you mean very good or excellent, that is slang at its worst if used by a professional communicator. Snail mail is the emailer's slang for mail by post, but usage has put it in everyday vocabulary. Nevertheless, there is no place for ginormous, couch potato, fab, must-have (a must-have bag) in any formal sense.

Much modern-day slang owes its popularity to the advertising copywriter. Night becomes nite, you is U, clean changes to kleen, flow slides to flo. Slang has contributed to confusion about spelling and yet, despite the protestations of purists, much of it is finding its way into the language.

Computer technology, multimedia, interactive television, even healthcare have all provided their own slang expressions, much of them pure jargon, intelligible only to those working in the field. Slang is for the voice, not for the pen. If you must use it, restrict it to informal writing – the sales leaflet, emails or staff memos; but it should never go in the annual report or the corporate brochure.

Slangy words like punter, donned, luvvies are deleted by journalists. But text messaging and the internet have been responsible for much of today's slang. We hear in speech gonna for going to, wanna for want to, lippie for lipstick, terms that are simply soap opera solecisms.

Such abbreviations as gwp (gift with purchase item), lmk (let me know), nib (new in box) have no place in written work simply because they do not communicate what is meant. On the other hand, speech-writers might find inspiration in rhyming slang: mince pies (eyes), dog and bone (phone), dicky dirt (shirt), plates of meat (feet), if only to get a laugh. Hundreds of examples will be found in John Ayto's *Oxford Dictionary of Rhyming Slang* and in *The Oxford Dictionary of Modern Slang* by John Utah and John Simpson.

At a glance

- Cultivate sensitivity to clichés and jargon.

- Replace worn words and phrases with synonyms from thesauruses and dictionaries.

- Beware of jargon, the language of the specialist. It might not be understood.

- Jargon usually fails to communicate; use simple words instead of jargon.

- Put short explanation in brackets at first reference.

- Catchphrases soon become stale.

- There's always room for idiom.

- Avoid slang in formal documents and print.

06
Is it easy to read?

The words are as you want them, you have got rid of clichés and jargon, the punctuation is right – the writing is as good as you can get it. But there is more to it than that. No matter how much effort has been put into the text, it will be wasted if it is hard to read. Readability is a complex subject and is the province of the designer and typographer. There are, nevertheless, some basic principles to be considered now that so much copy is computer typeset in offices rather than by skilled compositors. And you want to be sure that when the proof comes back it will be right both textually and visually. If you can't read it, there's no point in writing it.

Even if the work is going to an outside consultancy before printing, the copy must be prepared so that the presentation style will be followed at the final stages of typographical design. For internal documents, too, care must be taken to see that the visual style is going to help the reader – in short, be easy on the eye. For if it isn't then there is an instant barrier to communication.

This section covers important factors in readability and concentrates on the overall appearance, whether you have a straightforward text document, website, or online job. The pros and cons of one design against another will not be considered here, nor will detailed guidance be offered on how printwork or online formats should be designed as these are subjective and largely beyond the scope of this book. However, some tips for online design will be found in Chapter 10 dealing with social media.

Edit with the reader in mind

Always consider the appearance of the page – whether in print or online – when editing. Avoid the 'grey' look which results when slabs of text are unrelieved by paragraph breaks or subsidiary headings and illustrations. Depending on the subject matter, make headings as lively as possible so that they not only drive the text forwards but make the page look attractive.

One sure way of achieving interest in printwork is to start the text with a drop initial letter, usually larger and bolder than the rest of the copy. This can increase readership by as much as 10 per cent. Some designers specify fancy and seldom-used typefaces for the drop initial letter, but these are usually unnecessary – the text type will normally suffice unless it is an 'arty-crafty' publication. If the opening paragraph can be kept to a dozen or so words then interest is sharpened and the reader is on the writer's side from the start.

Aim for short sentences

Short sentences aid readability: an average length of 20–25 words is easy to follow and assimilate. There are obviously occasions when this can and should be exceeded, particularly for technical and scientific subjects. But even here, aim for brevity unless detailed explanation is required.

Keep your paragraphs short if you are writing for the popular and tabloid press. Five-word lines – sometimes even shorter – will be seen in *The Mirror* and *The Sun*, but for general publication work – leaflets, brochures and the like – the aim should be for perhaps three or four sentences in each paragraph. The occasional one-line sentence of a few words is common practice in a sales leaflet.

Guidelines on paragraphing

One of the main factors affecting readability is the length of paragraphs and where they are placed in the text. Short paragraphs (pars or paras to journalists) attract and hold the reader's attention, while excessively long ones tend to be unreadable and fail to communicate. Just look at a page of typescript that is unrelieved by paragraph breaks: it immediately seems to be indigestible and stuffy. Compare that with a page broken up by lively headings which straightaway appears more interesting and inviting.

Paragraphs allow the writer to change tack or subject and, equally import-ant, give the eye a rest. When the text moves from one point to another that is the time for a par break. However, much will depend on the style of the publication or document and on the column width. For news-style print jobs, using double or multi-column format, paragraph breaks are usually needed after every second or third sentence – say about every 50 to 70 words. At make-up stage, this will allow subheadings to be inserted and columns to be equalised or space filled with displayed quotes. For single-column reports, books, manuals, leaflets and brochures, it is usually better to have slightly longer paragraphs with perhaps four or five sentences. There should be at least two par breaks per column, otherwise you are back to that grey look again.

FIGURE 6.1 Spot-on advice from Derby City Council's *Plain English Guide*, available on request from intouch@derby.gov.uk

PLAIN ENGLISH EDITING EXAMPLES

Before	After plain English editing
For the purpose of working with patients whose first language is not English a recommendation of good practice involves the utilisation of interpreting services. From social worker guidance	Please use the interpreting services when working with people whose first language is not English.
Consideration should be given to the identification of an individual to orchestrate access to funding and to develop programmes that contribute to the aims of specific regeneration initiatives. From a sports strategy document, written by external consultants	We must identify or recruit someone to access funds and develop programmes that contribute to the aims of our regeneration initiatives.
A co-ordinated approach to all marketing for sport and leisure in Derby is required incorporating innovative ways of marketing sports facilities and opportunities and use of language 'appropriate' for relevant target markets. From the same sports strategy document	We should co-ordinate marketing sport and leisure in Derby in a creative way, using language and publicity that attracts the groups we're targeting.
A charge is not normally made for the use of parks and open spaces if the event is for Charity or Fund Raising purposes but if the event is of a commercial nature the hirer will be advised of the hire charge after their application has been received. From the Council's Hire Conditions	The Council does not normally charge for the use of parks or open spaces if the event is for charity or fund-raising. If the event is commercial, we will contact you about the hire charge once we receive your application.
Evidence of Public Liability Insurance covering the event must be provided to the Council at least 3 weeks prior to the event. From the same hire conditions	You must send details of your Public Liability Insurance covering the event to us at least three weeks beforehand.

FIGURE 6.2 Comparison between a serif type (Baskerville) and non-serif (Gill Sans) in medium and bold styles, 8pt to 32pt sizes

8 Point
DESIGN AS APPLIED TO PRINTED MATTER IS THE MEANING
ful arrangement of the elements in a page or other visual area. The
arrangement serves as an invisible scaffolding or framework on which
to display meanings in print and picture. The contribution of the

9 Point
DESIGN AS APPLIED TO PRINTED MATTER IS THE
meaningful arrangement of the elements in a page or other
visual area. The arrangement serves as an invisible scaffolding
or framework on which to display meanings in print and pic

10 Point
DESIGN AS APPLIED TO PRINTED MATTER IS THE
meaningful arrangement of the elements in a page or
other visual area. The arrangement serves as an invis
ible scaffolding or framework on which to display

11 Point
DESIGN AS APPLIED TO PRINTED MATTER IS
the meaningful arrangement of the elements in
a page or other visual area. The arrangement
serves as an invisible scaffolding or framework on

12 Point
DESIGN AS APPLIED TO PRINTED MATT
er is the meaningful arrangement of the
elements in a page or other visual area. The
arrangement serves as an invisible scaffolding

14 Point
DESIGN AS APPLIED TO PRINTED
matter is the meaningful arrangement
of the elements in a page or other

16 Point
DESIGN AS APPLIED TO PRINT
ed matter is the meaningful arr
angement of the elements in a pa

18 Point
DESIGN AS APPLIED TO PRI

FIGURE 6.2 *continued*

20 Point

DESIGN AS APPLIED TO printed matter is the mean ingful arrangement of the

22 Point

DESIGN AS APPLIED T o printed matter is the meaningful arrangement

24 Point

DESIGN AS APPLIED to printed matter is the meaningful arrangeme

28 Point

DESIGN AS APPLI ed to printed matt er is the meaningfu

32 Point

DESIGN AS APP

FIGURE 6.2 *continued*

8 Point
DESIGN AS APPLIED TO PRINTED MATTER IS THE MEANING
ful arrangement of the elements in a page or other visual area. The
arrangement serves as an invisible scaffolding or framework on
which to display meanings in print and picture. The contribution

9 Point
DESIGN AS APPLIED TO PRINTED MATTER IS THE
meaningful arrangement of the elements in a page or other
visual area. The arrangement serves as an invisible scaf
folding or framework on which to display meanings in print

10 Point
DESIGN AS APPLIED TO PRINTED MATTER IS
the meaningful arrangement of the elements in a page
or other visual area. The arrangement serves as an
invisible scaffolding or framework on which to display

11 Point
DESIGN AS APPLIED TO PRINTED MATTER
is the meaningful arrangement of the elements
in a page or other visual area. The arrangement
serves as an invisible scaffolding or framework on

12 Point
DESIGN AS APPLIED TO PRINTED MAT
ter is the meaningful arrangement of the
elements in a page or other visual area. The
arrangement serves as an invisible scaffolding

14 Point
DESIGN AS APPLIED TO PRINTED
matter is the meaningful arrangement
of the elements in a page or other vis

16 Point
DESIGN AS APPLIED TO PRIN
ted matter is the meaningful arr
angement of the elements in a

18 Point
DESIGN AS APPLIED TO P

FIGURE 6.2 *continued*

20 Point

DESIGN AS APPLIED TO PRI
nted matter is the meaningful
arrangement of the element in

22 Point

DESIGN AS APPLIED TO P
rinted matter is the meanin
gful arrangement of the ele

24 Point

DESIGN AS APPLIED T
o printed matter is the
meaningful arrangement o

28 Point

DESIGN AS APPLIED
to printed matter is
the meaningful arrang

32 Point

DESIGN AS APPLI

Short paragraphs are best for news releases; if each has a significant fact, then the release will stand a much better chance of being used than a long, stodgy one. The same applies to speeches which may be issued along with the release. An occasional single-sentence paragraph can have an electrifying effect on the text, especially if it is a technical or heavy-going subject. But, on the other hand, too many jerky, staccato paragraphs can distract and confuse the reader. As with everything else, it is a case of moderation.

Where to place the par break? This requires some skill: it is no use hitting the return key and hoping for the best. A paragraph is a unit of thought, not of length, says Fowler. But in news-style publications and certainly in news releases, it is the other way round: the paragraph is essentially a unit of length with maybe six or seven par breaks per page of copy, possibly more in some cases.

The best place for a break is where the text can be neatly divided without upsetting the word flow, say three or four per page of typescript, with one linked to the other in a seamless way. If a natural link is not there, then use an appropriate conjunction like *but, moreover, however*; otherwise recast the sentence at the break and refer back. But you will usually be able to find suitable points to break the text without editing. Aim for a mix of short and slightly longer sentences to produce a change of pace and give colour to the copy. Too many short ones can irritate the reader, but too many long ones can bore and tire the eye.

Some final points in relation to computer typesetting: try to leave at least three words on the last line of a paragraph; avoid starting a new paragraph on the last line of a page. Indents for typescript and typesetting should not be more than three or four characters' width; if they go in too far the par break will be over-emphasised, although some designers may prefer to do this deliberately for special effect.

Intros and first paragraphs after headings usually go full out (to the full column width) with subsequent par breaks indented. Don't leave a 'widow' with a few characters or words dangling at the top of a page: *-ed* or *-der* hanging overhead look awful. Try to fill the line out by adding words, or cutting and taking the overhang back.

Line width and type size

As for column width, try not to have more than 50–60 characters per line, including spaces and punctuation in double-column format; anything above that tends to give a 'stringy' look. If the copy is set across the page, aim for between 100 and 110 characters per line. But remember that lines with only a few characters, those that run round a photograph or display heading for example, will be awkward to read and look messy.

Be careful when considering the relationship between line length and type size. Much will depend on your design objectives and the purpose of your printwork. As a general guide for ease of reading, font size should not be much smaller than 11pt, or perhaps 10pt at a pinch if well line-spaced. A line of 62 characters of 11pt Helvetica, for example, gives a very readable 110mm column width.

The eyes have it

Sadly, we do not all have the eyesight of youth, and for some, reading can be hard work. It is therefore crucial that the printed word can be read easily by the elderly as well as by the young. David Coates of the company 'to the point', says that the easiest print to read has good contrast against the background, and ideally that type should not be smaller than 11pt. 'An unfussy, plain typeface is preferable to an ornate one and should be printed black on a matt, off-white paper since shiny stock causes reflections and makes reading difficult. And never allow line after line of capitals: they are almost unreadable.'

It is obvious that the bigger the type, the better the readability. But there are limits: if it is too big, say much above 12pt as recommended by the DTI in its booklet *Read me*, the print begins to look like a child's big-print word book. The Royal Institute for the Blind advises that a minimum of 12pt should be used 'at all times'.

Doyen print journalist Pincus Jaspert says he is appalled by 'computer obsessed typographic dilettantes' who print green on blue or the reverse, even harder to read. 'A single blotch of colour designed to catch the eye instead confuses and irritates the reader.'

There is no single, clear-cut answer to what constitutes good legibility. So much depends on typeface, the size chosen, the column or page width and line spacing. It is the job of the designer to specify what is most appropriate for a given audience and medium – print or on-screen, magazine, newsletter, website or blog. It is the designer who is skilled in typographic principles and knows what is right for the chosen medium.

Crossheads and subheads

If you want to divide off copy into sections, if you are short of a line or two at the bottom of a page, or if there is a mass of grey text then you'll need the humble crosshead – probably several. For an A4 page in two columns, four or five are usually enough. But all depends on the style and layout.

Solid lumps of type will put the reader off. If for some reason you cannot break up the text with par breaks and/or illustrations, insert subheadings (also called crossheadings). These are of inferior weight to the main heading or title and give the eye a break from line after line of characters. They also add interest to the piece by flagging up new points the writer wishes to bring out.

Subheadings should be either in a larger size and/or perhaps in bold so as to stand out from the rest of the text. Make sure there are not too many on a page. If they are scattered about willy-nilly they look untidy, and might even look as if they are just there to fill space (which they might well be!). When you insert headings, balance them so as to avoid 'rivering' with one adjacent to another. In news-style publications, either in print or online, one-word subheadings look best, preferably of not more than seven or eight characters.

The best time to insert subheadings is at first proof stage or as you type a web page. If they go in too early you will not know where they will fall when the type has been set and the layout completed. If the job carries a second colour, you can use it for crossheads at no extra cost.

Avoid having a subhead above the last line of a column: put it in higher up or cut it out. Headlines can also go in at proof stage. It is useful to have a working heading when the copy is written to help with identification later on.

Line and letter spacing

Space between lines is called 'leading' (pronounced *ledding*) from the time when a strip of metal – usually a casting in lead – was inserted between each line of hand-composed type, or automatically added to the line in machine typesetting. Leading, or line spacing, is said to increase readability by 12 per cent as it introduces 'air' into the solid text, making it easier on the eye.

But avoid too much space between lines: that can be as bad as not enough, for the text will be harder, not easier, to read. And the wider the text is set, the more leading is needed for good readability. Where there is no leading at all, the text is said to be 'set solid'. The spacing is specified in point sizes (for example, 1pt or 2pt, with 72 points to the inch). Make sure that this line-by-line spacing is consistent; this is particularly important when setting text for reproduction.

Software packages enable the computer operator to select line spacing leading in point sizes and to perform many other typographical settings like line justification and widths, variable type sizes and a wide selection of typefaces, as well as extended and condensed styles. Underlining is another option, but care is needed in order to avoid it 'colliding' with the line underneath.

Pay close attention to the spacing between characters, or what the printer would call letterspacing. This is another software option and some computer software packages will insert letterspacing automatically in order to fill out the line, particularly when copy is set justified with both edges aligned. Letterspacing can be adjusted for readability or to fill a certain area, and is most often used for lines of capitals for display. Special typographic effects can be obtained by removing or adding space between characters to produce what is known as 'kerning'.

Where to break

End-of-line word division often causes trouble, and words can get misread if they are broken at the wrong place. Once the prerogative of the compositor, word breaks are now mostly computer controlled but they can still go wrong: at worst a single character gets turned over; at best a typographical eyesore. When the copy is keyed in, the operator tells the computer to hyphenate and take over a set number of characters for a given line width. Some software options allow the operator to override automatic hyphenation and insert word breaks manually.

Computers sometimes get it right but more often do not. And then the operator shuts off the automatic mode and goes to hyphensearch, relying on fading memories of how to break words at the right place. Avoid word

FIGURE 6.3 Good, clean design for a Royal Mail leaflet. It communicates well; note the lower case, sans serif type throughout

breaks if possible: one way is to set copy ranged left and ragged right; this will mean fewer word breaks than if the type matter is justified with both margins aligned and with the ends of the lines ranged with one another.

Unless you have lines ending with longish words (10 or more characters) there is seldom any need for a break when using ragged right setting. At proof stage avoid hyphenated line endings by simply taking a word over to the next line. Avoid uneven word spacing, when the computer struggles to complete a line and thus breaks where it can.

Where word breaks are unavoidable, etymology and pronunciation are the main determinants. Divide words at obvious syllable breaks, as in atmo-sphere or trans-port, or where two consonants come together like forget-ting, minis-ter and estab-lish. If there is one consonant at the break point, that character is normally taken over as with Euro-pean, popu-lar.

Do not divide two consonants forming one sound (calm-est, fea-ther). The endings -ism, -ist, and -istic are usually taken over and so are -ing present participles like target-ing. (But note puz-zling, trick-ling.) Do not carry over -ted or -ded. Be careful to reject divisions that could confuse or change the meaning: le-gends not leg-ends, re-adjust not read-just. A divided word should never end a page, especially a right hand one. A word should not be broken at the end of a paragraph to leave the last line with a hyphen and a few characters. Many more examples will be found in the *Oxford Style Manual* and in its A–Z reference section (also available separately as the *New Oxford Dictionary for Writers and Editors, New Hart's Rules,* and in the *Collins Gem Dictionary of Spelling and Word Division.*

Choice of typeface

Choosing the appropriate typeface is quite complex as much depends on the subject matter and style of the work. However, here are some ground rules worth considering: one is that serif types (those where the letter strokes are finished off like Times or Bodoni) are easier to read line after line than sans serif typefaces such as Gill and Helvetica.

Set type so that it reads with the minimum of effort and eyestrain; each job presents different problems depending on the type style being used. The professional designer or typographer will gauge the most appropriate font for any given job by taking into account the target audience and subjects covered.

Printing considerations

Without going into the broad – and subjective – subject of design, it is important to remember that ideas that might look great on a visual sometimes fail to work when they get into print or appear on-screen. For instance, it is next to useless reversing large amounts of text out of a solid colour (say white out of black) or out of a photograph as this guarantees non-readability.

A few lines of display type set fairly large can be read without difficulty, but when it comes to lines of text set solid in 10pt or smaller, there will be an immediate switch-off. The eye quickly tires and the reader turns to something else.

Similarly, don't specify a light typeface over a tinted page of equal strength. And don't allow yellow type on white paper, or any pastel shades on white for that matter. Tinted papers often give readability problems and it is generally better to stick to black on white, using colour either as solids or as tints for headings and display panels.

If the job is text-intensive and in danger of looking 'stodgy' it is advisable to include illustrations – either line drawings, photographs or perhaps explanatory panels in colour. You can always liven up a page with a bold draw-down quote from the text of just a few words. When printing a feature article or long news story, don't forget to include a short 'standfirst' saying in a few words what the piece is all about. This encourages the reader to read on. (See Chapter 7 for more detail on standfirsts.)

All illustrations should of course be captioned unless they are simply for decoration. The reader will often ignore the text and only look at the photograph or drawing. Captions are read twice as much as the text and turn glancers and page-flippers into readers. Annual reports are a typical example of this.

Break up the monotony of long blocks of copy by using the ornaments and symbols provided by most software packages. If there is a series of facts it is better to number them rather than trying to interconnect them. Always try to think of ways to attract the reader's eye, in ways appropriate to the content.

Justified or ragged right?

Both styles have their advantages, and all designers have their own ideas on whether the one is more readable than the other. It depends largely on the style of publication: if it is a 'newsy' one then the justified style would probably be better for that is the way most newspapers set their type. On the other hand, brochures and leaflets usually look more attractive and are easier for the reader to follow when set ragged right. But there are no firm rules and it is up to the designer to produce an acceptable style directed at the target audience and within the house style pattern of the publishing organisation.

FIGURE 6.4 Example of clarity and precision in the cover for the Royal Commonwealth Society's quarterly magazine *RCS Exchange*. Design by Fabrik, the branding agency

Putting on the stress

Bold type helps the reader to identify subject changes and gives the page visual interest. It provides focal points among roman and non-bold typefaces. But again it is a case of everything in moderation: too much bold type destroys the impact of a few carefully positioned subheadings. As a general rule do not use bold type in any great quantity, except perhaps for a display panel. Nearly all typefaces will have fonts in boldface, and computer software has the facility to change from 'plain' type to bold or italics, and to some other type styles as well.

Individual words in a run of text should not be set in bold just for stress, for that is the job of italics. But if too many words are italicised, or even whole sentences or complete paragraphs, this method of providing emphasis ceases to work. Fowler is scornful of overuse: 'Printing a passage in italics, like underlining one in a letter, is a primitive way of soliciting attention', says the second edition.

Bold to the rescue

Likewise, boldface is easy to produce on your PC from any font. Use it to give weight to a quote or announcement. Put titles of seminars or conferences in roman (or plain) unless it's a promotional leaflet. Use bold for headings, captions and draw-down quotes. But over-bolding fails to add force. Its best use is for limited runs of text especially if reversed out of a strong colour. It is easiest to read when white out of black, worst when white out of a pale tint.

Main uses for italics

Long, italicised paragraphs are out of place and look dated. In a release, troubles start: subeditors will not attach more importance to passages in bold or italics. Let the words, not typographical tricks, make the point.

Too many italicised words together upset word-flow and, at worst, confuse the reader. An otherwise neat newsletter can easily be spoilt this way. Excessive use of underlining, too, fails to add stress or emphasis. Underlining is the traditional mark for italics and looks awful when printed.

Foreign words and phrases not fully naturalised in English are usually italicised, but commonly used phrases like ad hoc, de rigueur and en masse are set in roman type nowadays. Once a foreign word gains wide currency in English, italics usage diminishes. This is particularly noticeable in titles of foreign publications.

FIGURE 6.5 The Link wins Gold Award in the 2011 Institute of Internal Communications best publication category. Strong headlines and clear text predominate. Design by Pressgang for G4S

For media titles carrying the definite article, write *The Daily Telegraph, The Times, The Economist, The Mirror, The Sun* but *Daily Mail, Daily Express, Evening Standard*. If there is *The* in the masthead, italicise that too. If in doubt check your media guide. When used adjectivally, drop the definite article as in '*Telegraph* reporters investigated…'. For textual references to titles of house magazines, use italics; the same goes for releases. Use sparingly everywhere.

The main uses of italic include titles of books, names of ships, newspapers and magazines, titles of TV and radio programmes and films. Check for others in your style manuals. As a general guide, avoid overuse of italics and bold in texts simply because the more there is, the less the impact. When you want to use bold and italics, let your designer decide where they will work best.

Choosing and using your designer

Choice of designer is crucial: use the wrong one and you have wasted valuable time and possibly spent money you could ill afford. It largely depends on building a friendly, warm relationship so that you both work together harmoniously and bounce ideas off each other. There is no finer working partnership than a writer and designer who each appreciates the other's experience and skills. You, as the writer, will have a basic knowledge of communicating to the reader. The graphic designer provides the expertise, the creativity, to get your message across in the most effective manner.

Start by collecting company websites, brochures and annual reports in a similar product or service area. First impressions count: before a single word is read, the layout, the colours, typeface and style must entice and excite the eye.

Seek out a designer who will be sympathetic to your objectives. Don't use someone who just sees your words as lumps of grey typematter to be balanced with illustrations and white space. Go for a graphics artist who understands typography and the printing processes and who has a flair for words; someone who has the ability to meld text, pictures and display type into an imaginative and satisfying whole.

He or she must be aware of the principles of branding and able to develop a consistent visual identity that will work throughout the communications spectrum, from websites and corporate brochures to letterheads and the annual report, from press and TV ads to vehicles and uniforms. It must go on presentation slides and appear on all kinds of materials and applications, paper, plastics or metal in a range of sizes from badges to shop displays. If these demands are satisfied, you have found the right one.

Basic knowledge of words is essential

The designer must be properly briefed on the objective, tone of the message and target audience of the publication, brochure or leaflet – no matter what it is. If the typography and layout reflect and support the message conveyed then the text stands a much better chance of being read. A 'busy' layout, possibly with a combination of complementary typefaces, would be suitable for a leaflet describing a new product; whereas a brochure describing an expensive management training course would project a more 'upmarket' image by using a sans serif typeface printed on high quality paper with plenty of white space.

A page of text without headings is uninviting and disorientating to the reader. Signpost headings in a different typeface or bullet points are effective in directing the reader to changes of thought or subject.

Readability is probably the most important factor in the design of any publication no matter how it is produced, whether printed or online. Paying attention to it is the communicator's first priority.

Now it's proof marking time…

The job of the PR professional is to spot the mistake, or 'literal', everyone else misses. Diligent proof-reading spells well-produced, fault-free print-work. And that largely depends on using the proper correction marks. You can avoid printing errors, usually known as 'typos', by marking proofs in the standard way universally understood by printers and their keyboard operators. Non-standard corrections only confuse and lead to more errors. Follow the marks approved by the British Standards Institution (BS 5261) – see Figure 6.6.

Typical typos: misspellings, wrong punctuation and transposed words or sentences; end-of-line breaks where a hyphen wrongly divides a word; layout faults such as mispositioned text, headings, captions; style slips like italics or bold instead of roman, capitals instead of lower case.

Mark all corrections clearly in ink, preferably by ballpoint pen. Use different colours to distinguish between errors made by the printer and your own corrections – red for printer's errors and blue or black for yours. Printers usually charge heavily for alterations, or alts for short; ensure you are not charged for theirs.

Put the change in the adjacent margin and a text mark showing the position. Where there are several marginal marks these should go from left to right in the same order as the textual marks. Put a diagonal stroke (/) after each marginal mark to show the end of the correction.

Where new copy replaces existing text line-for-line, count the number of printed characters in a line (including spaces) for the number of typescript characters needed to fill it. Get someone to read the copy while you check and mark the proof. Mark alphabetically each additional item of copy; check cross-references and the contents lists against page numbers. Take special care with headings and captions.

For heavy corrections, retype and attach a separate sheet clearly marked for position. Read and re-read, checking as you go. Remember that you read what you want to read. If you are checking proofs on your computer screen, all kinds of typos, poor sentence constructs and grammatical errors tend to be invisible. But if they are hard-copy proofs, mistakes like these tend to jump out at you. So, if you are sending copy by email or via web page, be sure to print it out first for a final check. That extra step is well worth it.

Another way to check what you have written is to read it out aloud. The ear will pick up any repetitions, clichés, jargon or awkward constructions the eye may miss. This applies just as much to proofs in front of you as it does to new copy.

The more time you spend on proof-reading, the better. It pays to look at every piece of work you see to check if there are any typos or style faults. I bet you will find something wrong or that could be improved. The main marks follow.

Standard proof correction marks

Extracts from BS 5261 Part 2: 1976 (1995) are reproduced with permission of the British Standards Institution under licence number 2001SK/0003. Complete standards can be obtained from BSI Customer Services, 389 Chiswick High Road, London W4 4AL (tel: 020 8996 9001). These extracts are also reproduced by permission of the the British Printing Industries Federation.

FIGURE 6.6 Standard symbols for correcting proofs

	Textual Mark	Marginal Mark
Correction is concluded	None	/
Leave unchanged	– – – – – – under character to remain	⊘
Push down risen spacing material	Encircle blemish	⊥
Insert in text the matter indicated in the margin	⋏	New matter followed by ⋏
Insert additional matter identified by a letter in a diamond	⋏	⋏ Followed by for example ⟨A⟩
Delete	/ through character(s) or ├────┤ through word(s) to be deleted	∂

FIGURE 6.6 *continued*

Instruction	Textual Mark	Marginal Mark
Delete and close up	⌒ through character or ⬭ through character e.g. charaᶻcter characᵃcter	⌒
Substitute character or substitute part of one or more word(s)	/ through character or ⊢———⊣ through word(s)	New character or new word(s)
Wrong font. Replace by character(s) of correct font	Encircle character(s) to be changed	⊗
Change damaged character(s)	Encircle character(s) to be changed	✕
Set in or change to italic	——— under character(s) to be set or changed	⊔⏌
Set in or change to capital letters	≡≡≡ under character(s) to be set or changed	≣
Set in or change to small capital letters	≡≡≡ under character(s) to be set or changed	≡
Set in or change to capital letters for initial letters and small capital letters for the rest of the words	≡ under initial letters and ≡≡ under rest of word(s)	≡
Set in or change to bold type	﹏﹏ ·under character(s) to be set or changed	∿
Change capital letters to lower case letters	Encircle character(s) to be changed	≢
Change italic to upright type	Encircle character(s) to be changed	⊔⏌

FIGURE 6.6 *continued*

Instruction	Textual Mark	Marginal Mark
Invert type	Encircle character to be inverted	
Substitute or insert full stop or decimal point	/ through character or ∧ where required	
Substitute or insert semi-colon	/ through character or ∧ where required	
Substitute or insert comma	/ through character or ∧ where required	
Start new paragraph		
Run on (no new paragraph)		
Centre	enclosing matter to be centred	
Indent		
Cancel indent		
Move matter specified distance to the right	enclosing matter to be moved to the right	

FIGURE 6.6 *continued*

Instruction	Textual Mark	Marginal Mark
Take over character(s), word(s) or line to next line, column or page		
Take back character(s), word(s) or line to previous line, column or page		
Raise matter	over matter to be raised / under matter to be raised	
Lower matter	over matter to be lowered / under matter to be lowered	
Correct horizontal alignment	Single line above and below misaligned matter e.g. mi$_{sa}^{li}g_{n}$$_e$d	
Close up. Delete space between characters or words	linking characters	
Insert space between characters	between characters affected	
Insert space between words	between words affected	
Reduce space between characters	between characters affected	
Reduce space between words	between words affected	
Make space appear equal between characters or words	between characters or words affected	

At a glance

- Consider the appearance of the page when editing.

- Avoid long slabs of type and a 'grey' look.

- Go for short sentences and paragraphs.

- Edit out 'widows' with just a few words at top of page or column.

- Include plenty of crossheads and subheads.

- Try not to have too many word breaks at line-ends.

- Choose typefaces with care: the designer knows best.

- Think of older eyes: will print be legible? Keep to no smaller than 11 or 10pt size.

- Illustrations liven up dull text.

- Avoid long runs of reversed-out type.

- Don't overuse bold or italics.

- Learn the proof-reading marks and always use them when marking up.

- The more time you spend checking your proofs the better.

- Choose your designer with care.

07
Headlines: making them work

Headlines are a crucial element in printed communication. Short, punchy headings attract attention and take the eye to the text. However well the words have been crafted, they will not be read if the reader isn't encouraged to move on. That is the job of the headline: style will depend on the audience and type of publication. Newspaper-format house journals and periodicals demand a brisk, urgent approach. Websites and social media formats also demand a sharp, attention-grabbing style. On-screen copy tends to be scanned quickly: unless there are crisp, short headlines you'll soon lose your audience. Leaflets and brochures require a different kind of headline, as do internal and contact reports.

Whatever the type of publication or report, the headline must encapsulate the main points of the text in an interesting and eye-catching way. In fact, the livelier the better. Space will always be a limiting factor, and this is why it is often difficult to achieve a bright yet informative headline within the constraints of the column or page widths. That, of course, is where skill and experience come in.

House journals must be in tune with the audience to which the publication is addressed. A study of the many journal styles to be seen today will help when you edit and produce publications. Newspaper and magazine headings reveal many contrasting forms, with the tabloids shouting the news and the 'heavies' taking a more staid and thoughtful line. Trade press, professional and scientific journals adopt differing styles to reflect the varying needs and interests of their audiences.

There are no set rules for writing headlines, as every publication requires different treatment. The following basic guidelines for creating and presenting headlines will provide the foundation for a usable and flexible style, which can be adapted according to individual needs.

Use present tense, active verbs

The headline is essential for effective communication and to arrest the reader's attention. Its job is to take the eye to the story, to whet the appetite, to excite and inform. In-house newspaper or newsletter headlines should contain a present-tense verb, and thus generally follow newspaper style. Participle *-ing* endings should be avoided as in 'XYZ company is *launching* a new product.' It is much better to write 'XYZ company *launches*...' While the former is passive, slow and boring, the latter is vibrant and active. Most people read newspapers, and so it makes sense to follow their style whenever possible.

Headlines must be both impartial and accurate. They must give the news (or tell a story if a feature), not the opinions of the writer. They must not embellish the facts, but present them accurately and succinctly. If the story is about a person, name the person unless he or she is unknown to the audience. Brevity is your first priority, but don't sacrifice crucial detail on which the story hangs.

Headlines work best when they have an active, 'doing' verb, preferably single syllable ones like calls, tells, says, goes. The heading should say what the story is about in a few short words, enough to make the reader want to find out more, and there are plenty of examples of two- or three-word headlines that work well.

But there are occasions when just one word can have a dramatic effect and take the reader to the heart of the story like GOTCHA! (during the Falklands war) and GRABALOT (pay rises and bonuses for Camelot directors). Headlines like these, which appear regularly in the tabloid press, take much thought, but are extremely effective in telling a story in a punchy, pithy way.

It is important that headlines should stand on their own and not become part of the following copy; for example a house journal headline might read 'John Smith, new managing director of XYZ company,' with the first line of the copy running on directly from it saying 'Has plans for expansion...' Headlines should never do that.

Questions and humour

Another way to spark interest is to write question headings from time to time, starting with Who, Why, Where, What, or constructions like Is it, Was it. For publications containing mostly feature material, take a softer line. You can use longer headings and perhaps even leave out the verb. Jokey headlines, like HELLO TO GOOD BUYS, work best in tabloid-style newspapers and house journals, but can dilute the meaning of a serious message. If used sparingly, headings like PURRFECT ENDING for a story about cats about to use up their nine lives, and MONEY TO BYRNE for a news item announcing a two-million pound pools winner can get a story over far more effectively than a straightforward heading. Look for headings with a play on words, the double entendre. But avoid being facetious, and while there can be no objection to the occasional pun, attempts at being funny can cause a groan and be seen as a poor form of wit. It is all a question of balance, and fitting headlines to the audience and message. There is always room for humour.

Avoid 'label' headings

'Label' headings make a bland statement without verb or verve and hold little interest for the reader. They produce an effect of dullness and monotony. A heading which announces the winners of an awards scheme SMITH WINS TOP AWARD is so much better than the bland statement AWARDS ANNOUNCED – a typical label heading.

Do not use label headings above feature articles in house magazines or in newsletters – printed or digital. They can, however, be used as signposts for sectioning off a publication: labels like 'Latest publications' or 'Future events' are quite acceptable for this purpose.

Sometimes a label is unavoidable, particularly if space is short. In this case, use key words that are potent in themselves: anger, big, career, cut, gain, job, profit, loss, lose, new, win work well. Look for words that will arrest – and keep the reader reading.

One trick is to insert the occasional play on words, the double entendre, in headlines. You will notice such headings in tabloids and popular magazines, but if overused they can be painful for the reader. Avoid clever-clever headings in press releases; they are likely to backfire and cause unexpected problems.

Headings in sales leaflets and brochures

Sales leaflets, company brochures, catalogues and manuals require hard sell and persuasive messages. You can borrow a lot from the language of advertising. David Ogilvy, founder of the Ogilvy and Mather agency, writing in *Confessions of an Advertising Man*, says that five times as many people read the headline as the text. He goes on: 'The wickedest of all sins is to run an advertisement *without* a headline.' And then he adds something that could cause the writer of a sales leaflet to take a deep inward breath: 'If you haven't done some selling in your headline, you have wasted 80 per cent of your client's money.'

The two most powerful words in a headline are free and new. Other words and phrases useful for headlines are: advance, advice/help on, bargain, big/great/huge, development, easy, fast/quick, gain, hurry, important, just out, profit/loss, quality, says/tells, win, want/need. Avoid superlatives like amazing, magic, miraculous, revolutionary, sensational, superb, startling unless they are for an advertisement.

Emotion can play a significant part in a successful and memorable headline: Ogilvy suggests that headlines can be strengthened by words like darling, love, fear, proud, friend, baby. He quotes a headline of a few decades ago for a range of soaps and moisturisers with a girl talking to her lover on the telephone: 'Darling, I'm having the most extraordinary experience... I'm head over heels in Dove' as being one of the most provocative headlines ever to come out of O&M. More recent examples of memorable headlines include 'Catisfaction' (Whiskas petfoods) and 'It's good to talk' (British Telecom), 'The future's bright, the future's Orange', 'No child born to die' (Save the Children), 'Because you're worth it' (L'Oreal).

For sales leaflets and other promotional material, a good headline is one which makes a stated promise and a well-defined benefit, is not set at an angle so that the reader gets neck-ache trying to read it, and is set in easy-to-read type. Headlines using an unfamiliar typeface and those that are buried in the text and printed upside down just to satisfy a creative whim should be ruled out immediately.

Style and presentation

While short, snappy headings are suitable for newsletters and magazines, longer ones are sometimes more appropriate for sales leaflets and brochures. According to Ogilvy, when the New York University School of Retailing ran headline tests for a big department store, it found that headlines of 10 words or more, and containing news and information, consistently sold more merchandise than short ones.

Presentation is important. Bold type, at least seven or eight sizes larger than the text type (or up as subs would say) makes the headline stand out from the rest of the text. For instance, if the copy was set in 10pt, 2pt leaded, headings of 18pt or larger would provide sufficient contrast. Although it is a matter of individual style and taste, most headlines look better if set upper and lower case rather than in full capitals. A long headline of four or more words in capitals adds nothing to the effectiveness of the message. Do not underline or put capitals in an attempt to add emphasis: this will not have the desired effect and will look old-fashioned and clumsy.

Don't put a full stop at the end of a headline. Make sure that if a headline runs to more than one line that the first is not broken with a hyphen: that looks not only ghastly but thoroughly unprofessional. Either shorten the line so that there is no need to break the last word or rewrite the whole heading. Try not to exceed three-line headings for house magazines (three-deck in journalese) although a four-deck heading in a large size, say 42pt or more, would not look out of place in a tabloid format.

Computer typesetting allows great flexibility in choice of headline styles and sizes, and there is no limit to the creative possibilities that can be achieved. The time taken on the writing and presentation of headlines is well worthwhile and deserves as much care and attention as the story itself. Subheadings, or crossheads, are just as important as their bigger brothers and demand just as much care in their wording and presentation.

Standfirsts to entice the reader

The good standfirst – a few lines in bold type above the heading or within a feature article, say between two columns – helps to 'sell' the story to the reader. Writing one that works is a problem not easily solved: it's one of the hardest jobs a newspaper subeditor faces.

Do not think of it as an introduction that simply duplicates the first paragraph. Its job is to persuade the reader that the piece is worth reading, to give a flavour of the subject. In just a few words it should show, for example, what benefits will be gained and explain how the information might be used. Look at it as a kind of taster to entice the readers to find out more and to show what's on offer rather than leaving readers to work it out for themselves.

Humphrey Evans, of the NUJ magazine *The Journalist*, says: 'Standfirsts work best when they pay attention to readers' concerns'. He points out that the standfirst offers the chance to address readers directly, 'to positively persuade them' they want to read this particular piece.

The crucial point is that the wording must be short – in fact the fewer the words the better to get the point across. Phrases like 'look behind the scenes', 'the writer argues/says...', 'he/she examines...' and, where applicable, a brief direct quote from the article, all provide a fast start. Just think you are writing a blurb, an advertisement in a pithy and creative way that will entice the reader to read on. Forget any idea of writing a précis: that's the last thing you want for an effective standfirst.

Subheadings

Subheadings (also called crossheadings) can be centred or ranged left and are a good way to break up long stretches of type. Pages look better with subheads and they can be handy for filling space, for instance when you have difficulty in equalising column depths. Too many subheads will look messy, particularly if the page is no larger than A4.

FIGURE 7.1 Helvetica medium in sizes suitable for headlines

28 Point

DESIGN AS APPLI ed to printed matter is the meaningful ar

32 Point

DESIGN AS APP lied to printed matter is the mea

36 Point

DESIGN AS A pplied to print ed matter is the

Subheads should consist of one or two words of not more than seven or eight characters each; they should never go into a second line. Do not have them in the same type style as the text. They work best if they are in bold or in italics. Sometimes they look well in a second colour: it will not add to the cost if they are printed in one of the colours already being used. Like headlines, subheads do not require full stops at the end, but there is no objection to question or exclamation marks.

Stuck for an idea? Take a single, but significant, word out of the text and put it as a crosshead. A few of them judiciously placed can make a dull page look interesting and alive.

Extra emphasis can be given to a passage by inserting side-headings in the margins. Insert these at layout stage and do not attempt to write them in

FIGURE 7.2 Contrasts in type sizes and styles in Helvetica medium and bold

DESIGN AS APPLIED TO PRINTED MATTER IS THE meaningful arrangement of the elements in a page or other visual area. The arrangement serves as an invis ible scaffolding or framework on which to display mean

DESIGN AS APPLIED to printed matter is the meaningful arrangeme

DESIGN AS APPLIED TO PRINTED MATTER IS the meaningful arrangement of the elements in a page or other visual area. The arrangement serves as an invisible scaffolding or framework

DESIGN AS APPLIE d to printed matter is the meaningful arra

when the body copy for the text is written. Style and layout design will dictate how many there should be and where they should be positioned.

Never overlook the wording and presentation of headings. Time and trouble spent getting them right will always pay off: improved communication will inevitably result.

Slogans for brand recall

A memorable slogan is the mainstay of successful advertising campaigns: but it is not always the panacea that agency and client expect it to be. Often it is the slogan that is remembered, not the product, and with slim relationship to sales. Even so, slogans like 'Guinness is good for you', 'Go to work on an egg', 'Drinka pinta milka day' and the wartime security slogan 'Be like dad, keep mum' worked brilliantly.

Research showed that wherever people went, they thought that Guinness actually *did* do them good (the slogan was dropped in 1963 as it was a claim that could not be adequately substantiated); the Egg Marketing Board ran its slogan for decades and it became advertising folklore. Despite objections by purists, the National Milk Publicity Council's slogan over 50 years ago soon found its way to respectability, eventually gaining entries in dictionaries.

The snappy slogan, like a news headline, can bring lasting recall and has a significant influence on the target audience. But extra sales are hard to prove.

The best slogans are those with words of one syllable, as the first two examples illustrate. Another critical factor is choice of typeface: it should follow that used in advertising and in all printwork for the company's products. If colours are used, they should also follow those in promotions and corporate literature.

Lettering style, whether in bold or italics, should be consistent – from signs on vans and lorries to display cards and posters. And the slogan can go on releases as well, providing it is not too obtrusive. It should never overshadow the headline, and should be positioned well away from the story itself.

Above all, slogans must be simple and clear. Once they become overwordy and clumsy, they will not be remembered and it would be better to use other forms of publicity. The slogan that produces instant recall is the one that is short and to the point, that is repeated and repeated, that makes you laugh, the one that is emotionally charged. That is the one to aim for.

Elements of corporate identity

Recognisable corporate identity depends on the design and execution of the communications process in all its aspects. That means a consistent type style and colours for everything from vehicles, website, printwork of all kinds from letterheads, memos, visiting cards to the annual report and publicity material, to press and TV advertising, to packaging, to the sign outside office or factory – easyJet is a good example of how a strong brand identity can lead quickly to marketing success.

Building an effective and memorable corporate identity of a company and its brands is largely the responsibility of the advertising agency, but at the design stage and for subsequent publicity, the PR practitioner has a critical role to play.

FIGURE 7.3 Broad use of the easy brand: easyJet (top), easyInternetCafé (bottom); also in easy.com and easyeverything

Headlines for websites

Most people tend to scan web pages rather than read them as they would a newspaper or magazine. They tend to pick out individual words and so the headline performs a critical function in communicating the message. The rules for writing them are much the same: active verbs, punchy yet meaningful headings that tell the reader something. But there's one big difference: the designer can use any number of colours – and photographs – at no extra cost.

Since the headline is such a significant aspect of web-page design, size is crucial. It is no use using a typeface or size that looks apologetic. Similarly, bold colours are essential to make the words stand out and be memorable. Headings in a wishy-washy colour look dreadful and don't work. Treatment of web-page headlines to achieve the best combination of size and face is the job of the designer, just as it is for a print job.

Your designer must ensure that the final 'look' of the website is in tune with overall marketing objectives and branding strategy. Leave it to him or her and don't interfere more than you have to. (See also Chapter 19 for advice on writing for the web.)

At a glance

- Make headings short, punchy and pithy.

- Present tense and active verbs work best.

- Go for single-syllable words whenever possible.

- Introduce humour but don't overdo it.

- Avoid slow, boring 'label' headings.

- Short standfirst 'sell' the story to the reader.

- The most powerful words are 'free' and 'new'.

- Bold type in larger size provides contrast with text.

- Use upper and lower case, not capitals.

- Subheads of one or two words are effective.

- Maintain corporate identity in product branding.

- Website headlines must catch the eye.

08
Dealing with figures and abbreviations

Figuring out the numbers

The way you treat numbers is as important as the way you treat words. A mixture of numeral styles can confuse the reader and make the production look amateurish. A set style for numbers should be a priority for everything produced whether for print, presentation, release or correspondence.

Style manuals set out a number of guidelines and provide plenty of examples. Individual publications adapt these and expand on them to suit their own needs and audiences. While rules of this nature are open to interpretation, they provide a starting point and this section draws attention to some of the important points for house style.

Basic considerations

The first rule is not to start a sentence with a figure. Spell it out instead. The reason for this is that the style is followed almost universally in newspapers and magazines and in most professionally produced publications and websites. It is something we have all become used to and any diversion immediately stands out and looks 'wrong'. But it would be clumsy to spell out a multi-digit number; either write out The year 2012 or else recast the sentence completely. However, there are occasions when it is difficult to avoid a figure at the beginning and when this happens, say in an annual report or in giving statistical data, then there may be no alternative but to start with a figure.

The second rule – and this is for numbers *within* a sentence – is to spell out numbers up to and including ten; above that write figures. But if there are sequences of numbers, some of which may be higher than ten, use figures throughout for the sake of consistency and clarity. Write out hundredth but after that put 101st and so on. For decimals, use a full stop on the line as in 1.5, and do not attempt to centralise it as if writing a decimal by hand. (In other languages a decimal comma is used.) There is no point in putting a single zero after the decimal point unless it is called for in tabular matter, but a nought should go before the point as in 0.75. Numerals should be used for page references, currencies and for groups of statistics.

Symbols, abbreviations and punctuation

Next: avoid using the % sign in text, unless it is for a specialist audience; spell out *per cent* as two words, but use *percentage* of course. The symbol should be kept for tables and charts and for text where figures predominate. Fractions should be hyphenated (two-thirds) and do not mix (or compare) fractions with decimals. When both a whole number and a fraction are spelt out, only hyphenate the fraction (one and three-quarters). It is better to write (in formal text) twentieth century rather than 20th. Note that one in three is singular but two in five are plural. Some newspapers will prefer to write a mile and a half instead of one and a half miles, but seldom, if ever, print $1^{1}/_{2}$ miles!

Avoid a combination of the to/from style (when comparing years, for instance) with hyphens as in from 2008 to 2012; put from two to three, or from 12 to 13, but not a mixture of the two styles. Reserve hyphens or dashes for numerals and never use them for spelt-out figures.

A billion at one time meant a million million but modern usage suggests that it means a thousand million – a definition accepted by national newspapers. It is better to spell out a million and a billion, but if m and bn are used do not put a full point after the abbreviations unless they come at the end of a sentence. Full points should not follow units of weight and measurement (cm, ft, kg), and do not put hyphens in combinations like half an inch or half a dozen. With temperature put the degree symbol immediately before C or F. No punctuation is necessary in dates (12 March 2011). In compounds, put a hyphen in half-hour and two-day.

Nouns of measurement: singular or plural?

All nouns of measurement remain singular when used attributively before another noun: a six-foot man, a five-litre can. But plural feet or inches are used when an adjective follows (he is six feet tall). Similarly, stone stays singular in plural expressions (she weighs nine stone). Metric measurements take the plural form when not used attributively: six kilos of potatoes.

It is worth noting, says the *Oxford Guide to English Usage*, that the use of the plural form after a plural qualifier when nothing follows after it is incorrect: there is a temptation to write the audience is 10 millions when it should be 10 million.

Nouns of quantity always take the plural when referring to indefinite quantities and are usually followed by of: there are hundreds of trees.

Detailed advice on the treatment of numbers will be found in *New Hart's Rules* (OUP).

Abbreviations: the long and the short of it

Now let's look at abbreviations and how to deal with them. First, the abbreviation everyone uses without hesitation: *OK*. What do the letters stand for? Unless you have seen it in my 'Last Words' column for the CIPR or made a study of the subject, the chances are that you don't know – and that is the trouble with using abbreviations: readers may not know what a given set of initials stand for and that means communication not working.

OK, here are some answers. Take your pick: originating from the nineteenth century, it could come from Old Kinderhook, the upstate New York birthplace of eighth American president Van Buren who used the initials as an election slogan; or perhaps a contraction of American slang *Orl Korrect*, or of Orrins-Kendall crackers, according to Bill Bryson in *Mother Tongue*. Even though the origin may be obscure, we all know what the letters mean.

Few abbreviations are as familiar and instantly understandable as OK. Abbreviations are often used without hesitation, but are meaningless to the reader, simply because the writer is used to them and they have become part of the company's jargon. Get them wrong and your message fails. So what are the rules for dealing with them?

Avoid overuse

The first point, to quote a well-known saying, is familiarity breeds contempt. If you overuse abbreviated sets of initials they quickly tire the eye. Unless the initials are sufficiently familiar to be part of the language (BBC, CBI, TUC) the name should be spelt out in full before using abbreviations. Otherwise, spell it out in full after the initials at first reference. It would be equally tiring to see a repetition of the full name when a contraction would be more suitable and convenient. There would be little point in explaining the initials BMW, because besides being a well-known brand, there is usually no *need* for the reader to know what they mean.

Do not continue to use the same set of initials. For example, in references to the BBC use 'the Corporation' or possibly for informal speech or tabloid publication, 'the Beeb'. Again, for the CBI, it could be called after the first reference 'the employers' organisation' or just 'the organisation'. In other cases, use a shortened form such as institute/association/federation/body or, in the case of firms, company/consultancy/firm/group/shop/store, or name by product or service type. But keep clear of slang words like *outfit/shop* for public relations or advertising companies.

Be careful of ambiguities

Watch out for ambiguities like PC, which could mean personal computer, Police Constable or Privy Counsellor. You may be *in* PR, but don't describe yourself as *a* PR, even though *a* PR or PRs are in common use. You see an *ad* but not an *advert*, you join a *demo* and you get *flu* not *the* (and no apostrophe). Ensure that descriptions are accurate. A common mistake is for BSI to be written out as the British Standards *Institute* instead of Institution; it was the Public Record Office, not Records, before it became the National Archives. Writers wonder how to write PLC (Public Limited Company). It is up to the company: it can be shown in caps, or lower case or a mixture of the two, although the all lower-case style is now generally favoured.

Capitals and full stops

Most house styles require all abbreviations to be set in capitals, but some organisations are read as acronyms and take lower case (Aslef for instance), while others are set upper and lower case for the sake of clarity (BSc, Dr). In general, full stops are not needed in abbreviations of company names, titles and civil honours, academic qualifications, and the courtesy titles of Mr/Mrs/Miss/Ms.

No full point follows numerical abbreviations (1st/2nd), units of length, weight or time (cm/ft/cwt/lb/kg/min/sec); am/pm; days of the week (Mon/ Tues); months (Aug/Dec); or in points of the compass (NE/SW) unless used separately (N.S.E.W.). They are seldom necessary in acronyms (laser) and if there is no way of avoiding etc (never &c) don't put a point after it.

Make sure your text or office-produced documents have all abbreviations typed or set in a consistent way without (or with) full points as may be dictated by house style. Get out of the habit of using eg, ie, pa – they are what might be termed 'lazyisms'. For *etc* write a short listing of what the items are; for eg/ie just put a comma, for pa spell out per annum or annually or every/each year. Note that *eg* is not the same as *ie*: *eg* means 'for example', while *ie* means 'that is'.

Ampersands and definite articles

The ampersand is a useful and convenient abbreviation for *and*, but it should be restricted to company names (Marks & Spencer) and never used as an alternative to *and* in text. A check with the telephone directory will confirm whether or not a company name contains an ampersand.

The omission of the definite article has caused heated debate: the Queen's English Society has blamed this on advertisers, headline writers and bad teaching. But it is not something to be too bothered about unless *the* is there to describe a specific thing or event. It would be tedious to describe Joe Bloggs as *the* managing director of XYZ company. Drop it and you make the copy run faster. Name plus title in lower case is all you need.

The is certainly not needed when talking about branded products: you would say, in a release or article, Ford motor cars, not the Ford motor cars, in a general context, but the Ford when referring to a specific model, say in comparison with other vehicles.

When a title such as *The Times*, or the CIPR for that matter, is used attributively, you can drop the *the* as in *Times* reporters investigated..., CIPR policy decisions were made.... There is no objection to using *the* with less and more (the less/the more you have); nonetheless (not none the less) is preferable to not any *the* less.

You need *the* when referring to the particular, the specific. Keep it for titles of books, plays and films when it is part of the recognised title and when mentioning a person by title as in the Prime Minister, Tony Blair, not the American way Prime Minister Blair.

If a shortened word is pronounced, do not put a definite article before it (the CIPR but not the M&S). Hence the rule: *the* goes with abbreviated organisations but not the company names. You wouldn't write the ICI would you? Be careful in exchanging phone for telephone, photo for photograph, as both contractions are more comfortable when used informally and in speech.

Use facsimile, telephone in full for printed address details, fax/phone as a verb ('I will fax/phone you'). In formal contexts write telephone.

A full guide to abbreviations (but only those covering the larger commercial organisations) will be found in the *Oxford Style Manual*; advice on setting abbreviations for printed material is given in another section of the manual. Most dictionaries will indicate what abbreviated titles, honours and qualifications stand for.

And, by the way, OK in capitalised form is mostly preferred to okay or ok. It is all a matter of house style (and context) whether you write OK or okay, or whether to use all lower case for both abbreviations. (For anyone who wants to know more about this abbreviation, there's *OK*, a book on how it was coined, what it stood for and the extent of its influence worldwide by Allan Metcalf (OUP).)

At a glance

- Don't start a sentence with a figure if you can help it.

- Spell out numbers up to and including ten within a sentence.

- Avoid the % sign in text; spell out per cent as two words.

- When comparing years use either *from/to* or hyphenate; don't mix.

- 'Number' takes the plural when referring to a group.

- For sets of initials spell out the full name at first reference or put it in brackets.

- No stops in abbreviated company names or titles.

- The definite article (the) is not needed for branded products.

- Consult style guides such as the *Oxford Style Manual* for guidance on abbreviations.

09
Keep it short, simple – and plain

Some of the strictures of purists who insist upon rigid adherence to rules of grammar are little more than mythology and have no place in everyday usage. Those who believe that it is always wrong to split an infinitive, end a sentence with a preposition, or start with a conjunction are in a linguistic straitjacket and unable to communicate as well as they might.

Likewise, unnecessarily long words, complex sentences and lengthy paragraphs confuse the reader. Double negatives, needless jargon, faulty or misplaced punctuation, and constant repetition of words and ideas can all lead to nonsensical, hard-to-follow text. And that means that the reader quickly loses interest in the face of endless waffle.

Plain English, written in a simple and straightforward way, is the recipe for clarity of expression. More than that, it is the basis of good style. Earlier chapters have discussed some of the ingredients for securing and keeping the reader reading, and, without trespassing on that territory, this chapter looks at writing with economy of language, a crucial factor in getting your message understood.

Aim for brevity

Brevity is the essence, particularly for the media. Complicated constructions and lengthy, unwieldy sentences not only bore the reader, they provide an instant barrier to effective communication. More important still, brevity spells time saved for the reader. Copy must be clear, concise and unambiguous. Whether the piece is for publication in a newspaper or periodical or for a brochure or leaflet, it should be written so that it grips the reader from start to finish. What are the best ways of achieving this?

First, use short words rather than long, and plain language instead of complex terminology. Try to keep sentences down to 25 to 30 words, fewer if you can. Use full stops liberally: they are the writer's best friend. Aim for not more than three sentences per paragraph for releases and news-style publications. But variety is the spice: an occasional longer paragraph gives colour and balance to a piece. And the one-liner can be effective – it jerks the reader to attention.

Sentences can of course be much longer than this; indeed, those of up to 60 or so words are acceptable for technical or legal contexts where detailed explanation is required. If a sentence is starting to 'look' too long, and tops the 60 mark, break it up with stops, or insert quotations if appropriate. With feature articles and corporate brochures you can be more generous with words. But even then, be aware that the longer the sentence the more likely the reader will tire and skip the copy you have tried so hard to get right in terms of style and fact.

As you write, get into the habit of asking yourself 'Is there a shorter word that means the same thing? Is there a better word? Are any words sheer verbiage and should be cut out? Is every word doing a job and telling you something?' In short, write tight to write well.

Plain words

Your search for plain words and the removal of unnecessary ones will be aided by reference to the Plain English Campaign's website (**www.plainenglish.co.uk**) where advice and information will be found on keeping language simple and easily understood. Further help is available from the Plain English Commission (**www.clearest.co.uk**). Martin Cutts, Research Director of the Commission and author of the *Oxford Guide to Plain English* says there are three main techniques for dealing with 'dross' to allow your information to 'shine more clearly': strike out useless words and leave only those that tell you something; prune the dead wood, grafting on the vigorous; rewrite completely. In his book, Cutts gives many examples of the overlong word or phrase, the useless word, and the officialese that defies understanding; as well as advice on how to rewrite lengthy and tedious text. When editing down copy it is essential not to alter the sense in any way and to follow the basic rules of grammar.

With a little thought it is easy: see how 10 words in the following sentence can be lost without altering the meaning:

> XYZ company *had as its main objective the need* (wanted) to increase output by at least 10 per cent *in* this *current financial* year.

Here, the words in italics can be deleted without changing the meaning. The single word 'wanted' takes the place of seven needless ones. Verbiage like this throughout a piece of several hundred words would turn off the reader after only a few paragraphs. Expressions that can easily be shortened include: the question as to whether (use whether); there is no doubt that

FIGURE 9.1 Online issue of *Plain English* magazine now published annually. Quarterly issues back to 1999 can be read online

Plain English

Action for plain English   December 2011

Our guest speaker

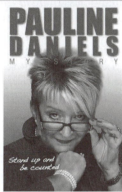

Birkenhead-born Pauline Daniels made her name as Britain's best female stand-up comedian, noted for her spot-on comic tim

Peter Grant, Liverpool journalist and writer of Pauline's biography, marvels at her effortless communication with her audience.

Pauline is frequently involved in raising funds for worthy causes, on several occasions playing Shirley Valentine in aid of charities.

She proudly pronounced during last year's Capital of Culture celebrations, "Look out World, we are on the up. We are brimming with culture, but we have something no other city has … Scousers". Scousers she describes as "friendly, helpful, funny – and bloody good at football".

Plain English Campaign are honoured that Pauline has given her time to support us at this year's awards and share her love of plain talking with our audience.

Pauline's biography available now.

100,000 plain English names for action

UK Plain Language Act

The Campaign has recently launched an 'e-petition' to persuade the Government to pass a Plain Language Act for the UK.

If passed into law, this would make public bodies use language in their documents which the public can understand and use.

This would be a great leap forward and shows, once again, that the Campaign is at the forefront of demands for crystal-clear communication of public information.

Be an important one in 100,000 – add your name to the e-petition at http://epetitions.direct.gov.uk/petitions/17809

Sign your name and make it plain

Addressing down

A letter correctly addressed to the Plain English Campaign office was wrongly delivered. It eventually arrived at its intended destination with this message on the back of the envelope.

"Notwithstanding his usual exemplary service, the deliverer of Her Majesty's mail has seen fit to insert said envelope into my portal opening constructed for this purpose, albeit the obvious misrepresentation of residence. Felicitations of a personal nature. In other words, "not known here".

Sent to the Manchester Evening News and published in Readers' Digest August 1999

Plain English Campaign - working for clearer communication
PO Box 3, New Mills, High Peak, Derbyshire, SK22 4QP
Phone: 01663 744409   Fax: 01663 747038
E-mail: info@plainenglish.co.uk   Website: www.plainenglish.co.uk

(put no doubt or doubtless); in spite of the fact that (replace with though); owing to the fact that (write since or because).

Cutts includes helpful lists of plain and short words and phrases. For example, he advises facts/details not particulars; help not facilitate; idea not concept; buy not purchase; start/begin, not commence. Do not let long-winded phrases get the better of you: for instance, write although or despite instead of 'despite the fact that'. Sir Ernest Gowers in *The Complete Plain Words* demonstrates that simple prepositions can often replace wordy phrases: if for 'in case of' and to for 'with a view to'.

From my file of unnecessarily complicated words and phrases (preferences in italics): concerning, *about/on*; currently, *now*; donation, *gift*; in addition to/as well as, *besides/also*; conclude, *end/decide/stop/deduce*; duplicate, *repeat*; endeavour, *try*; fluctuation, *change*; general (adj), *broad*; give rise to, *cause*; in the course of, *during*; heterogeneous, *mixed*; intercede, *plead*; journey, *trip*; not less than, *at least*; language, *tongue*; master (v), *grasp*; principal, *main*; persons, *people*; remuneration, *fee/pay*; stipulate, *state*; subsequent to, *after*; tendency, *trend*; understand (v), *see*; virtually, *almost*; with reference to, *about/regarding*; warehouse, *store*.

Look for the shorter, simpler – the plain word: check for alternatives in the *Oxford Dictionary of Synonyms and Antonyms*, the *Penguin Dictionary of English Synonyms*, *Roget's Thesaurus* and similar reference books.

Local government communication

Local government with its many different publics from householders to businesses, from contractors to social services, faces communication problems arising from a range of departments with widely differing staffing arrangements. A council's messages, anything from Council Tax demands to rubbish collection, must be widely understood and acted upon by the numerous publics. To achieve effective communication across such a broad audience, words and phrases must be written and presented in a simple, straightforward way. Take the North Lincolnshire Council for example: its guide on plain English and house style is a concise and effective aid for its officers and staff.

The council's *Style Guide*, now in its fifth edition, updates much of the advice to staff on written communications. Particular attention is paid to the internet since its website is now a key channel for detailed information on services. The latest edition of the guide, produced by Paul Harrop, includes hints on content and structure of web pages as well as detailed guidance on how to set up and use the readability tools in Microsoft Word. It has tips, extra dos and don'ts, an expanded reading list, and 'before' and 'after' examples of letter and report writing.

The guide emphasises the need for short words, avoiding the abstract and concentrating on the specific. It recommends the active voice, not the passive, and using the first person (I/we) rather than 'the council' in publications and correspondence. It is emphasised that good writing depends on facts not waffle, without repetition, coupled with correct punctuation and delivered in plain and simple English.

FIGURE 9.2 Needless phrases and expressions only fit for the delete key. From the Plain English Campaign's *A-Z Guide of Alternative Words*

V

variation . . . . .change
virtually . . . . .almost (or edit out)
visualise . . . . .see, predict

W

ways and means . . . . .ways
we have pleasure in . . . . .we are glad to
whatsoever . . . . .whatever, what, any
whensoever . . . . .when
whereas . . . . .but
whether or not . . . . .whether
with a view to . . . . .to
with effect from . . . . .from
with reference to . . . . .about
with regard to .about, for
with respect to .about, for
with the minimum of delay . . . . .quickly (or say when)

Y

you are requested to . . . . .please
your attention is drawn . . . . .please see, please note

Z

zero-rated. . . . . .free, free of
zone . . . . .area, region

Words and phrases to avoid

The words and phrases below often crop up in letters and reports. Often you can remove them from a sentence without changing the meaning or the tone. In other words, they add nothing to the message. Try leaving them out of your writing. You'll find your sentences survive and succeed without them.

- a total of
- absolutely
- abundantly
- actually
- all things being equal
- as a matter of fact
- as far as I am concerned
- at the end of the day
- at this moment in time
- basically
- current
- currently
- during the period from
- each and every one
- existing
- extremely
- I am of the opinion that
- I would like to say
- I would like to take this opportunity to
- in due course

- in other words
- in the end
- in the final analysis
- in this connection
- in total
- in view of the fact that
- it should be understood
- last but not least
- obviously
- of course
- other things being equal
- quite
- really
- really quite
- regarding the (noun), it was
- the fact of the matter is
- the month(s) of
- to all intents and purposes
- to one's own mind
- very

FIGURE 9.3 Useful before-and-after editing for plain English from the Derby City Council guide

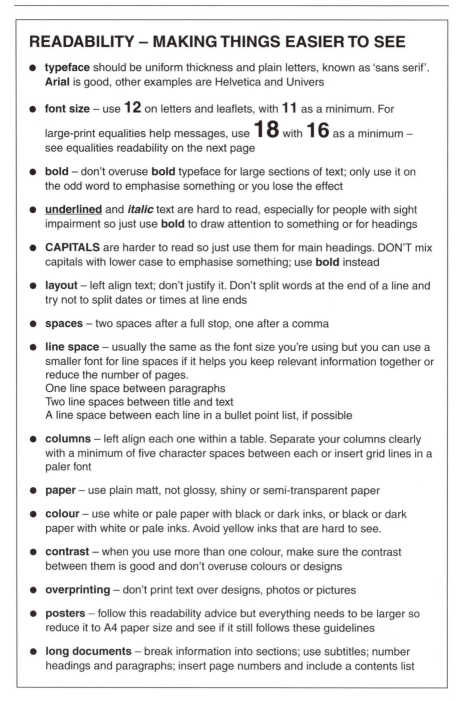

READABILITY – MAKING THINGS EASIER TO SEE

- **typeface** should be uniform thickness and plain letters, known as 'sans serif'. **Arial** is good, other examples are Helvetica and Univers

- **font size** – use **12** on letters and leaflets, with **11** as a minimum. For large-print equalities help messages, use **18** with **16** as a minimum – see equalities readability on the next page

- **bold** – don't overuse **bold** typeface for large sections of text; only use it on the odd word to emphasise something or you lose the effect

- <u>underlined</u> and *italic* text are hard to read, especially for people with sight impairment so just use **bold** to draw attention to something or for headings

- **CAPITALS** are harder to read so just use them for main headings. DON'T mix capitals with lower case to emphasise something; use **bold** instead

- **layout** – left align text; don't justify it. Don't split words at the end of a line and try not to split dates or times at line ends

- **spaces** – two spaces after a full stop, one after a comma

- **line space** – usually the same as the font size you're using but you can use a smaller font for line spaces if it helps you keep relevant information together or reduce the number of pages.
  One line space between paragraphs
  Two line spaces between title and text
  A line space between each line in a bullet point list, if possible

- **columns** – left align each one within a table. Separate your columns clearly with a minimum of five character spaces between each or insert grid lines in a paler font

- **paper** – use plain matt, not glossy, shiny or semi-transparent paper

- **colour** – use white or pale paper with black or dark inks, or black or dark paper with white or pale inks. Avoid yellow inks that are hard to see.

- **contrast** – when you use more than one colour, make sure the contrast between them is good and don't overuse colours or designs

- **overprinting** – don't print text over designs, photos or pictures

- **posters** – follow this readability advice but everything needs to be larger so reduce it to A4 paper size and see if it still follows these guidelines

- **long documents** – break information into sections; use subtitles; number headings and paragraphs; insert page numbers and include a contents list

Guidance on reports and documents, and results for using the council's name, are included. Any county council or local authority, or indeed any organisation wanting a set of basic rules on style and usage, can get an online copy from the council's website **http://www.northlincs.gov.uk/NorthLincs/ CouncilandDemocracy/policyandperformance/NorthLincolnshireCouncil StyleGuide.htm**.

Another style guide comes from Derby City Council. Its useful *Plain English Guide* includes a directory of short words for long, a list of meaningless and patronising phrases, plus helpful grammatical and punctuation points. There's a four-page list of abbreviations and acronyms for spelling out at first reference.

Of special interest to local government communicators are examples of how copy can be improved by using simple language. Latin words and expressions are out, as well as long-winded and obscure wording in correspondence and documents. Even so, this guide insists on a capital initial letter for council and has yet to ban the verb 'to be', a signal of the passive voice, although implicit in some examples. An email version of the Derby guide is available on request by emailing **intouch@derby.gov.uk** (the communications team).

Computer software for plain English

It is now possible to test and measure your ability to write plain English if you have access to Microsoft Word. Once the user has finished spell-checking, Word can display information about the reading level of the document based on the number of syllables per word and words per sentence in three ways.

It rates reading ease on a 100-point scale; the higher the score, the easier the text is understood (aim for a score of at least 70). Second, the Flesch-Kincaid test ranks text on a US grade-school level, suggesting a minimum acceptable score of 7–8. Third, the most useful score is for passive sentences, the prime barrier to clear, concise language essential for effective communication. Here, writers should aim for a nil percentage score for press releases.

Once the figure starts to climb above 0 per cent for news items and articles, swap round to the active voice with the subject or 'doer' immediately before the verb ('Bob wrote the report', not 'the report was written by Bob'). For publicity booklets, brochures and reports, try to achieve a score of below 10–15 per cent.

The program counts words, paragraphs and sentences, and gives averages for sentences per paragraph, words per sentence and characters per word. Aim for sentences of 25 to 30 words with not more than three per paragraph.

To activate readability, go to 'tools', then 'options', spelling and grammar and to the 'show readability statistics' box. For hard copy, scan into a document. Check out your last annual report, brochure or press release publication for passive voice, and use the program for your next printed message or even broadcast script.

FIGURE 9.4 StyleWriter software makes editing for plain English an easy task. With and without examples show simplicity of use. Editing problems are in bold; the lower example gives final result

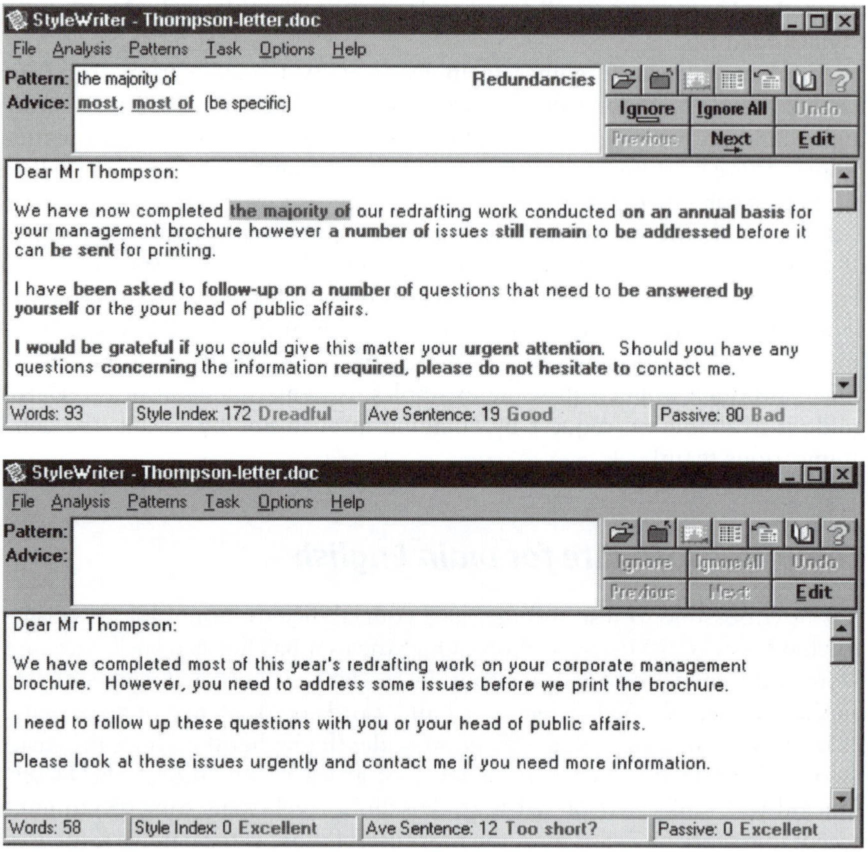

Another useful editing tool popular in local authorities is StyleWriter software. The program looks for overused language, passive verbs, clichés and confused hyphens. It cuts the number of words per sentence to the ideal 15–20 average and corrects grammatical mistakes. All editing problems are displayed together, offering alternatives for the most appropriate word, phrase or sentence structure. Written work is analysed for 35,000 style and usage issues. Each problem is highlighted, with options for editing into clear, plain English.

CIPR Fellow Jenny Tozer, Assistant Director of Communications at Derbyshire County Council, says StyleWriter is used by everyone in the 15-strong press and publications office. 'Run alongside Microsoft Word readability tests and – my firm favourite – reading aloud what you've written, it's a good guide to clear and plain English.' However, the Plain English

Campaign would prefer people to learn the techniques of plain English writing rather than to rely on software. Go to **www.editorsoftware.com** for user examples and full details.

Watch out for tautology

If you use another word or words meaning the same thing in a single sentence or phrase, that's tautology: free gift, new innovation or that well-used cliché at this moment in time are typical. Repetition is seldom, if ever, desirable unless it is used deliberately for dramatic effect, perhaps for a speech or article. If you say you are going to *eat* lunch that is tautologous because what else would you do but eat it? You *have* lunch.

If you say someone died of a fatal dose, wrote a pair of twins, full and total exposure, or if you put 'he had nothing further to add' you are repeating yourself. Tautology abounds: early beginnings, added bonus, inside of, meet together, mutual co-operation, over again, past history, repeat again, revert back, unite together, whether or not easily reach type and tongue.

Don't risk repetition: it will never get past the good media subeditor.

Look for active verbs; avoid contractions

The verb drives the text forward. First, look for single syllable verbs: go, not proceed; send, not transmit; show, not demonstrate. You pitch rather than compete, know rather than comprehend, let not permit. To think is better than to believe, to ask is better than to enquire. And so on. As mentioned earlier in the section on plain English tests, choose active-voice verbs by putting the 'doer' – the person or thing doing the action – in front of the verb. It is much better to write 'XYZ consultancy wants new clients' instead of 'new clients are wanted by XYZ consultancy'.

Try to avoid using too many adverbs as qualifiers. They are an indulgence, often a sign that noun and verb are not working properly, *Times* journalists are told. Much the same can be said for adjectives; avoid those that are flowery and expansive: rather, very, little (unless referring to size), pretty for example – especially in news stories. Never use them in releases, unless they are part of a quote, and even then it is better to cut them out if you can.

When you need to save words and shorten copy, do not fall into the trap of using contractions of modal or auxiliary verbs like will/shall/would; and so write you'll/you'd, or you're/you've, I'm. This is fine for speech and informal writing but not for formal contexts; it looks sloppy and chatty, but it can be admissible when you want to adopt a friendly, warm tone of voice. (Note that n't is an acceptable contraction of *not* for all but very formal usage.)

FIGURE 9.5 Help from the North Lincolnshire style guide for keeping sentences active and to the point

Part Two: Writing in plain English

Style Guide

Keeping sentences active

According to the Plain English Campaign (www.plainenglish.co.uk), active sentences are crisp and professional, passive sentences are stuffy and bureaucratic.

To make a sentence active you need to:

* put the doer (the person, group or thing doing the action), before the verb (the action itself)
* use 'I', 'you' and 'we'
* reduce the number of redundant or wasteful words
* avoid the verb 'to be' in all its forms.

The Plain English Campaign says it's easier to write active sentences once you've understood how a sentence fits together. It adds that there are three main parts to every sentence:

* the *doer* (the person, group or thing doing the action);
* a *verb* (the action itself); and
* an *object* (the person, group or thing that the action is done to).

So, if the sentence is 'Dave wrote the report':

* the doer is Dave (he's the author of the report);
* the verb is wrote; and
* the object is the report (it had been written).

To make a sentence active, simply put the three parts in the following order: *doer, verb, object.* An active sentence would read 'Dave wrote the report'.

In passive sentences, the order is different: object, verb, doer. So the sentence would read 'the report was written by Dave'.

Example

✗ Your bin will be collected by the council on a Monday

✓ We will collect your bin every Monday

✗ The new policy has been reviewed by the scrutiny panel

✓ Our scrutiny panel reviewed the new policy

✗ A meeting will be held by directors next week

✓ The directors meet next week

Page 8

Avoid foreign words or phrases – and Latin

Another barrier to understanding is using foreign words or phrases when an English one will do just as well. While it is true that many verbal imports are often just the words or phrases you want because there is no exact English equivalent, do not write above the head of the reader, who might think you are showing off.

Don't go Latin unless you have to: put among others not inter alia; yearly or annually not per annum; about, not circa; regarding, not vis-à-vis. Other Latin words to be avoided where English equivalents are available include ad hoc (for this purpose), a priori (from cause to effect), bona fide(s) (good faith), caveat emptor (let the buyer beware), et al (and others), ex officio (by virtue of official position), ex gratia (voluntary contribution), mea culpa (my fault) and quid pro quo (something given in return or compensation

FIGURE 9.6 Prime objectives of Derby City Council's *Plain English Guide* are clearly displayed on the cover

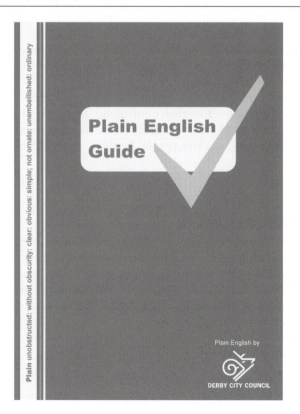

for something). As a general rule, don't go Latin and be safe! And be on your guard against pomposity: write before not 'prior to'; ultimately not 'at the end of the day'; but or however rather than 'having said that'.

Foreign words should not appear in releases. Put them in house journals and speeches, provided you think they will be understood. One or two will usually be enough. Once a word has become anglicised (as in role) it is not italicised and loses its accent(s). Nowadays, commonly used Latin words and phrases are seldom italicised.

Loan words needing care

Loan words and phrases include, from France, the italicised *bon mot* (clever saying), *déjà vu* (with accents, tediously similar), *de trop* (not wanted) and *tour de force* (feat of strength or skill). From Germany come the lesser known but useful *Sturm und Drang* (storm and stress), *Zeitgeist* (spirit of the times); anglicised words include achtung, angst, blitzkrieg (or just blitz), diktat, to join kindergarten, rucksack and waltz.

Italy brings us ciao (hello, goodbye), conversazione, espresso, in camera, incommunicado, prima donna – all well known, but not *alter ego* (intimate friend) to the same extent. Greece lends hoi polloi (the masses), Russia perestroika (reconstruction, reform) and glasnost (openness), and Spain the slangy vamoose, pronto, olé and the more formal adios, fandango, grandee, armada, machismo and quixotic.

Every writer's vocabulary should make room for these Jewish words, none of which have a direct English equivalent: chutzpah (shameless audacity), mazeltov (good luck), nosh (food, to enjoy food), schmaltz (chicken fat, sugary sentimentalism), shalom (peace be unto you), shlemiel (fool, inept person).

Double negatives

Guard against double or multiple negatives with too many 'unwords' like unnecessary or unless; or putting more than one *avoid* or *cease* or phrases such as *less than* and *not more than* in one sentence. Don't use constructions like *hardly* or *almost* followed by *without*, or there were no trees *neither* instead of *either*. If you do, the meaning can become obscure and the reader has to struggle with negatives (or too many positives for that matter) in order to understand what you mean.

Beware 'myths'

According to Cutts in the *Oxford Guide to Plain English*, some of the so-called 'rules' of grammar religiously followed by purists and scholars are little more than myths. It is these myths that are a further barrier to clarity of communication. They are the territory of the pedant and do not have a place in everyday writing and speech. The top-of-the-list myth says you should never split an infinitive. While most commentators agree that it is better to avoid a split, by putting an adverb or another word between *to* and the infinitive verb as in *to boldly go*, 'no absolute taboo' should be placed on it (*Fowler's Modern English Usage*). Cutts himself says: 'If you can't bring yourself to split an infinitive, at least allow others to do so.' There is nothing to stop you splitting an infinitive but be aware that it will irritate some people.

Another myth is the long-held theory that sentences must never end with a preposition. Cutts says a few 'fossils' still believe this, but agrees that some sentences do need to be recast, not because they break any rule but because they 'sound ugly'. It all depends on the degree of formality the writer wants to achieve: it would be pedantic to write or say 'To whom am I talking?' when 'Who am I talking to?' would be more natural. If the preposition looks stranded and unrelated to the word to which it belongs (or belongs to!) then rewrite the sentence and put it where it sounds natural. The more formal the piece, the earlier the preposition goes in the sentence. But do not move it back just because you think you should follow the schoolroom rule.

A third myth is that sentences must never begin with and or but. Authors throughout history have ignored this so-called ban: Cutts notes that Jane Austen begins almost every page with 'but', and *OED* gives several examples of sentences in English literature beginning with 'and'. In fact, sentences starting this way tend to have a sparkle absent in others, and are an effective way of adding emphasis to a point already made.

Some objectors demand justification from professional editors and stylists that sentences can start with *and* or *but*. Quite apart from the fact that the Microsoft Office grammar checker accepts this structure, most dictionaries and any style guide you care to consult confirms that writers down the ages, including Shakespeare, have used *and* and other conjunctions to start a sentence.

To quote from *Fowler's Modern English Usage* (third edition): 'There is a persistent belief that it is improper to begin a sentence with *and*, but this prohibition has been cheerfully ignored by authors from Anglo-Saxon times onwards.' Referring to *but*, *Fowler's* states: 'The widespread belief that *but* should not be used at the beginning of a sentence seems to be unshakeable. Yet it has no foundation.'

Cutts sums up the position neatly with this comforting thought: 'In short, you can start a sentence with any word you want, so long as the sentence hangs together as a complete statement.' Objectors please note.

Tips for writing tight

Writing tight in a plain, easy-to-read style is hard work and demands ruthless pruning. Try to keep cross-references to a minimum; divide complicated copy into vertical lists rather than having a succession of semi-colons or commas; don't bury key words or phrases in slabs of text unrelieved by headings; don't confuse the lay-reader with jargon or technical terms and don't use slang words in any formal sense.

Cut unnecessary words and choose verbs to achieve crispness. Make the punctuation work for you by dividing the copy into short manageable sections with liberal use of full stops. Create interest by asking questions – a technique more commonly found in articles and feature material than in news items – and include quotations if appropriate. Keep your sentences short, and have plenty of paragraph breaks. In a report or internal document organise points under headings.

Be careful not to duplicate words and phrases in the same paragraph. Repeating technical words may be unavoidable, but nothing is more off-putting than reading the same word over and over again. Look for alternatives in *The Oxford Thesaurus*, *Roget's Thesaurus*, the *Penguin Dictionary of Synonyms* or *The Wordsworth Dictionary of Synonyms & Antonyms*. Sometimes you can find the word you want in a good dictionary.

There is still much to do...

Don't think that once you've finished the piece that is the end of it. The work should not get anywhere near your out tray until you have edited and polished it over and over again and convinced yourself there is no way it can be improved. The whole piece might need rewriting. (There's more about this in Chapter 13.)

Sometimes you will be rushed and get no chance to recast a piece. But don't despair – if you are quick you will undoubtedly have time for a bit of editing. Unless you are up against a tight deadline, there is usually time for another draft. And don't think, 'Oh well there is still time to look at it again at proof stage.' That is fatal and can lead to mistakes.

Out with redundancies and wasted words

Don't allow redundancies (unnecessary words in italics): *advance* planning, *brand* new, *concrete* proposals, divide *up*, *join* together, filled *up*, follow *after*, *general* public, *penetrate* into, limited *only* to, petrol *filling* station, *total* extinction, *revert* back, *watchful* eye.

Cut out those wasted words: *actually, basically, hopefully, really, kind of/ sort of* and that favourite ploy of speakers starting a new thought with

FIGURE 9.7 Crucial points for writers in the Queen's English Society newsletter. The sub-heading says it all

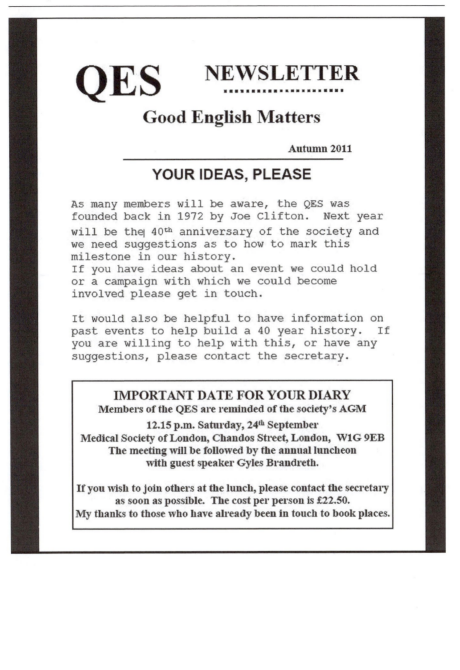

QES NEWSLETTER

Good English Matters

Autumn 2011

YOUR IDEAS, PLEASE

As many members will be aware, the QES was founded back in 1972 by Joe Clifton. Next year will be the 40th anniversary of the society and we need suggestions as to how to mark this milestone in our history.
If you have ideas about an event we could hold or a campaign with which we could become involved please get in touch.

It would also be helpful to have information on past events to help build a 40 year history. If you are willing to help with this, or have any suggestions, please contact the secretary.

IMPORTANT DATE FOR YOUR DIARY
Members of the QES are reminded of the society's AGM

12.15 p.m. Saturday, 24th September
Medical Society of London, Chandos Street, London, W1G 9EB
The meeting will be followed by the annual luncheon
with guest speaker Gyles Brandreth.

If you wish to join others at the lunch, please contact the secretary
as soon as possible. The cost per person is £22.50.
My thanks to those who have already been in touch to book places.

'Well...' Phrases like *lodged an objection, in many cases,* and *tendered his resignation* can be replaced with *appealed, often* and *resigned*: in each case one word is doing the job of three. And there's 'then' after everything, or 'to be honest', almost as bad as the favourite terminator 'ah right'. Plenty more wasted words are in James Aitchison's *Cassell's Guide to Written English* (Cassell).

Be aware of confusables – words that look and sound alike but have different meanings (Appendix 1).

Revise and revise again

Even when close to deadline give your copy one more read. Take a break and come back to it: there will always be a fact to check again, a word to lose, a better, shorter one to find. Every minute you spend on revision will be rewarded by brighter, brisker copy. And I bet you will have saved at least one mistake!

Swapping paragraphs, changing words, even rewriting whole passages, are easy. Writing takes time and effort: here are 10 rules for making it better:

1 In headings, use the present tense and an active verb.

2 Check the facts; put them in a logical order and rewrite non-sequiturs.

3 Edit to cut, not add. Put in plenty of paragraph breaks.

4 Confirm that there are no ambiguities.

5 Replace long words with shorter ones; avoid repetition, redundancies.

6 Correct grammar but don't be pedantic.

7 Delete clichés and jargon.

8 Watch for legal pitfalls, particularly libellous statements.

9 Check that there is no vulgarity.

10 And ensure that spelling and style are consistent throughout.

You may not have a chance to see your copy again before it is published: check, check and check again. Only when you have satisfied yourself that all the above rules have been met, do you hit the PRINT or SEND button.

At a glance

- Be brief. Long, clumsy sentences only bore the reader.

- Cut out dross, verbiage, no matter what you write.

- Use short, simple words. Plain English communicates best.

- Don't repeat yourself. That's tautology.

- Choose active verbs, put the 'doer' first.

- Avoid Latin words and expressions.

- Kill redundant and wasted words.

- Write tight, prune ruthlessly.

- Software programs can do it for you.

- Revise as you go along. And again at the end.

10
Social media: the X-factor for PR

Social media sites dominate: tweets by the billion worldwide – around 7,000 tweets per second when big stories break; Facebook with more than 750 million users globally; blogs by the hundred thousand every day; LinkedIn – dubbed as the 'Facebook for suits' – grows by a million users a week. On the Royal Wedding day in April 2011 there were over 70 million viewers watching live streams on YouTube, some 140,000 Clarence House followers on Twitter, and nine million Facebook views.

Companies rely on new technologies for sales growth. *Management Today* reports that sales uplifts of up to 20 per cent and improved profit margins result from employing the new technologies of the digital age. Brands need to join the online conversation in order to remain competitive and meet consumer demands.

To this end there has been the emergence of the social media manager in PR consultancies and companies whose job is to ensure that clients or customers get the best possible experience from using the new digital platforms through monitoring results and implementation where requested. There is now software such as Syncapse to record every Facebook posting and tweet about a brand and its users. Just do a Google search of social media software companies: you will find many useful sites to guide you through the mass of data available.

For the public relations business it is largely tweets that count. News desks throughout the world rely on tweets for breaking news. Journalists get and send tweets on mobile smartphones and a news story can be in their hands within a matter of seconds. With links to websites, tweets can provide a mobile press centre for consultancies and brands while the journalist is on the move or in the office. Write a blog, tweet it and it's out for everyone to see.

Facebook and LinkedIn can be used as platforms to publish information and press releases, while Flickr can host pictures to support news stories. Vimeo is a site specifically set up as a community for sharing video content, which is directly hosted on the site itself. Images and video, of course, can be embedded in Facebook messages or linked via Twitter. But in the end it is the words and how they are written and presented that count. Let's now see how the main social media platforms work in practice, with hints and tips on finding the right words for the digital era.

Essential tools for journalists and brands

The seismic shift in the media landscape from mainstream to digital media has meant that the communications business – public relations practitioners in consultancies and companies, journalists and advertisers – have had to learn how to set up, implement and use on a daily basis the social media platforms alongside traditional media, news agencies and wire services. Take Twitter to start and see how it works for PR.

Easy set-up for your Twitter account

Signing up is easy: go to twitter.com, choose a username, password of your choice and email address so that Twitter can contact you, then hit the 'create account' button.

When setting up your Twitter account consider search engine optimisation (SEO), advises Michael Carnell, a consultant at Edelman Digital. 'SEO is the process of working out the keywords with which people will try to find you online. Use your Twitter biography to say something about who you are and your interests, which should then be reflected to some extent in your tweets'.

Avoid using punctuation in your username and don't restrict tweets to just one word. Messages (including the person you are tweeting and any website address) must not exceed 140 characters.

How to keep to character limit

The character-count drops down as you type and you cannot go beyond the 140 limit. However, tweets can be made longer if really necessary. Keren Haynes, of Shout! Communications in London, says that there is software, TwitLonger (**www.twitlonger.com**) for this, but you then get a line of ellipsis dots (…) once you have exceeded the character limit allowed by TwitLonger. Shout! recommend keeping to the 140-character limit as that is what Twitter is about – punchy, attention-grabbing posts.

To help keep the character-count down, words can be shortened (u for you, ovrlk for overlook) but make sure they are clear and don't confuse the reader. For instance, the u pronoun could be taken for an adjective or noun starting with that letter and give a completely different meaning.

Ideal for contacting journalists

Tweets come up on the author's profile page and are sent to all the followers who have registered an interest in his or her work. If you want to communicate with someone directly, say a journalist – but note this will be public – you write *@username* (for example the BBC technology correspondent Rory Cellan-Jones's Twitter name is @ruskin147); then put a hash tag sign # (for my Apple keyboard it's alt+3) which goes before a word or phrase if you want to make statements to your followers on particular subjects. The idea here is to identify tweets by subject by using an easy abbreviation that doesn't take up too many of the tweet's character limit.

How to shorten website addresses

Twitter now automatically shortens website addresses, but there are other ways besides. A popular method has been to use Bit.ly software (**www.bitly.com**) to give a unique code of characters and numerals for a website address. This is particularly useful if, for example, you want to show a website link where a video can be seen. It costs nothing once you have signed up.

Bit.ly is also useful for tracking the click through rate (CTR) – the number of people who clicked on the Bit.ly link in your tweet. This metric can help you measure the success of a campaign.

Establish lists of tweeters

Most practitioners set up lists of journalists using Twitter in specialist groupings so that selected writers can be identified. Twitter allows the user to see what subjects that person is discussing and so provides an easy way of feeding information such as blogs or references to press releases on company websites. It is an excellent way to start and build up a relationship with a journalist since 'it fits in nicely with their lifestyle', says Haynes.

Consultancies and in-house PR staff use it extensively to respond to journalists' requests: the 'smart' mobile phone gets the story to them in a flash. The days of the press conference for high-volume product launches are long gone: tweets, Facebook videos and blogs have taken over big time.

An online directory of all of Twitter lists is Listorious (**www.listorious.com**). Enter your search term, press 'Search' and then click 'Lists' to see lists of tweeters for the subject you need. This is a great tool if you want to identify a target group of tweeters.

PR professionals should use Twitter to search for the hash tag journorequest (#journorequest). Journalists consistently use this hash tag to attract the attention of PR people and brands: it is therefore a good way to track correspondents seeking people to interview or looking for details of products and news stories.

Nevertheless, Twitter in no sense replaces text, picture and video feeds from traditional media sources, such as agency news feeds, backup data and from PR consultancies and company media centres (see Chapter 11). It provides a broad-brush approach for newsgathering for instant transmission, besides monitoring social trends and breaking stories worldwide. But its efficacy depends, as always, on users' ability to express their tweets in an understandable and succinct way and yet say it all in fewer than 140 characters.

TweetDeck (**www.tweetdeck.com**) is essential software for anyone needing to monitor content on twitter, says Carnell. After downloading the desktop software, you can open multiple columns of search terms, and each time a tweet is published matching your criteria, you are instantly notified. This is perfect not just for monitoring tweets to your own Twitter feed, but for tweets around a person, brand or subject.

Facebook – the PR marketing platform

Of the 750 million users worldwide, nearly three-quarters of the UK population are either fans or are online to the site every day. The average user has 130 friends who converse with each other. The dramatic growth in the medium is exemplified by the fact that more than 30 billion items of content such as web links, news stories and blog posts are shared each month by Facebook members. According to the *Insider White Paper* published by MediaCom, part of Sir Martin Sorrell's WPP group, Europeans spend more time on Facebook than any other site and 60 per cent of users follow a brand in social media.

In developing a marketing strategy, brands and PR consultancies need to know their audience. It is important for your fans to like your page so that they will return to it and share it with others. Sharing means connecting with other Facebook members and engaging with that community. That means sending and sharing videos, news stories, pictures, blog posts and advertising messages.

Content is king. In this regard Facebook and other social networking sites are no different from traditional media. Your messages must be clear and precise with no wasted words. A snappy headline perhaps in the form of a question is a good starting point. Attract attention by referring to the audience or sections of it that make up the whole. One approach is to be breezy and informal by calling them by their occupation, something like 'Hi, white van driver' and leading on to 'hit the link for news of the latest satnav'.

Include illustrations, particularly product photographs, pictures of fans and their messages on your Facebook wall. Use colour liberally with text against a solid tint background, but a strong tint for PR and sales messages. The Facebook page should show links to basic company information, details of specific products, choice of videos with running time of each, posts by customers or clients, pictures of current products and site usage monitor stats.

This is not to say that Facebook and other social media platforms gain at the expense of print, TV, outdoor advertising, exhibitions and direct mail promotions. Facebook provides that extra push through online conversations between users that is essential to meet the challenges of today's highly competitive global conditions, from high street to trading park.

Content that is interesting generates likes, more so than a brand connecting with people over Facebook which should be seen as a place to bring people to your website. Most people will like a page if they feel the content is relevant to them: they will interact with you when, for instance, you post questions.

And don't forget to include the Facebook logo f on stationery, press ads, website – everywhere.

Designing and writing blogs

Hundreds of thousands of new blogs are created daily worldwide, literally millions can be found on the web. Popular websites that could host your blog include Wordpress (**www.wordpress.com**) or Blogspot (**www.blogger.com**). However, with these hosts your blog address will be something like 'myblog. wordpress.com.' This is a sub-domain. Companies should look at integrating blog services with their websites instead of using a third party website. Third party websites take users away from the company's own website (which is not a good idea).

Once you have created your domain name, your first task is to ensure what you write and how you present the words and pictures is understood and acted upon, just like a press or TV ad. Take a look at Whispers, the Shout! Communications regularly-updated blog for stories and events as well as Twitter feeds.

Most blog designs follow a single-column format with sidebars on either side which can be used for the blogger's photograph, links to other websites, frequently asked questions, company information or personal biography, a search box – you name it. Choose a 'readable' typeface like Verdana and set it in at least 12 point size. Other fonts suitable for online use are Times Roman and Arial.

Make sure that the fonts you choose are clear and easy on the eye – particularly when there is a large amount of text to be read (see also Chapter 6

'Is it easy to read?'). Most of the type is pre-defined by the blog template if you use one. The user will be selecting 'styles' such as 'paragraph', 'heading 1' etc.

A better idea might be to adopt a two-column layout and using part or all of one of the sidebars. This would give a 'newsy' feel to the page and opens up the chance of strong headlines that would help to get the message over in a reader-friendly way. Call in your website designer or print typographer for advice on visual presentation. Good design is just as important as getting the words right.

Create visual interest with a side-blog, in effect a blog within blog which goes alongside the main page to give quotes, links to background information, perhaps music or videos, without cluttering up the main page. You can add a sidebar without much trouble; if your blog host can't provide it there are services available to help: just Google sideblog service.

Content is key

As with all forms of communication, consider your audience before anything else. Find out who is visiting your website, who your Facebook friends are, the tweeters and their followers. Write with the audience in mind at all times. To quote from Jonathan Yang's *Rough Guide to Blogging*: 'A blog is only as strong as its content. Posts that are entertaining, informative, inspirational, humorous or memorable will always touch a chord with readers'.

Since blog posts are largely expressions of the writer's personality, it is crucial that you develop a writing style that will chime with the audience. Provided that you are cheerful and friendly, the rest is relatively easy, says Yang. Blogs full of clichés; crammed with jargon; wordy and boring are a waste of time. Since on-screen text is usually briefly scanned and not read word by word, you need to catch the reader's attention and hold it with sharp copy that means what it says.

Put headlines in bold, several sizes up from the text and specify interline spacing to at least 2 or perhaps 3 points (leading to the typographer) to open up the text. Line after line of closed-up text is virtually unreadable. Make sure there are plenty of paragraph breaks, keep sentences to 25–30 words maximum. Never, never type words in capitals and don't underline as it may lead the reader to think that it is a link to another site. Short sentences along with short paragraphs are key.

Insert cross-headings at major changes in thought so as to avoid a grey, solid look to the page. Pictures, cross-headings and specific points in boxes help to liven up the dullest subject. Make sure there's plenty of 'air' throughout, otherwise your reader will soon lose interest and move on to something else.

Edit as you write

Think of the reader as you type your copy. If you see the same word or phrase in close proximity, find a different word or expression that means the same thing. Ensure your grammar is spot on, for instance that verb agrees with subject, and spelling is correct. Most computer software now provides automatic spelling and grammar checks: if there's something amiss in the spelling there's usually a line of red dots underneath the word.

The golden rule for all bloggers: cut, cut and cut again to ensure snappy, lively copy. Online readers have a much shorter attention span than print readers – just a few seconds per page in some cases. If it's dull and stodgy you might as well forget it.

And finally...

Say who you are, and what you do. Journalists keep a close watch on blogs for news and features, so ensure your press and broadcasting contacts know about your blog output. Post blogs regularly. Unless there are new posts at least once or twice a week, you may be forgotten. And that is the last thing you want.

Now get started

You write a profile of yourself, provide a head and shoulders picture, upload your CV, send out invitations to connect with you or your firm, join relevant specialist groups. Use the search engine tool to find people you know or those who might be of help to you or your employer. You don't have to be at your desk to use it.

Social media tools are fully mobile: use them on the move with a BlackBerry, iPhone or Android. Smartphones have apps for LinkedIn as well as for Twitter, Facebook and blogs. So, wherever your work takes you, with your mobile and LinkedIn you can keep up with your contacts and your audience, post updates and find out about relevant news items.

LinkedIn is the business

This is the social networking site for business across the board. For us that means PR professionals, consultancies, journalists, news outlets, media companies, print and video production companies – the complete mix. The so-called 'Facebook for suits' has over 120 million users worldwide, more than six million in the United Kingdom alone. The emphasis is very much on networking rather than being a social media platform for chatting and gossiping.

On this site you make connections with people with whom you might want to do business, or to provide leads to business opportunities. You invite them to connect with you and then you link into their network of friends and contacts. In this way you can get help for a business start-up, career advancement, seek advice on dealing with problems such as HR questions and finance. LinkedIn could enable you to get a better job. Since LinkdIn has more than two million company pages, few executives with an eye on their future can afford to ignore it. It is becoming an essential tool for the recruitment agencies. Last year there were nearly two billion people searches on LinkedIn.

Footnotes

David Phillips, co-author of *Online Public Relations*, another title in the PR in Practice series, says that this year is the time when using online content has become a must. Bridge Farm, in *The Archers* Radio Four soap, offers a fictional but a perfect example of this shift to a need for Online Reputation Management **http://bbc.in/nqyN4o** and an agency view: **http://bit.ly/p6XAIM**.

'The whole idea of using social media is now a mainstream act of marketing and PR faith', says Philips. 'The big difference is that PR people are now expected to communicate directly with the public and, in order to be understood or accepted, in their language (my test for students is to explain what Twitter is in the style of Enid Blyton)'.

'However, in my view, this does not mean the practitioner has to abandon good English. Sentences still need a subject!'

Philips's co-author, Philip Young, considers that it is important to appreciate that social media/digital communication is having a 'profound impact' on the creation of narrative. 'People are drawing on information from many different sources, almost simultaneously, and it is highly unlikely that this will reflect a "conventional", sequenced transmission. At the very least, this suggests it is beneficial to make communications self-contained, but it invites a more sophisticated view of storytelling'.

It is important to know who you are talking to is online, far more so than in traditional media. Digital communication channels are inherently porous. This means communicators need to be cautious in message content, for instance something you say in private may be read worldwide.

Careless conversation can become a public relations nightmare. Grammar and punctuation matter greatly online: even if the original recipient of a sloppy message is forgiving, those further down the line have no need to be and this can impact on organisational reputation. So be warned.

FIGURE 10.1 Significant page from the *Insider White Paper* discusses social media targeting through the new Google+ platform. Published by Mediacom, part of the WPP advertising and marketing group

WHY SOCIAL MEDIA MATTERS (CONTINUED)

Social media targeting
The new Google+ platform illustrates the power of the data that lies behind social media. In just three weeks it has attracted an estimated 19 million global users and includes a host of innovative features.

These include: Sparks, which lets you specify the content you like, such as cars, and create a bespoke news feed; Hangouts, which enables group video chat; and Circles, a feature that lets you define different groups of friends who are generating comments.

By combining the social power of the connection with the data provided by Gmail registration, Adword targeting and knowledge of search keywords, brands can find out more about their customers than ever before.

Imagine a consumer searching for products and retailers on Google Maps and getting results that show them recommendations from their network of friends about what to buy, where to shop and, more crucially, where to avoid.

Paid for messages from recommended retailers might prove highly powerful. Imagine consumers searching for a restaurant on their mobile and the results showing redeemable vouchers that match their taste preferences, serviced by recommended outlets nearby.

Brands are already establishing themselves on Google+ - Ford has a page, for instance - but the real potential is in the power of the data fusion mentioned above. It's the opportunity for advertisers to use the power of Google's reach and targeting in a new, richer, more personal way.

Of course, everything hinges on Google+ reaching the kind of penetration/usage its more established brethren currently enjoy. ■

The new Google+ platform illustrates the power of the data that lies behind social media. In just three weeks it has attracted an estimated 19 million users.

THE INSIDER WHITEPAPER BROUGHT TO YOU BY **MEDIACOM** JULY 2011 8

Author's note

The social media scene changes by the day if not the hour. What is relevant today, may well be outdated when you read this chapter. For the latest updates and trends, a thorough Google search is essential. Members of the Chartered Institute of Public Relations should go to the CIPR website (**www.cipr.co.uk**) and log on to the social media page for any help they may need.

Facebook and Twitter are 'social networking' sites. The content on them is classed as 'social media'. There is a massive difference between the two.

At a glance

- Social media platforms and new technologies have transformed communications strategies. Now seen as a mainstream act of marketing and PR faith.

- News desks worldwide rely on tweets for breaking news.

- Twitter does not replace traditional newsfeeds: tweets provide a broad brush approach to news gathering for instant transmission.

- With links to websites tweets provide a mobile media centre for firms and consultancies.

- Tweets can be shortened to reduce character count.

- Most PRs set up lists of journalists in specialist groupings.

- Software is available for reducing length of website addresses – a unique code of characters and numerals.

- Facebook members share some 30 billion items of content – websites, news stories, blog posts – each month.

- Messages must be clear and concise with no wasted words. Put a snappy headline or question to attract attention. Content is king.

- Don't forget to include illustrations; use colour liberally.

- Blog format is usually single column with sidebars for photographs, FAQs and links to websites. Choose a 'readable' font in at least 12 point size.

- Consider your audience before anything else. Find out who your website visitors are, Facebook and Twitter users.

- Write short sentences, insert cross-heads, enliven text with boxes highlighting specific points.

- LinkedIn is a useful social networking site for making business contacts – practitioners, consultancies, journalists, news outlets, print and video companies. It might enable you to get a better job.

11
Writing for the media

There are special requirements for preparing written material for publication in newspapers, consumer magazines and trade journals, and also for broadcast in news outlets. The news release – whether emailed, faxed or on a website or blog – is still the basic form of communication between an organisation and its audience, and there are various rules and conventions that should be followed to ensure the material gets published and does not end up in the bin. In this chapter I uncover important points concerning the writing and issuing of news releases, and then turn to commissioned articles.

News releases: basic requirements

When you send out a release you want it to be published. National and regional newspapers, consumer magazines and trade journals receive hundreds or perhaps thousands of news stories every day all vying with press releases for every inch of space. Virtually all releases are emailed these days by companies and organisations or through consultancies and online press centres. Each release must catch the eye, be instantly interesting and newsworthy at first scan of the screen, otherwise it is a no-hoper.

Broadcasting media – BBC, ITV and other commercial television programmes and the many national and local radio stations – also have huge demands on their airtimes for news items and, like the press, need information presented in a succinct way.

What the press don't want

The release that is wrongly targeted or lacks news value is worse than useless. If you issue a release for a new kind of shelving or for a breakfast beverage to a national daily, there is no chance that either will be used: you have

FIGURE 11.1 Part of online BBC Media Centre page. Gives full information for journalists searching for BBC news stories. Releases are available in nearly 40 subject categories

wasted time and money. The only hope for the shelving story is a paragraph in a DIY magazine; for the drink, a paragraph in a catering paper. And even that's doubtful if there are similar products on the market.

Peter Bartram, author and journalist, says that most of the releases he receives are not relevant to the subjects he writes about. A survey among 89 editors and senior journalists from consumer and business magazines as well as national and regional newspapers identified the top three problems: 81 per cent of respondents said that 'too many' were irrelevant to their publication, 79 per cent said too many did not contain a useful news story and 76 per cent found too much self-promotion and 'puffery' in releases.

Targeting and news value are critical factors. So is timing. Popular nationals will look for a 'human' storyline with the accent on people rather than things. Broadsheets need items that stretch the intellect, specialist papers the subjects they normally cover. Anything else will be binned. Journalists receive hundreds, possibly thousands, of releases daily but few will be printed. Even those getting as far as the news desk will be rewritten or used as background material.

Never telephone or email editors or their staff to find out if they are going to use your story. Even worse would be to ask why not. Did they want more information? Asking that tops the horrors. If journalists want to follow up a story, they won't be long contacting you. That's the time to start adding to the facts you have given, or suggesting someone to interview.

Your news will be in competition with information from many other sources, not least stories coming in from staff journalists, freelances and news agencies. The essential points are that releases must be worthy of publication and able to attract the journalist's attention. Here are the main points to watch.

Headings

The release should be clearly identifiable as a communication for publication or broadcast, and should carry a heading such as 'News Release', 'Press Release', 'Press Notice', 'Press Information', 'Information from XYZ' or just 'News from XYZ'. If sent out by a consultancy, it must be made clear that it is issued on behalf of the client company or organisation.

Such headings should be in bold capitals or upper and lower case of at least 14pt so as to stand out from the mass of other material on subeditors' desks and computer screens. Show the heading in the corporate colour, typeface and style of the issuing organisation.

Essential information

Put the full name and address of the issuing organisation, with telephone, fax numbers and email/website address in a prominent position. Type the date of issue. Give a contact name for further information, together with his/her contact details if different from the main switchboard numbers. Be sure to include the contact's email address.

Always include an out-of-hours telephone number since many journalists are still working when you have left the office. It is not necessarily good PR for the managing director or chairman to get your calls when you should be talking to the media in the first place!

Titles

The title of the release should be in bold but not underlined. (Don't write a too-clever-by-half or facetious heading – it won't work.) It should say in as few words as possible what the release is about, and should not, if possible, run to more than one line. Use a present tense verb. If secondary subheadings or side-heads are needed, then these should be in upper and lower case, preferably in bold face.

Content

Be brief and factual and keep sentences short. Two sentences per paragraph are about right, and often just one sentence will be enough to get a point over. The opening paragraph should contain the essence of the story and display the news. Here you must answer who?/when?/where? questions in the same way that a reporter is required to do. For example, if a company chairman has made a statement, give his name and position, the date (if you say 'today' put the date in brackets afterwards so there can be no mistake), where the statement was made, and, if at a hotel, name it.

A trick here is to put the last two details in a second paragraph saying Mr So and So was speaking on (date) and (where) to save cluttering up the opening paragraph with detail that might easily obscure the point of the story. Never write 'recently', always say when.

Following paragraphs should expand on the story. Try not to let the copy run over to a second page. It will make the subeditor's job much easier if you start with the main point, fill in the detail in the succeeding paragraphs and end with the least important point. Your news release can then be edited down with far less trouble.

FIGURE 11.2 BBC press release. Related links enable journalists to check for further details on the Children in Need appeal

FIGURE 11.3 While this is a well-structured release, journalists would expect 'announces' in the opening paragraph. Use present tense whenever possible. Full contact details are on the RCGP news page

RCGP announces changes to the Specialty Training Curriculum

25/11/11

The Royal College of General Practitioners (RCGP) has announced changes to the GP training curriculum to make it more user-friendly and easier to navigate.

The changes will apply to trainees beginning their training programme in August 2012 and are part of the College's ongoing response to feedback gathered from trainees, trainers and the wider training community.

Largely presentational, the majority of changes are structural and linguistic to make the curriculum easier to understand. Individual curriculum statements are more focused and more clearly linked to the core curriculum statement Being a GP.

Revisions beyond the normal annual update are minimal and learning outcomes will not change significantly, though they may be expressed differently to make their meaning clearer or to bring them up-to-date with latest thinking and learning.

A new user guide and glossary has also been posted on the RCGP website at http://www.rcgp-curriculum.org.uk/curriculum_documents/future_changes.aspx

> The main differences are: The curriculum has been arranged into three parts: The Core Curriculum (Being a GP); four contextual statements (exploring the core statement in the context of general practice) and 21 clinical examples of how to work with the Core Curriculum.

> The current 10 statements labelled 2 to 4.1 have been reorganised into the four contextual statements, which are now: The GP consultation in practice, Patient safety and quality of care, The GP in the wider professional environment and Enhancing professional knowledge. This allows the NHS Leadership Framework and the importance of sustainability in general practice to be integrated. Statement 4.2 (Information management and technology) has been integrated into all of the new contextual statements.

> Language has been changed from the passive to the active tense to better engage the reader. The use of educational terminology has been simplified and clarified. Case studies and questions for reflection have been added to the statements. Better cross-referencing and linking to the core statement.

The curriculum is the first of its kind for general practice in the UK and was introduced in August 2007. It defines the learning outcomes for the specialty of general practice and describes the competences required to practise medicine as a general practitioner in the UK NHS. Primarily aimed at the start of independent work as a general practitioner, it must also prepare the doctor for a professional life of development and change.

FIGURE 11.3 *continued*

The College has been reviewing the usage and impact of the Curriculum, both formally and informally, since its introduction. In addition to the direct feedback received, the College commissioned the University of Birmingham to conduct a three year evaluation of the curriculum and its impact on training. Please contact the RCGP Press Office for a copy of the report.

Dr Charlotte Tulinius, RCGP Medical Director of Curriculum, said: "It's really important to have ongoing feedback so that the Curriculum remains contemporaneous, fit for purpose, relevant to the trainee and relevant to patients.

"The response so far has been very positive and most people acknowledge that it is important to have a curriculum so that the skills, knowledge, attributes and behaviour required by a GP are clearly defined."

"However, some trainers and trainees have told us that it could be more user friendly and that its structure and how it should be used could be more clear. We hope that the revised version addresses this and that all users will find it beneficial."

Ends

Write in a factual style without flowery adjectives and superlatives or emotive words when you are describing products and services (*exciting* development). To repeat the point, don't put *recently* in a release if you can't be precise: say *last week/month* with the date in brackets. Avoid clichés, jargon words and comments as expressions of opinion. If you wish to make a comment about something, put it as a quote from someone in the organisation. Just stick to the facts and let them stand on their own without embellishment. It will be up to the journalist to put his or her interpretation on the story you are issuing.

If there is a lot of technical data to be included put this as an attachment. Similarly, you can attach a verbatim speech, providing reference to it is made in the covering release.

Layout and style for the posted release

While most releases are emailed nowadays, there are still some that are sent by post. In that case, the copy should be typed double-spaced so as to give the subeditor plenty of space to make changes.

Put at least a couple of lines between the heading and the first paragraph. Put extra space between paragraphs.

Do not underline any of the copy. This is the universal mark for copy to be set in italics. Do not set any of the text in italics or bold in the forlorn hope that it will be seen as more important. If a title of a book, film or article is used within the text, put it in single quotes.

FIGURE 11.4   Well-written news release from the AA, the advertising industry trade body. Note short paragraphs, crisp quote, concise notes to editors

PRESS RELEASE

AA signs up to Public Health deal

15 March 2011: The Advertising Association (AA) has signed up to Department of Health's Responsibility Deal, with a specific focus on the food, physical activity and responsible drinking pledges.

The Responsibility Deal seeks to tackle public health issues through partnership between government, health professionals and industry. The AA has worked with the Portman Group, advertisers, media owners and agencies to pledge further action on alcohol advertising, including an industry commitment to avoid advertising of alcohol on static poster sites within 100 metres of schools.

The AA also hosts business4life - a coalition of organisations that support the government's Change4Life programme by playing an active role in improving the nation's lifestyle through better diet and physical activity.

AA Chief Executive Tim Lefroy said:

"This is a government that thinks we will get further, faster by working together rather than imposing the heavy hand of regulation. We agree, which is why we have signed the deal and will be supporting its delivery through our members and our networks."

- ends -

For more information please contact Ian Barber: 020 7 340 1107 / 07828 656298

Notes to editors

The Advertising Association is the only body representing all sides of the advertising and promotional marketing industries. Its membership represents advertisers, agencies, media and support services in the UK. The advertising industry employs nearly 250,000 people, and has a Gross Valued Added (GVA) of £6.2bn to the UK economy each year. Further information about the organisation is available at: www.adassoc.org.uk

Type on one side of the paper (white, A4) and if there is a continuation sheet, type 'More' at the foot of the page. Do not break a paragraph at the end of a page; if necessary take the whole paragraph over to the second page rather than leave a few words dangling (as a 'widow', printers would say) at the top of the second page.

Leave a decent margin on each side, about 30mm ($1^1/4$ inch). Do not try to achieve justified type where both sides are aligned. It is a waste of time.

Use double quotes for direct quotations (the actual words spoken); this is standard newspaper style. For reported speech follow the style in *The Times*: [name] *admitted* yesterday... he *suggested* there *were* some signs...

At the close of the copy, type END or ENDS in capitals. If there are special points to be made for the attention of the editor, such as explanations of technical terms or how to obtain follow-up information, put these against a side-heading 'Note to Editor'. If possible, give a word count. This is usually easy to ascertain with reference to the spellcheck facility provided by most software packages. The subeditor can then easily calculate the amount of space the copy will occupy when it is typeset.

Press releases – the essentials

There is little difference between an emailed press release and a posted one. Almost all are emailed nowadays. The same principles apply: keep them short, snappy and simple. Mike Atchinson, a partner in media consultancy Clark Brown Associates, says few nationals and particularly broadcasters see posted press releases as anything but 'quaint, begging the question, if it's so ****ing urgent why are they sending it by snail mail?'

Atchinson, who was formerly night foreign editor of the *Daily Mail* after working on the *Sun*, *News of the World* and *Daily Express*, says the release first goes to the copy taster on the relevant desk: news, features, consumer, city, sport or women's. They will look for one thing: reader interest. Perhaps the story will contain a line in it that sparks special interest and that will be enough to take the story forward. They have little or no interest in the technical side: they leave that to the subs who will later 'knock it into house style'.

Copy tasters have a low boredom level. Get the news angle, the point of the story, in the first couple of paragraphs. If you don't it's a no-hoper. 'If you cannot rattle out the story quickly, they won't wait for your bombshell ending,' he says. 'Keep to bite-size parcels of information and use familiar fonts like Times and Helvetica as most people are comfortable with them.' But as Michael Watts says later in this chapter, if you go down the brazen route with fancy typefaces and gaudy colours, your carefully-crafted release will look like spam and be deleted without a second thought.

FIGURE 11.5 Judi Goodwin, approved CIPR trainer on press releases, picks this release as a 'good' example

Date: 4 April 2011

Brooklands looking for the "corner shopkeeper of the future"

The developers behind two and a half thousand homes in Milton Keynes are looking to the past to create something new and exciting for the future.

Places for People have plans for a village shop at Brooklands on the East of the city and they are looking for a local entrepreneur to take it on and make it a centrepiece of the new community.

"We want it to be a real village shop at the very heart of the community," says Project Director, Simon Elcock. "Our vision for the store is that it should draw everyone together and be a place where people meet their new neighbours and form the kind of friendships which knit villages together."

Mr Elcock is so keen to get the right person in place that he is offering a remarkable deal to whoever takes it on. "We want to make it possible for someone to come in who has not necessarily got huge funds at their disposal but *has* got great ideas and drive. The right candidate could have a profit share rental arrangement and hopefully that would be a great incentive for them to really get the shop buzzing."

It is hoped the shop will sell all the traditional things one would expect like milk and news-papers but will also specialise in stocking high quality, locally-grown produce. There may even be scope for including a coffee area within the store.

"We've already worked so hard to make Brooklands a wonderful place to live and unusually for a development of this kind, we've already put in the parks and playgrounds and planted many acres of trees."

Budding shopkeepers who think they might be up to the challenge of Brooklands new village store should contact Anna Dodson by email at Anna.Dodson@placesforpeople.co.uk, or by telephone on 01908 608476.

ENDS

For further information please contact: Carolyn Jardine, Jardine Michelson Public Relations Tel: 0845 1651651/07734 837912

About Places for People:

- Places for People is one of the largest property management, development, and regeneration companies in the UK. It is made up of 14 businesses focused on providing all the facilities and services a community needs to thrive.

- The Group builds and manages homes, provides job and training opportunities, runs affordable childcare centres, supports new and existing businesses, offers financial products such as mortgages and loans, and specialist care and support services that enable people to live independently in their own home.

- It works in over 230 local authorities across the UK, with a portfolio of over 63,000 properties working with 200,000 customers.

FIGURE 11.6 Judi's comments on the Places for People release

Judi Goodwin comments:

A good example of a concisely written press release that has a story of real benefit to the community. The first quote from the project director is relevant, heart warming and it sounds like real speech. Journalists can often spot the quotes written by PR people and usually find them predictable, repetitive and uninspired. The release received almost word for word coverage in the local paper, the *Milton Keynes News* but the reporter re-wrote the intro like this.

"A developer is looking for a traditional shopkeeper to help build a new community." Which is an improvement as it gets to the point faster.

The second quote was dropped from the published version, possibly because it smacks a little of "blowing our own trumpet".

FIGURE 11.7 Judi Goodwin's top ten tips for writing a winning press release

Judi Goodwin's Top Ten Tips

1   Don't try to be too clever in the intro. Just sum up the story in a nutshell.

2   Write like a journalist, not a PR person. Write in the style of the publication/s you are targeting.

3   Lead with the news and how it will benefit the readers – not "ABC have discovered a cure for the common cold." But "A cure for the common cold has been discovered by ABC Pharmaceuticals."

4   Avoid advertising jargon like 'fabulous', 'fantastic' or 'amazing' – these words are part of the copywriter's toolkit and don't belong in a press release.

5   Don't put basic facts in quotes. Tell your facts in the text and use quotes to give insight, opinions, revelations or predictions, or something that will inspire and enlighten the readers.

6   Quotes should sound like real speech and should not repeat anything already stated.

7   Make sure your email subject line tells the journalist what the story is about.

8   Keep to a minimum any mentions of the name of your organisation. The sub-editors will probably edit them out anyway.

9   Use bullet points where appropriate to convey essential information concisely.

10 Dig deeper. Talk to the people involved. Probe for quirky angles, surprising outcomes or any anecdotes that would strengthen your story.

If you have pictures, send them separately to the picture desk: copy-takers will tend to ignore them as they will think it is nothing to do with them. If there is sufficient interest in the story, then they will come back to you to ask for an illustration. And of course it will give you a valid reason for calling the publication to tell them that illustrations are available if needed. If you have an attachment, check with the relevant desk for advice on formatting. It helps if you put it in the bulk of the email rather than an attachment that may cause problems and delay in opening it.

FIGURE 11.8 Tightly written release drawn from Ofcom for Media and Analysts

Ofcom

Search...

Independent regulator and competition authority
for the UK communications industries.

| News Releases | Analyst relations ▾ | Speeches & Presentations | Facts & figures | Images |

Home / News

The state of the communications nation
November 1, 2011

New report reveals communications coverage and capacity in the UK

Ofcom today launched digital communications coverage maps, including outdoor mobile coverage and mobile broadband availability, using data supplied by communications providers.

The maps, available at http://maps.ofcom.org.uk, are part of Ofcom's first report on the UK's communications infrastructure which it is now required to submit to the Secretary of State for Culture, Media and Sport every three years. Ofcom's report also refers to the coverage and capacity of the UK's landline network, digital radio and TV.

Each of the 200 areas of the UK has been ranked according to a score given for coverage and colour coded with green ranking highest and red lowest.

Ofcom's data shows considerably better household coverage compared with geographic coverage. This is because mobile providers tend to prioritise investment in network infrastructure where the maximum number of consumers and businesses can be served.

The maps show that 97% of premises and 66% of the UK landmass can receive a 2G signal outdoors from all four 2G networks. This means that approximately 900,000 UK premises do not have a choice of all four 2G mobile networks.

For 3G, 73% of premises and 13% of the UK's landmass can receive a signal outdoors from all five 3G networks, with lower coverage in less densely populated areas. This means that approximately 7.7million UK premises do not have a choice of all five 3G mobile networks.

The areas of lowest 3G geographic coverage are in the highlands of Scotland and mid-Wales which are both sparsely populated with hilly terrain.

Ofcom is currently working closely with the Government to consider how the £150m that it has allocated to help address mobile not-spots, can deliver the greatest benefits for UK consumers. Working to address mobile not-spots is one of Ofcom's priorities as set out in its 2011/12 annual plan.

You must also put it on your website with a link to the media or information page. Your press release archive must be updated daily. Atchinson again: 'Until the media know all about you and your organisation, and use you regularly, always tip them off that you have an archive.'

Says Chris Wheal in *The Journalist*, the NUJ magazine: 'If you want a story found by search engines and selected by the searcher, the first line must include key words and phrases and no unnecessary words. At the BBC where the web and Ceefax are one service, the rules are strict: one sentence per par, minimum two lines but no more than four, headlines in 31–33 characters and so on. All sites need their own such rules.'

Production points. Avoid different type sizes and colours, no indents to paragraphs and set your copy ragged right. If you try to justify the type-matter with both sides aligned, you will have trouble with hyphenations that go wrong or, worse still, unsightly gaps in the text. There's no need to double-space: on-screen editing makes it easy for the subs to sub. At the click of the mouse, there's the copy for editing.

Confirming Atchinson's point, typographers and designers say you should keep to a sans serif face to help readability and therefore aid communication. These things can of course be corrected and changed by the operator, but in the rush of getting the release out, such finer details can be overlooked.

The emailed release will give you the opportunity to use corporate colours and typestyles, but avoid lengthy runs of reversed-out copy and pale colours on a white background which look even more dreadful on a press release than they do in print. It is less than useless to go in for typographical tricks like these.

Embargoes

Journalists dislike embargoes – which is a request to withhold publication until a specific time and date. Avoid them if possible, as they are not binding on the media and are there to give the journalist time for research or follow-up before a speech, or in advance of an announcement by a company or organisation. If you decide to issue a release under embargo, make this clear above the title of the release. A suitable form of words would be:

> **EMBARGO**: NOT FOR PUBLICATION, BROADCAST, OR ON ANY MEDIA OR ELECTRONIC COMMUNICATION BEFORE (TIME) ON (DATE).

Alternatively the embargo notice could simply state, 'Not for use before 00.00 hours (date)'. The wording of embargoes for releases giving advance information on winners of awards requires care to ensure that details do not leak out in advance of the presentation event.

A simplified embargo notice with just the time and date can also be used provided the restriction is absolutely clear and unambiguous.

FIGURE 11.9 Ofcom online media centre directs journalists to information sources and contact details for follow-ups

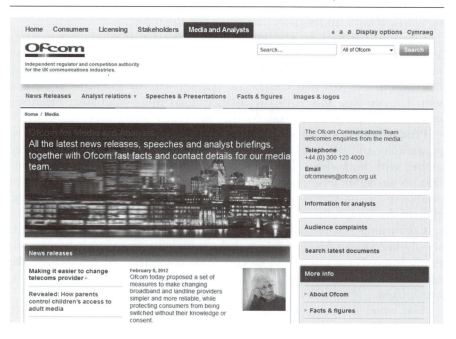

Issuing the release

Most releases are on company websites or as links on media centres. Others are emailed or are on social media platforms. Only a very few go by post these days: if you do send one out by 'snail mail' ensure it goes by first-class post and reaches the chosen news desk(s) the next day.

Since journalists have to sift through hundreds if not thousands of releases daily, yours must stand out as a good story both in content and visually. Make sure the subject is clear and concise, one that says in a nutshell what the story is about. If you do this, the search engine will alert the journalist for instant follow-up.

A telephone call to the news desk saying a release is on its way to their screens might help, but only if they know you. See Chapter 19 on websites for more help.

Is it news?

There is no point in sending out a news release if it is not news. You will only annoy the journalist if you do and your hard work will be wasted. So has your release got news value? The short answer is: does the news editor think it will interest the reader? News is something not known before.

To quote Pat Bowman, former head of public relations for Lloyds Bank:

> News value is relative; minor stories make news on a slow day. Only big news counts on a busy day. A boring product story may be valuable news to a trade paper, but no publication with a general readership would look at it. How it is written will make all the difference in perception of a story: if it is written in a lively, interesting way it is more likely to be seen as important; if it is expressed in a boring fashion, using tedious, hard-to-grasp, waffly words and phrases then it will be considered dull. Then the only future for it is the waste bin.

Tabloids, says Bowman, are likely to be influenced by the entertainment and novelty value of a story, while the quality press will be more interested in stories that are stimulating, topical and relevant in today's society. Immediacy can also have an effect: it can outweigh importance in the assessment of news value, particularly for TV and radio. 'Don't try to bamboozle journalists into thinking that the story you are putting out is a good one when there is nothing new in it at all,' says Bowman. It could be an utter waste of time.

Robert Hornby's *The Press in Modern Society* gives penetrating thoughts on news and news value. To summarise Hornby: what may appear as news in a provincial newspaper holding a dominant position in a city will bear little relationship in presentation to the same news splashed across the front page of a national daily. It is like comparing a seaside revue with a West End musical. So what are the basic elements of a news story? First, it must be something new. Other factors can be grouped under three headings – importance, human interest and topicality.

Importance can mean a well-known person connected with the story, perhaps a politician or public figure, especially if they have been in the news before.

Human interest is exemplified by something that is interesting to the many rather than the few. Anything pathetic, or that causes indignation, and the topics of prices, crime or abuse of privilege gets read. Other people's big financial gains, rags-to-riches stories, romances, children, animal welfare, good/bad luck items, the unexpected, the surprising and the unusual always attract attention. Most people prefer reading about people to things: many column inches of publicity can easily be lost if releases ignore the human angle.

Journalists' requirements are changing in line with the instant delivery of news on television, radio and on social media networks, particularly Twitter. In consequence, newspapers are increasingly filling their pages with background stories and feature articles on such subjects as lifestyles, health, entertainment, sport, home and garden. These subjects are all fertile ground for human interest stories.

Topicality means facts about a subject of intense current interest, with excitement, danger and rapid movement (like chases and police hunts); well-known faces must be photographed in easily recognised places and backgrounds to provide maximum impact and make for easy recognition.

A great deal of the trivial derives its news value from such topicality, especially in the popular press.

Study newspaper style

Look at newspapers to see how journalists write: whether broadsheet or tabloid, extremes of style determine the way different newspapers approach a given story. The former will probably give far more detail, while the latter will tend to oversimplify, leaving little room for intelligent interpretation.

Write to catch the eye of the reader in the same way as the journalist does. One thing is certain: a 'new' story or one that has not been published before has got news value; and if it is exclusive it will have an even better chance of publication.

No puffs please

Releases must not become blatant advertising messages on behalf of the client company or other organisations. If you put out an advertisement under the guise of a news story it is sure to put the editor off and ruin your reputation as a public relations professional into the bargain.

These so-called 'puffs', which attempt to gain editorial space, should properly be paid-up advertisements. But a new product or service can of course be a news story for release to the specialist press covering the industry sector you are covering.

Releases to the specialist press

If you write a release containing technical matter there is no profit in using jargon meaningless to the average reader, or writing in a highbrow way to woo white-coated boffins.

Where releases to the national media are on scientific or financial subjects, write in simple, concise language that will be understood by a lay audience. The only place for the technicalities and jargon of the industry or business is the trade press. Few technical journalists are specialists and fully trained in the technologies they write about. If you provide copy that needs little editing your release is far less likely to be changed than if you give them gobbledygook, however well intentioned that may be.

What journalists want: a specialist view

Diana Thompson, managing director of PlusPoint PR, a specialist consultancy for the graphic arts industry, constantly monitors the needs of editors

FIGURE 11.10 Short sentences and paragraphs feature in this specialist release. Where's the job title of quote author?

HEIDELBERG

Press Information

www.journalist.heidelberg.com

Heidelberg Graphic
Equipment Limited
69-76 High Street
Brentford Middlesex
TW8 0AA

Graphico selects Polar to replace Wohlenberg machine

Riots in Croydon left Graphico unscathed but delivery of its Polar 115 X Plus guillotine had to be delayed a week.

Set back behind the London Road and just opposite the much-publicised shop where the lady leapt to safety, Graphico saw neighbouring businesses burnt and vandalised.

"The London Road was closed for four days as fires were still simmering but we were alright and we did get our Polar in when the road re-opened," says Shaukat Dungarwalla.

It is the company's first Polar guillotine and replaces a 17 year old Wohlenberg. Graphico has always had Heidelberg presses and two years ago added a Suprasetter 74 Computer to Plate device. Confidence in the service support that Heidelberg provides was a key element in the company's decision to change guillotine supplier.

The company shopped around for a machine. It liked the Polar technology, the robustness of the machine, its touchscreen and programmability but it was the peace of mind in knowing how and where to get speedy service back up that was convincing. Without a working guillotine work cannot be completed.

The Polar 115X Plus will operate a 12 hour day on national and international work, including contracts for many leading hotels, restaurants and banks. The business offers a concept to delivery service, including offset and digital printing, and it has extensive print and storage logistics to enable users to call off products as needed.

14 September 2011

and freelance journalists and has seen a rapid and complete move from post and faxed copy and photos to a reliance on email distribution. At exhibitions or for press conferences, hard copy plus a CD with digital stories, backgrounders and photographs work best.

Says Thompson: 'Everyone wants memory sticks or CDs with press packs or emailed news shots these days. These provide the opportunity for higher resolution images but for releases 300dpi and 1Mb as a Jpeg file is safe for transmission and an acceptable quality for most trade papers. Increasingly video footage is required as well as still images, a reflection of the great emphasis on multi-media publishing.' Never send a picture in a Word file, she advises, simply because they take a long time to download and are often unusable.

Some freelances and websites do not want photographs but in these cases she notifies the recipient that photos are available on request. Good illustration that is well captioned really can make the difference between being published or not, or the size of story that results.

It is crucial, she says, that public relations people send copy and pictures in a way that is acceptable and helpful to the journalists. The worst thing they can do is to send a press release and pictures in several versions by post, fax and email all at once. 'That just duplicates work and can even result in a story being written twice. Imagine the time and waste that involves.'

Only good stories will reach news desks

Most releases go by email or via websites to newspapers and broadcasting outlets these days. Only a very few are sent by post: gone are the spikes and dustcart-sized bins for dud copy. This means that copytasters are faced with a thousand or more stories on their screens every day: only the ones that are newsworthy, or have some human or perhaps financial angle, will be read and passed to the news desk. If it is about a specialist subject, then send it to the correspondent dealing with it, say the one covering financial, health or media stories.

Releases that come from news agencies such as the Press Association (020 7963 7000), Reuters (020 7369 7000) and Bloomberg UK (020 7330 7500) have a good chance as they will have already been sifted and sorted first by agency subs.

It is important that releases have short headlines giving the main point of the story, preferably in the present tense with no fancy typography or gimmicks in a vain attempt to attract attention. The originating firm or organisation should be clearly shown with embargo details (if needed) and background information and contact details. Even more important is for mailing lists to be kept up to date: it is next to useless sending a release to a named correspondent who left a year ago.

Freelance journalists, on the other hand, usually work on home computers and increasingly find their in-boxes clogged up with emailed press releases. Says freelance Michael Watts: 'For that reason, releases in the post can often, when appropriate, still have more impact.

'This is because they appear more of an "event", as it were. Indeed, the very ubiquity of emailed releases is increasing making their "success" more apparent than real. Sure, they go out OK but the more that arrive to clog up one's inbox, the less impact they have. Indeed, how many are even being *read* [his italics]?'

It is a waste of time to use unfamiliar typefaces and garish colours. Watts thinks gimmicks like these have 'a note of desperation' about them. The more straightforward, the more authoritative it is, the more like 'proper news' the release looks and the more likely to be used, he says.

Watts says all this is producing a 'grand paradox'. He points out that there are exceptions (for example when an instant announcement has to be put out immediately), but otherwise PR people just 'click the mouse and spew the stuff out everywhere'. And with no postage, it doesn't cost a bean, he adds. 'Trouble is that in this respect it becomes precisely like spam. And we all know what happens to spam.'

It is important to remember that if the story is a good one, it will have a chance of publication. And on a slow news day, it has an even better one.

Words and phrases journalists hate

Journalists' pet hates include enormity (doesn't mean huge), the chattering classes, ironically (unless in the proper sense), luvvies, crippled/disabled or any kind of disability, punter, legendary, luxury, fulsome, 'creeping' American-isms, blocks (verb), 'gender' words like career girl, signal or signalling (unless a transport story) and, needless to say, needless to say.

They also reject any needless or wasted word. Redundant words (in italics): appear *to be*, *brand* new, *close* proximity, crisis *situation*, *frown* on his face, few *in number*, include *among them*, merge/join *together*, *more* preferable/ superior, if and *when*, *invited* guest, *new* tradition, penetrate *into*, *on the question of*, *passing* phase. The reader will find plenty more in *Essential English for Journalists, Editors and Writers* (Pimlico Random House) by that master of style, Harold Evans.

Journalists are always on the lookout for clichés, flowery adjectives and overused expressions. If something can be said or written with fewer words or in a shorter way, they will cut without hesitation.

Don't forget the internet

Most large companies and organisations now make their press releases available on the internet, and they can be printed out if required. Leading organisations in the communications field, such as the Chartered Institute of Public Relations, the Institute of Practitioners in Advertising, the Advertising Association and the national media organisations all have internet sites

FIGURE 11.11 Short, snappy release on Press Complaints Commission news and features page. Link takes reader to full results

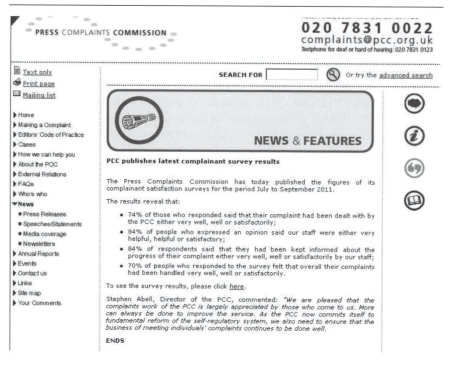

from which their press releases can be downloaded. Again, it is important that contact names and day/night telephone numbers are included, as well as background information.

If you are setting up an online media centre or want to provide a 24-hour service for journalists on the internet, ensure that access is simple and that contact details, including email addresses, are included. Allow for pictures and graphics to be downloaded, and update regularly.

Information on setting up and using an online media centre is later in this chapter. PR professionals – whether consultancy, client or in-house – should also consider providing a regular news feed on their respective websites.

A news feed lists current news items. Visitors to your site will be interested in anything relating to your product or service, especially up-to-date news. You can add the necessary code to your website that will update relevant news by the minute. Go to the Yahoo News Feed site: **http://news.yahoo.com/rss**. See also Chapter 19, Writing for the web.

News releases – for broadcast

Video news releases. On a slow day, airtime can take some filling, particularly for TV and radio stations transmitting 24-hour rolling news. Video news releases, or VNRs, may be the answer. Often dubbed 'fake news', they are meant to be indistinguishable from independently-produced news reports. This may be so, and have proved useful as a back-up for PR campaigns and background information for journalists. TV stations occasionally include parts of VNRs in their newscasts, but there is always the danger that they will be seen as 'puffery'. Consequently, no broadcaster would ever play one in full.

A VNR usually consists of a short tape or CD-ROM of a minute or two, ready for transmission, often with a second tape carrying interviews and background. It can also be uploaded to the station's website. Costs from a specialist VNR company vary: from £5,000 upwards for UK transmission depending on production time and method, besides extra cost for overseas distribution.

A word of warning: you may not get the results you expect or want. Unless the story is a heart-stopping one the VNR has little chance of success and money may be wasted. Question the specialist producing company carefully before signing up.

The B-roll – a better solution? Television networks want to put material from PR people in their own style. Cut it to bits if they want to. Otherwise it would be seen as free advertising and killed on the spot. The answer is the B-roll. For those outside the broadcasting loop that is meaningless jargon, but for TV producers and journalists it spells a taster of what might be possible when fully developed. Andrew Harvey, one of the first presenters for BBC TV news programmes, says they can be a 'big help' in today's high-pressure news reporting.

Let Keren Haynes, joint managing director of Shout! Communications, explain. The B-roll is 10–15 minutes of roughly edited footage, filmed on behalf of the client and distributed to broadcasters. 'Clients should give the station material they can't easily film for themselves and if it is a news story, it must be shot the way journalists would. That means straight-forward shots without slow documentary-style pans and no graphics.'

Costs. Shout! Communications would charge about £3,500 for a B-roll, based on a day's filming and a further day's editing. A UK satellite feed would start at a few hundred pounds, globally to 500 stations from £2,400. Hard copy goes by broadcast format tapes, normally DVCam. Find out more on their website (**www.shoutcommunications.co.uk**).

For a list of VNR and B-roll specialist companies, simply Google video news releases source.

Website press pages not full answer

According to studies by Benchmark Research reported in *PR Week*, 88 per cent of journalists writing about a company visit the firm's website for information. Just over half of them feel that enquires are better handled by websites than by traditional press offices.

While it is true that most websites provide immediate access to press releases and statements, it takes time and effort on the part of the public relations staff to post it on the site, and this may not be all that well executed if deadlines are tight.

Very often the needs of the journalist are not provided for, with the 'press room' page of websites being regarded by management as something of a poor relation, even though it is often believed by the PR department to be the be-all and end-all of its communications objectives. On the whole, the website press room will only be able to supply a 'scattergun' distribution, with no ability to target specific media and audiences, and with 74 per cent going straight to the screen wastebin.

The answer lies in the online newsroom such as that provided by Glide Technologies, a firm acquired by NASDAQ OMX Corporate Solutions in 2011. The service is a software tool used to build state-of-the-art newsrooms for a company's website. In short, this allows the PR department to publish press information such as releases, photographs, interviews and so on to the web quickly with minimal technical overheads.

Says Glide Technologies founder Sam Phillips: 'With this service, PR staff can build multimedia press communications giving them the opportunity to enhance their services with sound, video and photographs. Once published on the site, any release can be automatically distributed to a targeted press list to named journalists if required'.

Developing an online newsroom

New technology and the internet have transformed facilities for journalists and public relations practitioners alike. Online newsrooms make the work of the journalist easier and provide prime support vehicles for the PR operation of any company or organisation, small or large. It extends the facilities of the traditional press office by providing a round-the-clock service at a fraction of the cost, enabling instant access to journalists following up a story and providing automated functions, such as tailored news distribution, that increase efficiency.

FIGURE 11.12 Section of Comet media centre. Their press site gives latest news stories, image gallery and latest awards

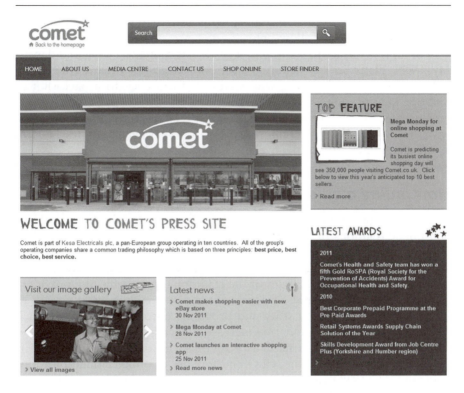

Furthermore, news published to the site primarily for the attention of journalists is now increasingly of interest to a wider audience looking for this information on the company's website. For example, investors will often be interested to know what campaigns a company is running and what their involvement is in local communities, or what they are doing to minimise their impact on the environment.

These are all the sorts of things that might be communicated through the PR team but investors want to know they are investing in a socially responsible company. Customers and even employees may also be just as interested in a company's PR output as members of the media.

An online newsroom allows the PR team to communicate these important corporate messages to audiences on which they are not directly focused or communicating with via email or phone.

More information is available from **sam.phillips@nasdaqomx.com**.

Research has shown that journalists are more likely to use a release with links to high resolution photography and other 'add-ons' such as diagrams and video clips. More than half of those questioned have used blogs for research, but a large majority question their credibility.

Poor contact information, news that was irrelevant, bad deadline timing and mailboxes clogged with large attachments were among the most irritating scenarios reported by the journalists. However, the internet is highly favoured as a research source, with more than half the respondents using it for checks and follow-ups.

'For a press release to stand out, it really has to make a song and dance,' says Will Hans-Bevan, deputy editor of Telegraph Create (the *Daily Telegraph's* advertorial unit), who states: 'If I can click to a pack-shot at 300 dpi, I am far more likely to use it.'

Journalists are deluged with emailed press releases from PR practitioners, with the majority receiving hundreds every day. They need to be 'media-rich' as the jargon goes, to stand any chance of being used.

How online media services help journalists

New technology and the internet have transformed facilities for journalists and public relations practitioners alike. The online media centre or online newsroom makes the work of the journalist easier and provides a prime support vehicle for the PR operation of any company or organisation, small or large. It extends the facilities of the traditional press office by providing a round-the-clock service at a fraction of the cost, enabling instant access to journalists following up a story and providing automated functions, such as tailored news distribution, that increase efficiency.

Full advice on what is needed to establish an online media service is provided by Pauline Christie, CEO and founder of online communications company ://CORPORACT. An online media centre must be well planned and structured at the outset. It is crucial that the centre is fresh and up to date, otherwise it will reflect poorly on the communications team and the company itself. Christie describes the purpose of Corporact as follows.

How an online media centre works

Help to establish an online media centre is provided by ://CORPORACT (**http://corporact.com**). Their software will streamline communications with the media, and bring with it the functions of a traditional press office such as news releases, images, document downloads, corporate information. It includes RSS feeds, blogs, video clips, podcasts, webcasts, search engine optimization tools, social media and interactivity.

The service provides an easy-to-use single, coordinated communications capability that can deliver timely, targeted news to diverse media audiences, with minimal disruption and duplication of task and process (and in more than one language if required). The content management system delivers web-based real-time editing and support for documents, images, movies and flash content.

In addition, search engine-friendly features such as textual URLs and advanced metadata management, Google Analytics and Google advertising can be included. These news environments have been designed with both journalists and businesses in mind. They are easily managed without the need of technical knowledge, allowing the user to take direct control of online communications requirements, saving time and money and providing journalists with the information they need.

Built as a customisable, modular component, an online media centre can be adjusted to meet the needs and budget of any company. It will integrate with existing website design, matching its look and feel, providing up-to-the minute news, information and tracking capability.

A guide and full advice on what is needed to establish an online media centre is available from ://CORPORACT. Contact: **http://corporact.com/contact** or go to **http://corporact.com/building-media-centre** for further information.

Media centre features – a summary

An online press office (or VPO) can provide these services:

Latest news – a list of news items, in a latest-news or news-archive format.

Image gallery – photos with galleries of images, grouped by topic, slideshows and images hosted on Flickr.

Informational pages – all the details a journalist will need to write about your company including history, facts, awards, corporate responsibility and people.

Media contacts – names, contact numbers and emails.

Events calendar – an events calendar can help you to connect with journalists.

'In the news' – a list of headline links to stories about your client's brand that have appeared in the media.

Social media content – displayed in the company press office.

Subscribe – allows journalists to access your updates, by email or RSS.

Videos/podcasts – embedded corporate videos or podcasts of keynote speeches, AGMs, or interviews with the media.

News feeds – industry or share price feeds and third party news services.

News ticker – for displaying scrolling news on your website.

Scheduled publishing – schedule or synchronise the publishing of any type of content at a time in the future.

The essential services such a centre must provide are the ability to access current and archive press releases, include facts and figures on the company together with background information, a facility to download documents and print-ready images (usually in JPEG format) and the provision of sound and video broadcasts.

It is important that the media centre can be updated by the public relations staff without relying on an IT specialist to do it for them. It must be easily accessible from the organisation's website at the click of a mouse.

Media centre for royal wedding at Foreign Press Association

The wedding of Prince William and Kate Middleton, who subsequently became the Duke and Duchess of Cambridge, attracted media attention across scores of countries. At the London offices of the Foreign Press Association a fully-equipped media centre was set up for the day in what is usually the restaurant of the Royal Commonwealth Society, the current location for the FPA. More than 150 overseas TV and press journalists used the extensive facilities provided. All were FPA members, some of whom had joined the association simply in order to be there on the day. There was no charge for any of the journalists apart from the annual membership fee.

There was wifi throughout (specially boosted for the day), four ISDN lines for radio broadcasters, live feeds of BBC coverage on multiple plasma screens on the walls. In attendance were two representatives from the Clarence House press office and one from the Ministry of Defence. They attended not specifically for interview but to supply information – such as about the uniforms worn, details of the bride's dress and background facts and figures about the royal family.

The Queen's former press secretary, Charles Anson, was there all morning. Peter Tatchell, a leading Republican, appeared twice. Both were extensively interviewed. Officials from Visit Britain attended as well as celebrity wedding planners and cake makers who came in and out throughout the day, answering a myriad of questions.

A significant feature of the media centre was that the FPA received no funding whatever for the operation, not from Government, Clarence House or anywhere else. Says Christopher Wyld, director of the FPA: 'In short, it was a huge success'.

A general email address without contact names and telephone numbers is not good enough, says Christie. It is also not generally a good idea to force journalists to register before allowing access to the centre.

Releases for radio transmission

Radio is equally demanding, if not more so. It is better to email copy to radio stations rather than sending audio tapes, though if you have close personal contacts this helps to get your story on air. The specialist video news release company can also arrange for syndicated audio tapes to be distributed to national and regional radio stations.

Again, research your audience well and try to provide items that will fit timewise in your chosen slot. Don't send a 15-minute piece that would take up half the allotted time of a current affairs programme, or a news story of a minute for a slot of only a few seconds.

Commissioned articles

If you are asked to write an article by a newspaper or magazine, or if you put up an idea for a feature, the content and prime thrust of the piece should be discussed with the editor well in advance. The brief subsequently agreed must be scrupulously followed. If you diverge from it then it is likely that the editor will ask for amendments, some of which may be substantial. Worse than that, changes may be made that you know nothing about until the article is printed – and then it is too late.

Write in the style of the publication and keep to the number of words requested. Nothing is more annoying for an editor if the article is well over the length specified and won't fit into the space allotted for it. If that happens, then your copy will be cut, and that may defeat your objectives. Similarly, if you commission someone else in the organisation to write the article, then be sure that the brief is followed, even if you have to exert some persuasion.

Don't forget to include illustrations. Most editors will require photographs, drawings, graphs or tables to support the points you are making or just to catch the reader's eye. Give the piece a title and put the author's name – the by-line – underneath. Make sure the article has shape: a beginning, a middle and an end. And if you type the number of words at the end, the editor will be a friend for life. But above all, keep to the deadline.

News and feature articles – the contrasts

The main difference between a news story and a feature has to be immediacy, says Robert Harland, formerly head of Coca-Cola international public affairs. 'A hard news piece covers an event either happening now or that has just happened. One must make sure who, what, when, where, why and how are answered. Language is shorter and one has to get to the point very quickly – no flowery words or phrases. The essential facts must be clear and high in the story. Always grab the reader's attention with a strong lead'.

With features, he tells me, there's a chance for creative writing. 'Topics can come from anywhere; an overheard conversation, a snippet on the news, personal experiences from the editor. Features can cover any subject, but the writer must always aim to grab the reader's attention with a topic presented in a captivating way whether it be deadly serious, amusing or slightly off the wall'.

Harland considers it's usually that one has the luxury of more time than with hard news story – more time for research, getting quotes, checking facts and playing with the language. 'More time also gives the feature writer opportunities for anecdotal and descriptive writing and in many cases to personalize a story'.

Presentation is critical. It's no use running a juicy news story or feature if it is not noticed. Headings need to be strong, short and pithy, text must be readable in at least 12 point size, well spaced with a picture or two as well as boxes to highlight particular points. For details, go to Chapters 6 and 7.

At a glance

- Make sure releases are properly targeted.

- Give full contact details, and show the date of issue.

- Be brief, factual; type double-spaced.

- Embargoed releases: ensure clear publication restrictions.

- Is it news? If not, you've wasted your time.

- Don't try to turn a 'puff' into news.

- Write the way journalists do. Keep to the point.

- Follow newspaper style for snappy stories.

- Don't forget to send releases to news agencies.

- Put your releases on your company's website; ensure easy access.

- It's essential to keep mailing lists up to date.

- Most journalists trash wrongly targeted releases.

- Develop an online media centre.

- Agree the content of feature articles in advance; keep to the agreed wordage.

12
Captions: how to handle them

Always provide captions for any photographs or illustrations accompanying news releases and websites; these are used extensively in company annual reports and brochures. Care is essential in their preparation and handling: too often captions are left to the end, with the result that the caption lets down the illustration and the news story or article.

The important point about captions is that they lead the reader to the body copy. They provide an instant point of interest and will often turn a magazine 'page flipper' into a reader. Much thought should go into how a caption is written and presented, for if it misleads or contains errors, the communication can be irreparably spoilt.

Photo captions with releases

The caption to a photograph or illustration either accompanying a news release or sent separately as a caption story, is as important as the picture itself. If it fails to describe the person, product or service, all the effort and cost involved can be wasted. It can turn into a public relations disaster waiting to happen: once the photograph with its caption has left your hands there is little you can do to put matters right if you have misnamed someone or misspelt their name. If you are issuing a picture as an attachment to an emailed release, make it clear who or what the subject is.

Only when the picture is published do you realise that you have made a mistake – you go hot all over – but by then the damage is done. Although you may know who the people are in a picture, others may not, and will rely on you to tell them!

Caption content and style

Captions should be brief, certainly not exceeding 15 to 20 words, and reveal the content of the photo. Put a heading, typed double spaced, and give the name of the issuing organisation, company or consultancy with date, contact name, email and postal address and telephone/fax numbers. Refer to the source organisation, service or product.

If the photo shows a person or group of people, put job titles and names from left to right. When a well-known personality is featured, write the caption round the VIP, not someone else, even if you feel you ought to mention the chairman first. Photographic prints are expensive – it is much better to email the images.

Captions for the press

Most illustrations for press use go by email, media centres or via websites. The accompanying caption must explain in a few words what the picture or illustration is about and clearly name the person or persons involved. If you are emailing a photograph or other illustration for publication as an attachment, ensure that it is properly captioned, together with contact details.

If the illustration is going by post, always use a stiff-backed envelope when posting photographs or illustrations. Do not write on the back of prints as Biro or pencil marks can show through and make the picture useless for reproduction.

Captions should be attached with strips of Sellotape. Never glue or paste them to the backs of photographs; just stick them on lightly so they protrude from the bottom of the print and can be read in conjunction with the picture.

Points for websites

When designing websites remember that viewers are scanners, resistant to scrolling down the page as if it was text. The rules are strict and apply to captions to photographs and line illustrations just the same as everything else: short and punchy, no more than 10 words to include the names, in at least 12 point type and, if house style allows, in italics or bold. If it's in a box it will need a headline in fewer than 30 characters, set bold and seldom less than 18 point.

I have noticed lately that there is a tendency not to name people pictured in photographs. This can be infuriating to readers. Name them, even if it takes time to do it. See also Chapter 19.

Copyright issues

When you send out photographs to the press, always be aware of the copyright issue. News editors and picture desks will assume that photographs received from public relations people, especially when they accompany a release, will be free of copyright restrictions.

Photographs should be rubber-stamped on the back with a statement of the copyright position; ideally, similar wording should appear on the caption itself. Never issue a photograph or illustration unless you are sure who owns the copyright. The owner of the copyright is the author or creator – members of the Chartered Institute of Public Relations can obtain advice on legal points such as this by logging on to the member-only area of the CIPR website, **www.cipr.co.uk**, which provides much useful information. Otherwise, ask your solicitor or other legal adviser.

Captions in publications

Clear, concise captioning is the hallmark of a well-produced, stylish publication. In many cases, particularly with annual reports, shareholders get no further than the pictures. One way of getting the reader to take notice of the text is to have an arresting colour photograph with the caption leading on to a particular point.

Distinguishing captions from text

Set off captions from the text by using smaller type, different typeface, or by setting in italics or bold if the text is in plain or roman type. You can position captions in the margin, away from the bulk of the text. Sometimes it is possible to reverse out the caption on a photograph if there is a sufficiently dark area. There is a danger of the caption being unreadable if it is reversed out of a light-toned part of the picture.

An effective way to make captions stand out from the text is to print them in a second colour, preferably using one of the colours chosen for corporate house style. But take care that the colour is a strong one: if it is a pastel shade then the wording will be lost on white paper. If you set two- or three-word headings as intros to captions then you give added visual impact.

Always describe the picture or drawing, unless it is purely for decoration. State essential details, but not what the eye can see for itself. If it is an action shot say what is happening. Even if you think it is obvious, it might not be so to the reader. It is infuriating, for instance, to see an interesting photograph featuring a new product and management team, and not know what it illustrates or who the people are. Don't forget that a wrongly named person could mean a furious client, possibly a reprint, or even – horror of horrors – a libel action.

Draw-down quotes

The draw-down quote is a useful device for livening up a text-full page devoid of what is called 'colour weight' – ie with a total lack of light and shade provided by illustrations or headings. The editor takes a few words from a quote within the copy – usually a pithy or significant comment – and puts it in bold type positioned prominently on the page, perhaps between columns in the middle of the page, or at the top. This layout idea, which amounts to a caption or subheading to the text, also acts as a handy space-filler. But its prime use is to give sparkle to a drab page.

Lure the reader to the text

The caption should arrest attention and lure the reader to the text unless the photograph or illustration is there just to brighten up the page and not meant to tell a story in itself. Write crisply; you don't want just a 'label' making a bland, boring statement.

The caption might be read and understood while the text may not: the reader may not get as far as that. Make sure it contains a verb, preferably in the present tense, and with some news value. Journalists often get stories from the captions in annual reports, and from house journals and brochures.

Captions for charts

The chart caption should describe the essential finding or purpose and lead the reader to the relevant part of the text. With graphs and tables ensure that legends and headings are clear and unambiguous. Make sure that graph axes are explained and show the appropriate units.

Captioning groups of photographs

When you have several photographs or illustrations to caption, arrange the captions together in a block and number them. If there are several photographs of people, or a photograph of a group of individuals, it is convenient to have an outline line drawing showing people's positions, with a numbered key for identification.

Take time and trouble in the wording and presentation of captions. Increased readership and improved communication will inevitably result.

At a glance

- The caption can be as important as the story.

- Keep brief: confine it to 15–20 words.

- Be aware of the copyright issue.

- Distinguish captions from text by size and typeface style.

- Use draw-down quotes to fill space and add interest.

- Avoid verbless 'label' captions.

- Explain graph axes and show units.

- Include a numbered key with group photographs.

13
Why editing matters

The clue to good copy

The success of any newspaper, magazine, or current affairs broadcast depends on the skills of the editorial team from editor to junior reporter. But it has always been the subeditor, or sub for short, who gets the copy ready for printing or transmission. Traditionally, it has been the sub's job to ensure that news stories, articles and scripts coming in from reporters, foreign correspondents and freelances are written to style, make sense, are newsworthy, and above all are not only interesting but gripping to reader or listener, something that makes them read on or keep listening, no matter what.

What, in fact, *do* they do? To answer that you have to realise that editors are usually one step ahead of the daily (or weekly, perhaps monthly) task of producing the newspaper, magazine or programme. Their job is largely to decide what appears and how it will be presented, to set the policy, the tone, in relation to the audience.

The task of getting the words right is handled by the subeditors and finally the chief subeditor, who decides how long an item should be and how it should be treated, with perhaps a referral to the editor if there is a problem. Is it newsworthy? Is it of sufficient interest to be given a page, a column or two, a 30-second soundbite or a two-minute interview on the *Today* programme?

Individual newspapers and other media outlets organise their editorial offices in many different ways. There is no set system: it all depends on whether it is print or broadcast, trade or technical, or consumer magazine. The objectives are the same, to make the written and spoken word fit for publication or transmission.

With the universal use of computer-set type and graphics, most copy nowadays comes in to the news media by email or direct transmission of some kind. The old days of the sub with a Biro or pencil poring over piles of typewritten paper are long gone: copy is subbed straight on to computer screens where page layouts, headings and so on are all manipulated and organised for the next person in the editorial chain to take over. There may be a few instances where hard copy is provided, say a press release, feature article or letter to the editor, and in this instance the old-style sub comes into his or her own, editing and inputting from their own keyboards.

There are doubtless a few specialist journals and magazines that are so understaffed that there may be only minimal subbing – perhaps none at all. In such cases the sender, in this context the PR person, has to make doubly sure that dates, facts, names and places – let alone grammar and style – are all correct before the story goes out. If that is not done, there is a crisis designed to happen.

Let us now examine what the desk editorial team look for in every story or feature that reaches them by post, email, fax and telephone. Any readers wishing to delve deeper into the points raised in the following sections should refer to the relevant chapters in this book.

News stories

All copy coming in from whatever source is subject to editing. That is the kernel rule that applies throughout journalism and publishing. No story, no article, no script ever escapes the eye of the subeditor, news editor, even the editor. And no release will ever be 'used', as the jargon goes, without being subjected to severe editing or, more likely, a full rewrite. The only exceptions are the local freesheet desperate for free copy to fill the space round advertisements and small-circulation trade papers which also need to fill their pages with stories that are just, and only just, good enough for publication. So what do these subeditors and news teams look for in your carefully crafted copy?

Is it newsworthy?

This is the first hurdle for any news story. It must first get past the copytaster, the person who decides whether the piece has news value. Is it something that is not generally known? Is there a human angle? A financial success or failure? Is it, in fact, newsworthy? If your piece doesn't pass this test there's only one place for it: the trash can on the screen or the bin on the floor.

In the same way, if a news programme or paper receives stories that do not seem credible, or as journalists say don't 'stand up', 'have legs' (and will run and run) or are just plain boring, they will quickly be discarded. In trade papers, it may be the assistant editor, news editor or perhaps the editor who decides. The result is the same: if it isn't news, out it goes.

Accuracy

After news value, the editors and subeditors must decide if the story is credible, and consider whether it is factually correct. Accuracy is naturally the responsibility of the reporter, the writer, or whoever originates the story, article or script, but it is the sub who is always on the lookout for something amiss, that doesn't add up. Is the spelling of names correct: is it Clarke with an 'e' or not? Is the spelling of company names right? Are there any trade names that should be capitalised? If there are statistics or figures quoted, are they mathematically correct or are they doubtful in some respect?

The intro

Is the essence of the story in the opening paragraph(s)? Does the rest of it follow in a logical sequence, with following facts in descending order of importance? Can it be sharpened up to catch the reader's attention?

Grammar

Are the tenses right? Does verb agree with subject? Is there a verb missing; is it the right one? Are there any double negatives, and if so, do they make sense? Should it be who or whom, which or that? Are there too many adjectives, particularly flowery ones, or unnecessary adverbs? Has the writer used active 'doing' verbs and avoided the passive voice? Is it written in plain English? Is the text easy to understand? Have the basic rules of grammar been followed throughout?

Style

Has the writer stuck to the style rules of the publication? Are there needless capitals? Are there American -ize verb endings instead of the more usual -ise used in Britain? Is there over-hyphenation? Are the sentences and paragraphs too long? Should there be more par breaks? Has the writer followed the rules for numbers and dates?

Redundancies

The sub will be on constant watch for the wasted word, the one that can be deleted without any loss of sense or meaning. Are there any sentences or parts of them that can be deleted, shortened or rewritten to get rid of wording that adds little or nothing? Is there a single word that can replace a phrase? Is there inelegant repetition?

Non-sequiturs

Does one statement, word or phrase following another make sense? Is the sentence relevant to the preceding one? Does one paragraph follow on logically from the one before? Are there any ambiguities? Does the story itself make sense?

Punctuation

Are there too many commas in one sentence? Are there semicolons when full stops would be better? Has the writer a sense of rhythm, and given the piece balance by providing a mix of short and longer sentences? Are there exclamation marks to be deleted? Is the position of punctuation in direct quotes right?

Clichés and tautology

Are there clichés to be written out? Any repetition to be eliminated? Are there overused and stale words and expressions to be replaced? Is there a better word or way of putting something?

Jargon

Are there unfamiliar or foreign words that might not be understood? Are there any statements that will make sense only to specialist audiences? Are there abbreviations likely to be meaningless to the average audience?

A job to do

As you will have seen, the subeditors and the editorial team have a job on their hands once they get your copy, be it on screen or paper. And remember that newspapers and broadcasting outlets will have hundreds, possibly thousands, of stories to go through every day. Your story is just one of them, and it must be as newsworthy as it is interesting, as meaningful and as well-written as it can possibly be for it to have any chance of publication or transmission.

Feature articles

Journalists working on feature articles are not under the same pressure as those on the news desks. Nevertheless, the features editorial team on either a newspaper or magazine will be asking themselves much the same questions as their news colleagues, but with some significant differences. Sentences and paragraphs can run longer, there might be some photographs and illustrations to be accommodated and captioned so that pages will not turn out to be long slabs of grey type. The editors will make sure that the page is livened up by headings, crossheads, standfirsts (short wording above article titles), boxed paragraphs and draw-down quotes.

FIGURE 13.1 Busy day at the Foreign Press Association media centre for the marriage of Prince William and Kate Middleton. More than 150 journalists from scores of countries used the extensive facilities provided

The feature article will give creative opportunities for alliterations and play on words in headlines to provide both humour and freshness. These editorial tricks are not generally used in news pages apart perhaps from the tabloids once termed 'red tops'. In order to encourage the reader to go right to the end of an article and not give it a quick flip, the sub will try to make the article interesting by making it lively, relevant, arresting and, at the very least, worthwhile and useful.

Radio and TV broadcasts

You will certainly be a fortunate public relations practitioner if you can get your client's products mentioned on air, particularly by the BBC, which may cut out references to named goods and services. Other broadcasters also have restrictions on product mentions and you must be prepared to have them deleted.

Much the same applies to financial services and products which may be of interest to business programmes on both radio and TV. But you may be lucky if there is company news that is of sufficient interest for transmission to a range of viewers and listeners.

Many of the principles outlined above will be followed by the editorial teams involved with radio and TV broadcasts, with one exception: the words spoken on both radio and TV must be clearly enunciated so that they can be understood widely. If the script when read out is unintelligible to listener and viewer then there is no point in broadcasting it. This means that scripts must be free of words that are difficult to speak, for instance whilst and amongst instead of while and among (*whilst/amongst* are largely banned nowadays). Other sibilants, words pronounced with a 'hissing' noise (slippery slates), should be used with caution.

The first test for a script

Let Pat Bowman, former head of public relations at Lloyds Bank, once a frequent broadcaster and now presenter of an audio magazine for the blind, speak from his experience. He says that the first test for any broadcast script is to read it aloud, no matter who will eventually speak it. 'That will quickly show up any awkward words or phrases that need to be adjusted.

'Better still, tape the script yourself and play it back: that can be very illuminating. Most important of all, keep the structure simple, avoiding complexities like too many dependent clauses and, incidentally, allowing the speaker to breathe.'

Make the piece short and accurate

Another comment comes from Ken Brazier, a former BBC broadcaster and editor of the Overseas News Service. He says the way to get the best out of your script so that it appeals to the listener is to make the piece short, clear and accurate, just as you would for the press. 'Before starting to write, think the piece through, sort the facts into logical order so that they link easily from one to another. As a rough guide aim at one fact for each sentence.' Even if space is short, he says, it can be useful to repeat an essential fact such as a location or subject description: 'If the listener misses something he can't refer back in the way he can with the written word.'

On-screen editing

With so many stories and other copy coming in via emails and the internet, the subeditor must be skilled in on-screen editing. Public relations practitioners too must develop these skills, for they will be presented with on-screen copy from press officers, and from people in sales and marketing, customer service and financial departments. Some of this copy may be suitable and not require editing, while other material may have to be subbed, some of it heavily, and perhaps rewritten for a printed document or press release. On-screen editing may be the only way to turn a hopeless cliché-strewn, turgid article into a publishable piece.

The best way is to make a copy, paste it into a new document and work on that. There are software programs to make on-screen editing easier: check with your IT department. Sometimes it is easier to do a rewrite and paste it in – keeping the copy of the original of course.

Technical editing

Many of the attributes and skills of the features sub are also needed for editing technical publications, from trade magazines and brochures to sales leaflets and instruction manuals. The difference is that some knowledge of the industry or trade is needed so that accuracy is preserved.

There is no reason why a PR person with an enquiring mind cannot do the same and become an overnight 'expert', able to pump out copy just as well as a specialist journalist can. But the audience will inevitably know more about the subject than you do.

Special care will be needed when describing technical procedures, particularly in spelling unfamiliar terms; it is always worthwhile to spend time with the expert who can explain functions and how they work before you get anywhere near the keyboard. Then you can show the specialist a draft and get the OK. Take great care in the checking process: the more people who see the copy in advance, the better, and the less chance of something going wrong. Put plenty of leeway in the production schedule to allow for last-minute changes.

If the item is for publication in, say, the house magazine, mark up the copy clearly so that the operator has a clear run. And when the proofs come in, make sure a set goes to the specialists and technical staff for approval. The same goes for digital typesetting, news releases, websites, as well as for all forms of printwork.

FIGURE 13.2 Lively, informative E-newsletter from the History of Advertising Trust, widely circulated in the industry, and to volunteers and helpers

Edit yourself

Edit your copy as you go along. Since most of us type on computer keyboards, this is no problem; it is easy to switch round one word for another, change the position of sentences and paragraphs, or rewrite complete sections. It is no use thinking that you've finished that release or article after slogging away for an hour or more on it.

That is just the beginning: you must look at your work in the same way a subeditor would, deleting unwanted words, cutting the dross and sharpening up the copy. And then it's just a matter of starting all over again.

At a glance

- Most copy arrives at newsdesks by email and is subbed on-screen.

- All copy for publication is subject to editing.

- The first hurdle for releases is: is it newsworthy?

- Ensure copy is accurate and grammatically sound.

- No clichés, jargon or repetition.

- Provide illustrations and include quotes in news stories and in feature articles.

- The sub livens up slabs of type with headings and boxes.

- BBC producers usually ban brand names and products.

- On-screen editing requires special skills and computer software.

- Technical work ideally requires some specialist knowledge.

- Edit yourself as you go along.

14
Skills and styles for the office

Good, consistent style is just as important for correspondence, forms of address, wording for invitations and correct use of courtesy titles, as it is for publications and other printed matter. Good style is good manners, and that means answering – or at least acknowledging – letters no later than two or three days following receipt, and returning telephone calls and emails where possible the same day.

Presentation and layout are also key factors in getting your message across. Every letter, report, paper or printed invitation that goes out must reflect the style and corporate image of your organisation. If it is not up to standard or specification, then your public relations effort could well be wasted. If there is no set house style, then now is the time to establish rules for everyone in the office to follow.

Suggested style for correspondence

Most firms and organisations have style rules for letters, envelopes and other office stationery such as emails, invoices, order forms, fax messages and internal memos. A properly addressed and signed-off letter is the first point. Here are some of the basics.

Layout for letters

File reference and date should be ranged left and aligned with an element of the letterhead design. Do not put full stops, commas or other punctuation in addresses typed at the top of the letter. The following specimen layout style is commonplace:

Mr John Smith
123 Any Road
Anytown
Kent AN5 1ZZ

When addresses are set in a line, say in the body of a letter, then commas are used to separate the components as in Mr John Smith, 123 Any Road, Anytown, Kent AN5 1ZZ.

Courtesy titles

Titles at tops of letters and salutations are normally Mr/Mrs/Miss/Ms. When answering the telephone do not just say 'Hello' or even the modern but overused and insincere response 'This is Mandy, how can I help you?' Give just your surname or add your first name if you want. Do not give yourself a courtesy title and say 'This is *Mr* Smith speaking.'

Despite some past objections to the use of Ms, there is little sign of its decline. It has the advantage of a simplified style, but there is a trend nowadays for all courtesy titles to be replaced by first name and surname only.

Men are mostly given the title Mr in correspondence, but Esquire, Esq for short, is almost dead. Banks, insurance companies, accountants and other professional bodies retain it for fear of upsetting clients. Once Esquire denoted social standing, but by the middle of the 20th century it ceased to possess any sense of rank. Nowadays, it is hardly ever seen in the communications business.

The styles of Mr/Mrs/Miss/Ms are clean and uncluttered. But they are fast disappearing in everyday correspondence.

Honours and qualifications

Where style calls for the inclusion of designations such as civil honours and qualifications, these should follow the established abbreviations, ie, MBE, BA, BSc. No stops go between characters or after separate designations.

Dates and times

Separate the day of the week from the month, as recommended by *Fowler's*: 1 January 2008, not the American style January 1, 2008. The comma needed to avoid collision with the year looks messy. The th/st/rd/nd style for dates has mostly been dropped in business correspondence and printwork, along with deep paragraph indents and punctuation in addresses and salutations. Nevertheless, the style persists, principally in the professions and where there is no PR person to give the right advice. Avoid *nd/st/rd/th* after the day numeral.

When referring to times of day, type these with no space between the figures and *am/pm* as in 9am, 9.30am. Do not put noughts after the figure: for instance 9.00am would look cluttered and pedantic. The signee's name should be ranged left with the person's title typed underneath when needed. Do not underline the name or title, or put either in capitals. Use a fountain pen to sign letters. If you do, it is a sign that you have taken the trouble to make your signature stylish and not just dashed off. Get into the habit of using a proper pen: keep your ballpoint or felt-tip for memos and note-taking.

Copies

Where copies of the letter are sent outside the organisation, the addressee's name should appear beneath the signature, ranged left as in:

Copy to: Mr John Smith, XYZ Company

Details on people receiving blind copies, where the name(s) is not disclosed to the addressee, should ideally appear in a different position. Attach a compliment slip to the copy, with a note for that personal touch.

Letterheads

These should be printed in the same typeface, colour and style as all other in-house stationery. Postal address, telephone, facsimile and email and the website addresses should all be shown in a prominent position. Public relations department headings should carry, where appropriate, out-of-hours telephone and mobile numbers of senior executives, although many firms will prefer to show this information separately rather than have it printed with the heading.

Style for emails

The key to successful emailing depends not on informality (u for you) as once the case, but on treating emails just like a posted letter. By this I do not mean that all the rules for addressing, date and file reference need to be ruthlessly followed, rather there is room for a little levity that would otherwise not be prudent or desirable. In some senses, the email is just as significant as the typed, signed and mailed letter to clients, customers and suppliers. It demands the same degree of care in presentation and writing style as following the rules of grammar and punctuation.

An email is a legal document as witnessed in recent court cases. It therefore demands the same attention to detail in what and how the message is expressed. While the main benefits of the email are speed and allowing attachment of additional documents, photographs and illustrations, there are serious snags.

Once you have hit the send key there is no turning back: the email cannot be cancelled. If there is something in it you regret, your only hope is that it will not be read: it may have 'bounced' through using the wrong address.

Apart from that, an email can go anywhere with disastrous results. It might reach the client, it may go to an unsuspecting employee about to be made redundant, or worse, it could mean a libel action. If it is too informal, or if attachments mean little or nothing to the reader, you have not communicated effectively.

And since many email writers – and that probably means most of them – have never learnt to touch-type, messages can contain endless spelling mistakes that would normally be easy to spot in a printed letter. No self-respecting PR person would want that.

Many long attachments to emails are simply dumped without being read, says editorial consultant Roy Topp. 'Well-presented letters, on the other hand, have a physical presence and while they may end up in a tray, they are eventually dealt with and acted upon.' This, he adds, should be borne in mind by PR people. 'Communication is about talking to people and making them feel wanted. There is little to replace the carefully written letter for doing that.'

More advice on writing and sending emails will be found in Chapter 19.

Have clear, clean layout

If the layout of reports and documents has been well designed, then the message and information contained is more likely to be communicated and acted upon. The basic requirement for an effective layout is a legible typeface, following house style, and preferably the same as the one used for letterheads and other printed stationery. If the typeface, style and creative approach are used for everything, and uniform headings and subheadings are adopted, then all paperwork is immediately identified with the organisation. If it can follow the style for printwork as well, so much the better.

A distinctive 'look' to your correspondence and reports will be achieved if style is standardised: width of margins, number of words per page, page size, uniform space between the lines (leading), type and weight of paper. Put a little extra space between paragraphs, but do not try to squeeze too many lines into one page. Do not use italics or bold type within the body copy in an attempt to give added emphasis.

Writing a précis

A systematic approach is needed. To produce a précis, first read the report or article through to see what it is all about. Set down the important points with a target length, so you will not give too much or too little information. (Don't mark the actual document – you might want to make a photocopy and anyway the owner will not thank you for defacing it.) Do a rough draft, preferably on your PC, incorporating the main facts. Compare it with the original and fill in the gaps.

Check to make sure you haven't exceeded your target wordage. Aim for between a quarter and a third of the length of the original. Read through the draft carefully to see that the matter flows freely and is grammatically correct. Check for any departures from house style.

If you include quotations, they should be short. Quotes should be in reported speech, using the past tense in the third person: 'The committee/he *agreed* to do such and such' or the future past 'the committee/he *would* do...'. Don't use the present (*is/are*) or simple future (*will/shall*) tenses. Treat quotes in the same way as journalists write reported speech. Give it a heading, with your initials and date at the end.

Writing reports and minutes

A report can run from a short memo to any number of closely typed pages in a bound volume, perhaps an annual or interim report to shareholders. Minutes, too, vary in length and style, from a contact report to notes of a meeting.

Essentials of a report

A report must contain the important facts and, ideally, end with a conclusion and recommendations. Open with a title page, moving on to a list of contents, including illustrations or charts, acknowledgements and a short abstract. The body of the report should give the key points from research or investigations, quotations where appropriate and again be written in the third person. Conclude with appendices, if any.

Keep to significant points and comments; otherwise the reader will skip the detail and jump to the conclusions and recommendations. That is what journalists do: only if there is something that appears to be particularly interesting or might need additional information will they go back to the full text.

Start with a draft, then flesh it out with the detail, but only that which is strictly essential to the purpose and objective of the report. Make sure that there is a title and that the author(s) is/are shown on the cover and/or title page. Put the body of the text into numbered sections. Produce the report on a PC and use bold type for headings.

Restrict minutes to decisions

Minutes should be written and circulated within a week of the meeting, earlier if possible. They should be concise and restricted to decisions unless there is good reason to go into details. They should not be long dialogues of who said what. Use reported speech in the third person, and past and future past tenses. For example, in reporting a committee decision, you would write 'It *was* agreed that the company *would* pay a dividend' and not 'It *is* agreed that the company *will* pay a dividend'.

Set down the items in the order of the agenda. Distinguish between superior and inferior headings by underlining or using capitals, or by using bold or larger type sizes. Restrict italics to points of emphasis, though it is better to do without them if you can. Include an 'Action' column as a reminder for those who have agreed to do something.

Put the list of attendees, date of meeting and date of issue at the top and finish with date of next meeting. And get the chairman trained in returning your draft promptly. If you fail to achieve a quorum, just produce notes of the meeting, making it clear that it was not quorate. These notes can subsequently be put to the next meeting and taken as minutes.

Forms of address

Public relations people often have to decide how to begin and end a letter to royalty, and how to address government ministers, peers, MPs and civic dignitaries. Bad form – or at least insensitivity to tradition – can mean that your invitation to give a keynote speech or perform an opening ceremony will lead to a frosty reply. Care in addressing everyone with whom you are in contact, not just VIPs, is essential.

The British system of titles, forms of address and precedence is one of the most complicated in the western world. Nevertheless, most – if not all – answers are to be found in *Debrett's Correct Form*, which covers every conceivable situation in correspondence and in sending invitations to social and business functions. A few examples may be helpful to the reader, but for full guidance refer to *Debrett's*.

Writing to firms

When writing to firms, avoid 'Dear Sir/Madam'. When you do not have a name – it is usually easy to find it in telephone or trade directories – address your letter to the position, ie to the chairman, managing director or secretary. Follow the same procedure when sending an email. Finish off with 'Yours faithfully'. When writing to the press, write Dear Editor if you do not know his or her name. But it is always worth taking the trouble to write personally if you can, although a name on the envelope and letter will seldom ensure a reply or even an invitation acceptance.

Royalty

When writing to the Sovereign, all communications should be addressed to The Private Secretary to The Queen, to the office holder rather than by name, unless you know the person. For other members of the Royal Family, write to the Equerry, Private Secretary or Lady in Waiting as appropriate, the letter beginning Dear Sir or Dear Madam, again to the holder of the office rather than by name. In direct communications, start with Dear Sir or Dear Madam, with 'Your Royal Highness' substituted for 'you' and 'Your Royal Highness's' for 'your' in the body of the letter. Correspondence by email is not recommended.

Peerage

When writing to the peerage, put (for example) 'My Lord Duke' in the formal form and 'Dear Duke' in the informal, or the 'Duke of —' if the acquaintanceship is slight. Verbal address is 'Your Grace' (formal), 'Duke' (social). Special styles are accorded to the wives and children of peers.

Baronets

With baronets, letters begin 'Dear Sir John' (for example) with Bt added on the envelope. A similar style applies for knighthoods where the title is held for life, but the surname should be added if you do not know the person well. Should you meet a baronet or knight in the street or at a function, he should be addressed as Sir John, never 'Sir' on its own. The wife of a baronet or knight is known as 'Lady' followed by the surname.

Government ministers

Ministers of Cabinet rank and some other junior ministers are members of the Privy Council and have the prefix The Rt Hon before their names, with the letters PC after all honours and decorations awarded by the Crown. Privy Counsellors (the preferred spelling) are drawn from many other areas of public life, so watch out! Addressing letters to Government ministers is straightforward: Dear Sir (or Madam) for the formal style, Mrs or Miss for the informal with the option of Dear Minister when writing by his/her appointment.

Members of Parliament

Unless MPs are Privy Counsellors, they have just MP after their name plus any civil or military honours. They are addressed Mr/Mrs/Miss in the usual way. Members of the House of Commons do not have MP after their name once they lose their seat. Always check with the current edition of *Vacher's Parliamentary Companion*, *PMS Parliamentary Companion* or other reference source when writing to MPs and members of the House of Lords. These publications also include details of ministers and senior civil servants in Departments of State, and the names of officials in other Government departments and agencies.

Civic dignitaries

There are widely differing styles for civic dignitaries, depending on the particular town or city. The Lord Mayors of London and York are unique in that they are styled 'The Right Honourable' while the remainder are generally titled 'The Right Worshipful'. They are addressed at the beginning of a letter 'Mr Lord Mayor' and the envelope should bear the wording 'The Right Honourable the Lord Mayor of —'. Mayors of cities and towns are addressed 'Mr Mayor' and the envelope should carry the words 'The Right Worshipful the Mayor of (City of—/(Royal Borough of)' or 'The Worshipful the Mayor of —'. Letters should be signed off 'Yours faithfully' (or 'Yours sincerely' if a social occasion).

Debrett's should be consulted for checking titles of church dignitaries, officers in the armed forces, ambassadors, and for deciding precedence for table plans and guest lists.

Invitations to functions

Printed invitation cards should be sent for most functions, although in many cases – say for press conferences and for informal or social events – a well-presented letter, or an email if time is short, will suffice. Gold-edged cards are best and use of a script typeface is particularly suitable for formal occasions. The card must state the name (or office) of the person making the invitation, the nature of the function, where it will be held, the date and time and the style of dress. It should also state if decorations should be worn. The card must provide enough space for the name of the invitee, and an RSVP name and address, plus telephone number if appropriate. If possible, provide a prepaid reply card. The invitee's name should be handwritten in black ink. Those who do not bother to reply should not be invited again.

Replies to invitations

Replies should be sent out on the organisation's usual printed letterheads and ideally be written in the formal style, stating either acceptance of the invitation or regret at being unable to accept. State the reason for non-acceptance, examples being 'owing to a previous engagement/absence abroad/out of town that day'. Whether accepting or declining, the name(s) of the invitee(s) should be given, together with details of the function. If replying by telephone, send a written follow-up.

Acknowledging correspondence

Good style means good manners. And good manners is good PR. Nothing is worse than not replying to a letter offering or giving you something. It is usually possible to send a reply within a day or two. If you are too busy to post a typed letter, then a handwritten one will do just as well, even if you have to handwrite the envelope yourself.

An acknowledgement card is also helpful and should be sent as a matter of routine for all correspondence where a detailed and immediate response is not possible. This might simply state '(name of person of company/organisation) thanks you for your communication of (date) which is receiving attention'. It takes only a minute or two of your time to get off a reply of some sort: a telephone call or email will do the trick.

Replying to emails promptly is a courtesy not to be forgotten. It is not so important in inter-office memos, but essential for other messages – particularly those to clients and customers, if only a simple OK. Ensure that someone monitors your mailbox regularly for outstanding correspondence.

Setting out documents

The layout for reports, documents, agendas and minutes calls for a consistent and well-ordered style. A printed heading should give the name, address and telephone/fax numbers as well as website and email details of the organisation on all documents. Date and reference numbers to aid identification should be included. Insert extra space between items and leave generous margins (at least 25 mm on the right-hand margin, more on the left). Call in a professional designer to give you a template for keyboard operators to follow. That way everybody will produce documents to a consistent style, an essential requirement for developing a recognisable corporate image.

Writing a CV

Style for presentation of a curriculum vitae (CV) is important and could affect an applicant's chances of securing employment. It should be clear and concise, consistent in style, accurate, without spelling errors or wrong punctuation, use plain English and should concentrate on skills and achievements. There are several websites to help in the writing and design of CVs. A particularly helpful one is provided by the University of Kent Careers Advisory Service (**www.kent.ac.uk/careers/cv/cvexmples.htm**). Since most job applications are emailed these days, clear presentation and concise wording when applying online are crucial to success. Don't include a photograph: employers want to know what you can do, not what you look like.

If you post your CV, it should be on good quality white A4 paper with the text well spaced and not jammed up tight. It must have a well-written covering letter stating why you would like the position. Check for any errors.

Always address it to a named person, never Dear Sir(s) or Dear Madam. It only takes a minute to find a name through a trade directory or from the organisation's website. Unless you are applying for a creative job, do not use coloured paper or any ink colour other than black.

Pay special attention to the way it is laid out: use either the chronological style with latest job first and working backwards to junior positions, or the skills-based formula with your personal details highlighting the particular attributes needed for the job. Similar presentation styles can be used for emailed CVs, and make sure there are no spelling or grammatical errors.

Basic information needed

The basic details an employer needs are your name, home address, telephone number and email address, followed by academic and professional qualifications and the names of at least two referees. If your name does not immediately signify your sex, you may like to say whether you are male or female.

If your outside interests show that you have leadership quality, include those as well. Don't try to 'gild the lily', pretending that you are more important than you really are and including irrelevant information such as family history. If you talk about your ancestors, no matter how eminent they may have been, that is unlikely to influence the interviewers. All that will concern them is what you can do and how you will perform.

There are plenty of books on the subject and there are organisations to help. Trawl the internet for ideas. The CV Centre (**www.cvcl.co.uk**) provides a professional writing and advisory service. You can also get help from the Chartered Institute of Personnel and Development (CIPD) on 0800 064 6484.

What the employers look for

CIPR Fellow Robert Harland, former vice-president and director, international public affairs, the Coca-Cola Company, says the first thing he looks for in a CV is how relevant the candidate's current job is and length of service in previous ones. 'If someone only holds a job for around 18 months each time, I tend to think there is something wrong.' And he always looks to see if a candidate's shoes are clean and polished.

Restaurateur Prue Leith says that while core competence is the first essential, she asks herself if she would like to have dinner with them. 'Not Mr Angry, nor Miss Dragged-through-the-hedge backwards, but one who is engaging, courteous and well-presented.'

Their message is clear: manners, dress and voice count for much in the selection process. And find out as much as you can about the company before you go for interview. It works. I know.

Language for the telephone

Consider the way in which your telephone system is used, or perhaps abused. The operator is often the first point of contact. One bad experience can leave a lasting impression: business can be lost to a competitor simply because of ineptitude on the part of the receptionist.

If the operator is rude, offhand or at worst clueless about the firm and who does what, the organisation could suffer irreparable damage. Imagine a visitor having to compete with a gaggle of gossipers at the reception desk! Sloppy telephone technique and indifferent treatment of visitors can ruin corporate image faster than anything else.

Dealing with calls

Calls should be answered in no more than five or six rings, then automatically routed to an answering device if the line is busy. Better still if the call is answered in two or three rings, but unlikely. If the caller is holding on, the operator, or automatic answering service, should return every 30 seconds or so to check that the person hasn't been forgotten.

Modern systems take you through a list of touchtone options like 'If you know the extension you want, press it now.' This is a daft instruction because there can be few callers who know the number of the extension they want: much better to give numbered departmental options. Even so, these need to be kept to a minimum. Nothing can be more frustrating than having to listen to a long list to reach the extension you want. Worse still if it is a journalist seeking the press office for information on an important story.

Answering techniques

Operators should answer cheerfully, but without overdoing it and give the name of the organisation or its initials if well known. Don't say 'Hello', or 'Mr so and so', just give your name.

Voicemail messages should be brief, warm and welcoming, not bark at you like an angry dog. Check messages regularly and return calls the same day. If you are answering for a colleague, note down messages and take the number even if you think you know it – the call might be coming from somewhere else.

Provide a monitor at reception for website and email access; let visitors use it. Circulate press releases, news bulletins, house journals and reports to the receptionists, so that they are aware of new products and services. Don't let other people make your calls and tell you the person is waiting on the line. It's not only a waste of time, it's discourteous.

At a glance

- Establish a corporate style for everything.

- Omit courtesy titles (Mr/Mrs/Miss/Ms) on the telephone: just give your name.

- 'Esquire' is hardly ever used these days; mostly by banks and financial services companies.

- Agree style for dates, times, and correspondence format to be followed by all staff.

- Develop a clear, clean layout for reports and documents.

- Restrict minutes to decisions: long dialogues are not needed.

- Refer to *Debrett's* for guidance on forms of address.

- Use printed cards for formal invitations.

- Acknowledge all correspondence; respond the same day if possible.

- Update your CV regularly; keep it to two pages of A4.

- Ensure telephone calls are answered in no more than five or six rings.

- Keep voicemail messages brief, warm and welcoming.

15
Traps, snares and pitfalls

Appropriate choice of words is of paramount importance for imparting the sense and tone of any message. But for that message to be properly understood, and for it to be clear and unambiguous, not only must spellings and grammar be correct but the writer must avoid slang in formal texts, guard against overusing fashionable but sloppy phrases, and know whether words are hyphenated or not, or spelt as one word. This chapter examines some of these traps, which can lead to mistakes or even howlers that make your hair stand on end when you see them in print.

Spelling points

Difficulty often arises with advis*or* or advis*er*: the preferred spelling is *-er*; *-or* is pretentious, even old-fashioned. A useful rule is that unless preceded by a 't' or 'ss' verb (or less frequently noun) endings are usually *-er*. In order to avoid a spelling hiccup (not *hiccough* nowadays) you have to be on guard for mistakes like *practioners* – or literals and typos as printers like to call them. There is no 'd' in allege, it is contractual, not -ural, flotation not float-ation, hurrah/hurray not hoorah/ay unless you are talking about a Hooray Henry; idiosyncrasy not –acy; minuscule not -iscule; nerve racking, not -wracking. It is a gentlemen's agreement, not -man's.

Confusion often occurs between *passed* and *past*. The past tense and past participle of the verb to pass is passed as in it passed from you to me, whereas *past* as an adjective describes things or events that have occurred (past times); it can also be a preposition as in first past the post and a noun (memories of the past).

For words of more than one syllable ending in *-ed* or *-ing* and with the stress on the last syllable, the final consonant is doubled as in permit/permitted. But where the last syllable is unstressed, as in target and focus, the final consonant is not doubled: thus any argument on how to spell focused/ focusing and targeted/targeting is instantly resolved. In the same category go other favourite words in the PR vocabulary such as benefited/ing, budgeted/ing. Another way of telling whether you are right or wrong is to pronounce such words with a stressed double final consonant and so get fo*cussed* and targ*ett*ed. Or say to yourself mark*ett*ing, with a double 't' and the emphasis on the second syllable; it is obviously wrong and you will instantly recall the rule. (Get into the habit of looking out for a double 's' or 't' in these words – you won't have to wait long.)

With suffixes of words ending in a single 'l', the last consonant is usually doubled whether or not the final syllable is stressed as in labelled/travelled, but not appealed/paralleled.

Spellings of similar sounding or pairs of words frequently cause trouble. Take these examples: canvas (for painting pictures) but canvass (to solicit votes); dependant (relative) but dependent (upon). How many times have you seen these words misused and misspelt? Then there is the draughtsman (of a specification) but someone who drafts a document, the official who makes a formal inquiry, but a person who questions and makes an enquiry. Further has quite a different meaning from farther: the former suggests something additional to say or do, the latter increased distance.

Install becomes installation but instalment (sometimes with a double 'l'), all three having a totally different meaning from instil. A common mistake is to mix up licence (noun) with license (verb): how many times do you want to tell a shopkeeper to correct licenced to licensed? (In America, it is the other way round and 'practice' is both noun and verb.)

How often have you asked someone whether the first 'e' should be dropped in judgement? The rule here is that when a suffix beginning with a consonant (-ful, -ling, -ly, -ment, -ness, -some) is added to a word with a silent 'e', the -e is retained – but not always (exceptions include argument, fledgling). Judgement usually loses the first 'e' in legal works. In American spelling, the 'e' is dropped before a suffix beginning with a consonant as in abridgment, judgment. Another rule worth noting is when adding in- and un- to the beginning of a word; there is only one 'n' unless the word itself begins with an 'n' as in inseparable, unending, innumerable, unnecessary.

Other confusing spellings are principle (basis of reasoning) and principal (main); stationary (still) and stationery (paper stocks) – a way to remember this is 'e' for envelope. Note that the start of the last syllable in supersede and consensus is often misspelt with a 'c'. Keep a colander for straining and a calendar for giving the date; reserve program and disk for computer terminology, and resist the temptation to put an 'e' in whisky (whiskey is for the American and Irish, but never Scotch whisky – the Scots wouldn't hear of it).

More examples are in Appendix 1. There is a list of 100 top misspellings in the *Oxford A–Z of Better Spelling* (OUP). Every office should have a copy.

Be careful with foreign words

Take special care with foreign words. They are easily absorbed into English, but can just as easily be wrongly spelt. Even in newspapers we see fruits *du* mer instead of *de*, hors d'oeuvres (not plural) for *hors d'oeuvre*, crime passional for crime *passionnel* and bête noir for bête *noire*. Keep foreign dictionaries handy, particularly those covering English–French and English–German and vice versa for checking phrases like *couleur locale*, since computer spellchecks are not much help for other languages.

Errors can occur simply because you have seen the same words wrongly spelt before. It is easy to *think* you have got it right, but it's easy to miss, for example, the first u in *de rigueur*. Familiarity breeds contempt.

While occasional foreign words can liven up dull copy, keep them out of releases. When used in print or seen on-screen, the reader will quickly tire of them, particularly if the expressions are unfamiliar. Keep to anglicised words, otherwise you might be seen as showing off. The *New Oxford Dictionary for Writers and Editors*, the *Oxford Style Manual* and the *New Hart's Rules* handbook will confirm spellings of commonly used foreign words and phrases, and will show, by italics, those that are not yet accepted in everyday English.

Use your dictionary

It is difficult to remember different spellings for similar-sounding words, but being aware of the similarities and possible spelling errors encourages the writer to reach for the dictionary.

Before leaving the subject of spellings, one sure tip is always remember to use the computer's spellcheck for everything – websites, releases, articles, reports and letters; not only will it pick up errors that might otherwise not be noticed, it will often provide a word count by recording the number of questionable words. This is extremely useful information for both writer and editor, saving the tiresome task of counting up copy word by word to estimate the length when set in type. More examples are in Appendix 1.

-ise or -ize verb endings?

Both spellings are common in the UK, while the *-ize* ending is usual in North America. Readers in America may notice that -ise has been used throughout this book since this style is now generally favoured in the UK. There are

FIGURE 15.1 Local council gets it wrong: a warning sign is incapable of advancing or moving forward. Three years after this notice was photographed, the second 'd' was removed to turn 'advanced' from verb to adjective. Easy mistake to make

some words which must always end with *-ise*. These include advertise, appraise, apprise, arise, chastise, comprise, disguise, excise, exercise, franchise, improvise, incise, merchandise, premise, promise, praise, raise, supervise, televise. Few will object to *-ise* spellings throughout, although the use of capsize/sterilize/familiarize will seldom be criticised.

In the UK until a few years ago *-ize* endings were commonly seen in *The Times* and elsewhere, but as both the Oxford University Press and the Cambridge University Press switched to *-ise*, so newspapers tended to follow suit and thus another style trend was born. Even so, *-ize* appears to be as firmly embedded in America as ever. However much you may hate nouns becoming verbs, you have to realise that services are *privatised*, but most of us will object to being *hospitalised* or having plans *prioritised*.

One word or two?

Many words once happily hyphenated, and some two-word phrases, soon found themselves living together, joined without remorse. Thus we have seen railwayman/paybed/turnout enter everyday usage as examples of lost hyphenation. Many still persist in using alright ('Gross, coarse, crass and to be avoided', says Kingsley Amis in *The King's English*) instead of the preferred all right.

Underway as one word is gaining popularity. Jeremy Butterfield in his excellent *Damp Squid* (OUP, 2008) reports that the Oxford English Corpus of more than two billion words, found that the 'singleton' usage was 54 per cent against the popular two-word form of 46 per cent. Even so, who is to say that *underway* is any different from *anyway*? Website as a single word clearly has the lead with 82 per cent compared to a paltry 18 per cent as a duo yet, surprisingly, *anymore* claims 62 per cent contrasted with 38 per cent for the much preferred (in my view) two-word style.

There is constant confusion between forever (perpetually) and for ever (for always) as in 'He is forever complaining' against 'He will be in the same firm for ever'. Amis again: 'I'm forever blowing bubbles to be outlawed altogether'.

As Butterfield points out, nothing in spelling is permanent and since it was not that long ago that *nothing* and *otherwise* were two words, we have to accept the trends and go with the flow. It's just no good crying out for two words when one will almost always do just as well.

Many hyphenated words eventually end up as one for the simple reason that the style is modern and favoured by the popular press. We are used to them and no longer worry whether they are hyphenated or not. However, it is advisable to check with the usual reference sources such as the *Oxford Dictionary of English* and the *Oxford Style Manual* for recommended style for individual word-sets.

Puzzles and posers

When you accede to something you give assent to an opinion or policy; do not use it to mean grant, allow, agree. Rather than write accordingly, put so or therefore; adverbs like hopefully, admittedly, happily are usually unnecessary. It is better to write you plan or intend to do something than hope to do it, which suggests doubt that it will ever be done. Rather than adjust something, *change* it; you appraise it when you judge its value, not apprise which means inform.

Among is often confused with between. When writing about more than two things or people, among is usually needed. But when considered individually, between is preferred. Contrast 'food was shared among six people' with 'cordial relations between the UK, France and Germany'.

Avoid hackneyed words like factor which can usually be omitted without loss of sense. You can dispense with it easily, for example, 'in an important *factor* in the company's success' by recasting and writing simply 'important in the company's success'. Feature (as a noun) is another word that adds nothing and can easily be dropped. Meaningful has lost all meaning and is another candidate for excision. Also cut these out: one of the most, respective/respectively, currently, the foreseeable future, the fact is… and other words that contribute little except waffle.

Do not allow quasi-legalese such as persons for people, and over-formal terms such as notwithstanding, terminate or forthwith in correspondence.

Don't be old-fashioned and write amongst and whilst when among and while will do just as well. You should *try to* do something, not *try and* do it. Instead of writing *practically* all the time put almost, nearly, or *all but*. The world is populated by people, not persons; but that is not to say that there is no place for person. The noun person is normally only used in the singular as in 'he was a person of character'. Avoid using persons when people would be more appropriate.

Be careful not to add a qualifier to ungradable words like unique or perfect. You cannot have degrees of uniqueness or perfection: either something is unique or perfect or it is not. Other words like this are peculiar, sole, single, spontaneous.

Lookalikes need care

Is it big or large? While they are synonymous, you can't always swap one for the other. There's a big salary rise, not a large one; but you can drive a big or a large car. Differences are subtle: big is the colloquial and more familiar adjective. Amount of/number of goes better with large (a large amount of column inches, there was big publicity). Use whichever *sounds* right. Much the same applies to small/little.

Lookalike words with different meanings include simple/simplistic. The latter implies oversimplified, unrealistically straightforward; avoid when simple in 'easy' contexts will suffice. Biennial is once every two years, biannual twice a year; continual means frequently happening, continuous is non-stop.

To mitigate is to create conditions for reducing the severity of something, to militate against something is to have a significant effect against it. Affect is to have an influence on, effect to accomplish something. Discreet means circumspect, showing good judgement; discrete means unattached, unrelated. Practical is suitable for use, practicable able to be done.

Optimum means best or most favourable in a given set of circumstances, optimal is just a fancy way of saying it. Much the same goes for minimum/al except that minimal sounds old-fashioned. Masterful and masterly both suggest being skilful, but masterful hints at being dominant, commanding or with authority; masterly suggests a degree of expertise, say the special ability of a concert soloist. CD covers often err in this respect.

When it comes to loaning or lending, again the dividing line is not always clear. The verb to loan is an Americanism and is mainly associated with large sums and works of art. Take this example: the businessman loaned the party a million pounds but the chap down the road lent me a fiver. While lend is a verb, loan is used principally as a noun as in 'he is making me a loan'.

Chestnut time

Now that chestnut: is it less or fewer? The quick answer is that if the noun is countable, it's fewer; otherwise choose less. Fewer tables and chairs, less hope, less anger. Less/little goes better with size and quantity than few/fewer: thus for time, distance, money, reading, writing it's less than 10 minutes before we leave for home, there's less than 1,000 words to write, and less than £500 for doing it. Fewer or less people or miles? Since people take the plural verb, it's fewer than 20 per cent of the workforce who leave so early. And it's fine to write less than 25 miles away since it's a measure of distance, not individual miles.

Keep 'nots' out of attention-seeking standfirsts, those short intros to feature articles, as they can confuse the reader. There's no place for 'not for nothing'. Negative constructions should always be avoided: too many 'nots' and 'un' words joined with 'not' (for example 'not unwanted') can be brain-twisters. And as I've said earlier in this chapter, you can't be too careful when using a computer spellchecker: there's really no better way to check spellings than to use a good dictionary.

They're not right, they're not wrong

Watch out for get/got. While there is nothing actually wrong with them, they appear informal and should be avoided. Use obtain or possess instead, or consider rewriting. Also take care with to lay, to lie: the verb to lay takes an object while *to lie* does not (I *lay* my body on the floor as I *lie* resting). But you never have a *lay down* which makes a noun of it.

Like is another pitfall. Used parenthetically, to qualify a following or preceding statement, as in '*like* I was going to tell you something' is a vulgarism of the first order, *Fowler's* says. But resistance to its use as a conjunction and as a substitute for *as if* or *as though* is crumbling.

Keep clear of *nice*. *Fowler's* says: 'It should be confined in print to dialogue… ladies have charmed it out of all its individuality and converted it into a mere diffuser of vague and mild agreeableness.' It is better to forget *nice* and choose a synonym for it, unless you use the catchphrase 'Have a *nice* day.'

Arguments abound on whether to write (or say) compared to or compared with. The first is to liken one thing *to* another as in 'critics compared him to Olivier' while the second points to differences or resemblances between two things as in 'comparing the speaker's notes *with* what has been written'. Use *different from* in writing, keep *different to* for speech.

Another poser is the placing of 'only' in a sentence. Put it as close as possible to the word or words it qualifies: when it strays too far away, it can be obscure or remove the element of exclusivity. If, for example, you say you had *only* two drinks, that is better than saying you *only* had two drinks.

Avoid imprecisions such as lots of, many or things when figures or definitions can be given. Keep *an* for words beginning with a silent 'h' (an heir, an honour, an honorarium); otherwise it is a hotel, a harbour, a hero, a hope. Introduce a list of items with such as or for example, not eg.

Note that *anybody* and *anyone* are singular (anybody is able to visit the museum), as are every, everybody, everyone (every dentist *has* information on care of teeth; everybody is able to discuss his or her problems with a lawyer). *Each* is singular (each contributor should check his or her paper), and so is nobody or no one (no one is certain).

Vogue words and phrases

Numerous words are not only overused or become clichés but suggest the writer has not bothered to think of anything better. Top of the list must be 'or whatever' when it means in effect 'including many other things'. Don't say it and certainly never write it.

Then there are the clichés of having said that, at the end of the day, in-depth, ongoing and ongoing situation, geared to, in terms of, I'll get back to you, any time soon, name of the game, no problem, no worries, take on board, track record; and words like feedback, concept, consensus, lifestyle, viable, syndrome, validate, interface, scenario. Some, if not all, of these words are current coinage in the communications business and it is virtually impossible to avoid them. Try to find synonyms.

Getting in the mood

If you fail to distinguish between auxiliary (modal) verbs, and between relative pronouns, verbal inelegances and even mistakes arise. While sometimes interchangeable without loss of sense, look out for pitfalls. Here are a few examples.

Modal verbs shall/will, should/could, can/could, may/might possess different shades of meaning, expressed as moods or modes of action. Also within this category are *must* and *ought*. Unlike ordinary verbs, modals do not have *-s* or -*ed* added in present and past tenses; there can be no shalls, mighting or oughted apart from being *willed* to do something.

The general rule is that *shall* and *should* go with first person singular and plural; *will* and *would* the others. Thus, *should* accompanies *I* and *we*; and *would goes* with *he*, *she*, *it* and *they*. Both express simple future tense; *will* showing intention or determination, especially a promise to do something. You are more likely to be taken seriously if you say 'I *will* be in the office on Sunday.' '*Shall* be' somewhat dilutes the intention.

Care is needed in choosing *should* or *would* for there is a subtle but important difference between them. *Should* has moral force behind it, whereas *would* acquires mild conditionality. *Should* expresses three future possibilities: conditional, probable, and a less likely outcome as in, respectively, 'I *should* be grateful if you *would* answer my letter'; 'she *should* avoid the angry client'; '*should* you see him, remind him about the meeting.' *Could*, like *should/would*, indicates a conditional or future possibility, while *could/can*, used interrogatively, suggests seeking permission.

Difficulty often occurs in using *may/might*. Permission is expressed through *may* as in '*may I*', but both imply simple possibility in 'the client *may/might* come' and are indistinguishable. In some contexts *might* hints at uncertainty and suggests less optimism than *may* as in 'they might use the release' against 'they may be able to edit it'. Thus, *may/might* are often interchangeable where the truth of an event is unknown, but if there is no longer uncertainty, use *might*.

James Aitchison in his *Cassell's Guide to Written English* neatly expresses *ought* and *must* as 'duty, obligation and necessity'; *ought*, he observes, suggests likelihood of fulfilment, while *must* indicates strict or absolute necessity.

Another trap can arise in writing *which* and *that*. These pronouns are normally used with non-human nouns, otherwise write *who* or *whom*. While *which/that* can often be interchanged or even omitted without loss of sense, distinctions exist, particularly when sub-clauses beginning *which* are enclosed in commas. It is rare to punctuate *that* clauses in the same way. *That* defines, *which* explains.

It is a sound rule (says Sir Ernest Gowers in *The Complete Plain Words*) that *that* should be dispensed with whenever this can be done 'without loss of clarity or dignity'. Consult the *Oxford A–Z of English Usage* or *Fowler's* for examples of current *which/that* usage.

Genteelisms

Substitution of a normal, natural word for another that is considered by some as less familiar, less vulgar, less improper or less apt is defined by *Fowler's* as a genteelism. For instance, *assist* for help, *ale* for beer, *endeavour* for try, *odour* for smell are all genteelisms, along with ladies for women and gentlemen for men. A word that is simple and unpretentious is to be preferred to one that has a high-sounding, euphemistic ring to it. Words that were once listed as genteelisms (chiropodist for corn-cutter for example) have long since gained acceptance for everyday usage, and are no longer indicators of social class.

Here is a short but easily extendible list of other genteelisms for you to be aware of and preferably avoid: euphemisms such as *conceal* for hide, *corpulent* for fat, *ere* for before, *demise* or *passed away* for died, *dentures* for false teeth, *donation* for gift, *lounge* for sitting-room, *perspire* for sweat, *retire* for go to bed, *reside at* for live at, *sufficient* for enough, *take umbrage* for take offence, *toilet* for lavatory. And so on.

Keep clear of slang

Unless part of a direct quotation, say in a speech delivered at an event other than at an AGM, avoid slang words in formal writing. But you need to appreciate that today's slang is tomorrow's idiom. Slang words for 'publicise', drawn from the *Wordsworth Thesaurus of Slang*, include the following: promote, hype, plug, push, pitch, splash, spot, boost, build up, puff, ballyhoo, beat the drum for, tub-thump, hard/soft sell. If you are a publicity seeker, you are a hot dogger, publicity hound, showoff. Slang for 'publicity' includes hoopla, flack, flackery, big noise, ink, get ink.

While state of the art and cutting edge began as slang, these phrases have now found a place in the everyday language of communicators. Doubtless, many other spoken slang words will eventually find a final resting place in formal writing.

Keep mission statements short and simple

Mission statements can be a waste of time; those wordy, self-congratulatory, pretentious platitudes tend to be meaningless waffle. No one wants to know about your firm's passion, your destiny, even your vision for the future. Too many beliefs, aims, objectives fail to convince. It is almost like saying what life is for. A mission statement, if you insist on having one, should be a description of what your company is and does in a few short paragraphs.

It can be useful for background notes in a press release, provided it doesn't start talking about your commitment to excellence, your integrity, how enthusiastic your staff are. Look at it as your 'reason to be', a statement in plain language that will ring true with all your audiences, from employees to customers, from suppliers to opinion formers.

Top 10 tips for writers

1 **Brevity.** Restrict sentences to 25 to 30 words, three per paragraph maximum.

2 **Repetition.** Never repeat a word in a single passage. Look for synonyms.

3 **Clichés.** Kill stale, overused words and phrases. Consult a thesaurus.

4 **Jargon.** Cut out mumbo-jumbo. Will the reader understand?

5 **Facts, Facts.** Give facts, not waffle or comment, unless it's a quote. Always check your facts for accuracy.

6 **Qualifiers.** Write with verbs and nouns, not adjectives and adverbs.

7 **Accuracy.** Ensure the accuracy of everything. Watch for non sequiturs.

8 **Punctuation.** The full stop is your best friend. Use it liberally.

9 **Readability.** Make sure your copy is easy to read; does it look boring?

10 **Consistency.** Keep style consistent throughout.

At a glance

- Watch out for 'difficult' spellings.
- Keep two-way dictionaries handy for checking foreign words.
- Use your computer's spellcheck for everything you write.
- Keep verb endings consistent: -ise is mostly preferred in the UK.
- Most hyphenated words soon end up as one.
- Look out for differences and distinctions in lookalike words.
- Some words and phrases are not right, but not wrong.
- Avoid vogue phrases: they soon become clichés.
- Distinguish between modal (auxiliary) verbs.
- Avoid euphemistic 'genteelisms' where possible.
- Make mission statements simple, short, meaningful.

16
Americanisms – the differences

English is the dominant language in more than 30 countries: it is estimated that almost 400 million people across the world speak our mother tongue as a first language, the largest concentration being in the United States where there are some 250 million English speakers against the UK's 59 million. Around two-thirds of the world's population speak English as a second language.

English as a global language has important implications for the public relations practitioner. The indigenous differences between native speakers of American English and British English are significant. Global English, the way the language is spoken and written, is the voice of a national community: a mixture of accents, dialects, catchphrases and slogans coupled with grammatical and vocabulary variations.

Fewer than one in seven North Americans are able to read all the way through a newspaper article in another language. The part that language plays in the communications process is crucial, and the differences in style and usage between American English and British English must be recognised by all public relations professionals irrespective of their industry sector and the jobs they do.

Essential differences

American English differs from British English in vocabulary, spelling and inflection, grammar and construction, and punctuation. Familiar terms here are unknown in the United States and vice versa. Some Americans advise that releases, articles and other work going there should be in US style. Others say that it is better to write the way we do here and let editors change the copy to suit. That can be done for press releases and other computer-processed online documents but will not do for printed communications such as reports and brochures addressed to American audiences. And there are occasions when both styles are needed. Which to use for websites with global audiences?

Releases and websites

American PR executive Susan Stevens Boucher, who once worked here for National Grid as the company's director of corporate affairs, says that because news release messages are usually different in the two countries, separate versions are issued and language is not an issue. Where a single version goes out, it uses the language of the land where the release is being issued, regardless of where the news originates. American news issued in the UK would therefore be in British English.

It is a good idea to include a glossary of terms on websites carrying technical information so as to cover anything that might be misunderstood. For instance, with measurements the conversion rate must at least be shown and pounds also shown as dollars, particularly important for informing employees of financial results.

This is particularly true for a financial news release, where key terms like 'turnover' should be translated into the local language before issuing, so as to avoid confusion. (See under 'vocabulary and usage', later in this chapter.) For National Grid's website, both are used – American English for the US pages, British English for the UK. International websites should offer the user a choice of language, but that can be costly.

So the advice is when mailing or posting a release on your website for an international audience, keep it in British English and let journalists in other countries make the changes. If it's an internal employee communication or a publication, get someone steeped in US style to write it. Never let language get in the way of the message. Says Boucher: 'We found that even as our corporate writers became more proficient in the language of the other country, it was still best to have someone from the home country review the text to catch the nuances and subtleties that would otherwise be missed.' Just as it could take years of fluency in a foreign language to be proficient with its idioms and slang, so it could take years to learn American or Queen's English like a native, she added.

PR terminology

Where there's a communications director here, it's a vice-president there, but nowadays the terms public relations officer or public information officer are commonplace. In the United States you go to a clipping service; a video morgue; the local editor. Titles, as here, are changing fast: vice-president or manager replaces communications director/manager here. Over there, they're all communications professionals.

Vocabulary and usage

Here lie the main variations. To emphasise the main ones to US employees on being told about a merger, Susan Stevens says the National Grid simply printed a booklet *May I pinch your seat?* A few examples of US versus UK English: ground floor here is *first floor* there; flat/*apartment*; drawing pin/*thumbtack*; kennel/*doghouse*; receptionist/*desk clerk*; skip/*dumpster*; Joe Bloggs/*John Doe*. Here's a built-in recipe for a meeting disaster: if you write to *table* something, in the UK it means to discuss it, while in the United States it means to put it aside for later. It's turnover here, revenue there.

We write *and*, not additionally; *district*, not neighbourhood; *oblige*, not obligate. In Britain a parking lot is a car park, a hood is a vehicle bonnet, a truck is a lorry, a freight train is a goods train, a stove is a cooker. You go on the sidewalk in New York City, but in London you are on the pavement. There you buy gasoline, here petrol (gas stations offer both gasoline and diesel). The subway in a US city is the Underground in London. You go for a week's vacation if you work there; here it is a holiday. In America, you say first name not Christian name (a term that is also now removed from most style manuals here), inquire not enquire, billboard not poster, clipping not press cutting.

Americans normally give verbs *-ize* endings where we mostly use the *-ise* style. They prefer license/practice for both noun and verb, while here the 's' is for the verb only; the nouns defense/offense/pretense take a 'c' here and not an 's' as in the United States. Commas and full stops fall within quotation marks in press releases in US style, regardless of whether they are part of the quoted material. For any other communication, say a letter or brochure, punctuation marks go within the quotations, but only if they are part of the original quote. Americans use the terms parentheses for round brackets, and brackets for square brackets.

Co-operation is seldom hyphenated there, often here; while full stops are usually inserted in abbreviations there, but hardly ever seen here nowadays. A stroke is a slash over there; it's v. for versus here, vs. there. Here, your phone is engaged, for Uncle Sam it's busy. To an American, 'turnover' means the rate at which employees leave the company. To them 'natural wastage' means attrition. *To deliver on a promise* means to keep it. A hike is not only a walk, it can also be an increase.

Verbs inflect differently: *gotten* for got is commonplace (although not always considered to be good grammar), and so is *dove* for dived. Plural verbs and pronouns seldom go with words like audience, group. Do not write *meet with* nowadays, an old import from America, or say *outside of*.

Spelling

American English puts -er where we have -re, as in center, meter (measurement) but not always: theater and theatre are allowed there, and both forms permit acre and mediocre. Here, where verbs end in double 'l' (dialling/travelling) in American English there is one 'l'. But there are exceptions: the verbs distil and enrol have double 'l' in the United States. A cheque here is a check there, a tyre is a tire. There a word is spelled, here it is spelt; there's no 's' in towards in US style. Consult an up-to-date dictionary and usage guide if attempting to write and spell the American way – or better still consult an American.

Idioms and expressions

Some British and American idioms are similar in their phrasing whereas others are quite different. We say at a loose end, there it's at loose *ends*; not by a long chalk becomes not by a long *shot*. We write 'as sure as eggs is eggs', there they say 'you can put it in the bank' or 'it's a slam dunk' (a basketball expression, as 'hit a home run', 'hit it out of the park' and 'go the last yard' to finish something are baseball terms).

More recently we have heard in Susie Dent's *Language Report* of a smoke-easy where smokers go in order to escape the anti-smoking laws; a stained glass ceiling, an adaptation of the familiar phrase describing the barrier to promotion of professional women; a job spill, a situation in which job-related work encroaches on one's leisure time; a fake bake, the process of getting a sunless tan (also as a verb). If ever you wonder what POTUS means you will now know it stands for the President of the United States.

Many so-called Americanisms such as fall for autumn, candy for sweets, elevator for lift, will doubtless soon find their way into British English in the same way as truck, commuter and teenager have crossed the Atlantic with alacrity. The process is being reciprocated as more UK firms acquire US companies, and as UK ex-pats introduce Americans to the British way of speaking.

The habit of using British words and phrases is apparently growing apace over there. The late H W Fowler would no doubt be pleased and surprised, but perhaps dismayed if only he knew.

However, the two languages are still distinctly different, something PR people working with their American counterparts or with the media must not forget. If you are in a meeting or on a phone call and don't understand what the person is saying, be sure to ask what they mean. Otherwise, at best there can be confusion, at worst the spreading of misinformation. And for the public relations practitioner trying to get a foothold in the United States this could spell disaster and a quick flight home.

Understanding the media differences

Like their British counterparts, US journalists are busy, constantly looking for exclusives, and have little time for PRs who don't understand their individual needs and deadlines. American journalists often consider the public relations executive as an acceptable source, and will attribute quotes to him or her by name, rather than use the 'spokesperson' tag.

The media markets are quite different. Here, we are dominated by a number of major national newspapers. The US market has few newspapers with truly national reach, although most wire services cover nationwide news and the number of national cable TV stations and internet outlets has grown.

Anyone working over there will soon learn that the main targets of US publicists are the major regional news markets of print, television and radio and even the local media outlets, as well as the trade press.

While Sunday editions of major newspapers have different editors from the daily paper of the same name, they fall under the same corporate umbrella and often share reporters, so it is less likely that the same story can be placed in both the weekday and Sunday editions. Unlike here, you can usually get a photo editor on the phone.

The US media are generally more optimistic than here: they let go of a negative story when there is nothing new to report, and the writing style is more straightforward, with less dependence on intros and stand-firsts. Their attitude towards exclusives is quite different, and can spell trouble for a naïve PR person in Britain. Here, virtually every major news story is leaked to the media, and competing media then run it the next day.

Certainly, exclusives and 'leaks' are used in the United States, particularly in politics, but they run the risk of alienating other journalists who have long memories and will withhold coverage in return. In fact, if you give an exclusive to one media outlet, other media in the same market may refuse to run the story a day later. Exclusives must be justified to the other journalists whose interest you need.

The above section is based on advice given to a UK press officer by Susan Stevens (now Susan Stevens Boucher writer and PR consultant based in Central Massachusetts. She returned to the United States after living and working in the United Kingdom for nine years, two of which were with National Grid. Further information has been provided by Amy Atwood of Boston who also worked at National Grid with Boucher.

At a glance

- Appreciate and recognise the differences between American and British English.

- Use British English for one-version websites.

- For dual version sites, consider American English for US pages, British for UK.

- Keep releases in British English; let subs there make the changes.

- Public relations terms and titles differ.

- Check dictionaries for variations in definitions, spellings, grammar.

- Americans usually prefer -ize verb endings to -ise.

- There are wide variations in idiom and expressions.

- Be aware of the different ways American journalists treat exclusives.

17
The spoken word: pronunciation pointers

The way words are spoken is just as important as the way they are written. Well-enunciated speech, pronounced according to established guidelines, can help platform performance, aid communication between an organisation and its audience and make a significant contribution to the public relations effort.

Corporate image is not just the logo and visual impact of literature – the typeface, colours and house style. Much also depends on word of mouth and the mental picture of the speaker that is built up by tone of voice. And that picture is the one which can make all the difference between success and failure at a client presentation, a shareholders' meeting, a conference speech, or even a job interview.

No one wants to hear slipshod, careless speech like 'See yer layer', dropped or wrongly stressed vowels and syllables, missed consonants, a high-speed mumbo-jumbo of words shortened to the extent that they become almost unintelligible. Here are some basic points of pronunciation and a selection of verbal mishaps that are so easily made, but seldom corrected.

Received Pronunciation

Among the many varieties of English, Received Pronunciation (RP) is the standard most dictionaries follow. This is said to be 'the least regional being originally that used by educated speakers in Southern England' (*OED*), and the *Oxford A–Z of English Usage* takes it as 'the neutral national standard, just as it is in its use in broadcasting or in the teaching of English as a foreign language'. The new edition of *Fowler's Modern English Usage* makes specific recommendations based on RP and the pronunciations given are largely those of the *Concise Oxford English Dictionary (COED)*. It is from these, and other sources such as the BBC guide *The Spoken Word*, and the later *Oxford BBC Guide to Pronunciation*, that examples have been taken for pronunciation where uncertainty exists.

It is useful to differentiate between pronunciation and accent. As Kingsley Amis points out in *The King's English*, 'everyone's *accent* [his italics] is a general thing that depends roughly on a speaker's place of birth, upbringing, education and subsequent environment whereas *pronunciation* is a question of how individual words are spoken'. It can thus be deduced that pronunciation of a given word can be considered 'correct' while another may be 'incorrect'. RP provides a useful but limited yardstick by which pronunciation may be judged correct or not.

It should be noted that the main, hardback dictionaries including the *Oxford English Dictionary* and the *Concise English Dictionary* do not give pronunciations for everyday words like bake and baby since most native speakers of English do not, as a rule, have problems in using such terms. The principle followed is that pronunciations are given only where they are likely to cause difficulty such as foreign, scientific, technical and rare words or where stress patterns are disputed.

The International Phonetic Alphabet (IPA) is used to represent the standard accent of English as is spoken in the south of England, sometimes called Received Pronunciation or RP, states the preface to both dictionaries.

One of the most argued points is the placing of stress. If you know where it falls, the pronunciation of vowels can be determined. Look for the stress accent (like the French acute) after the stressed syllable or vowel sound in most popular dictionaries, even the well-thumbed pocket editions to be found in most office drawers. The stressed syllable (or vowel) is italicised in the following examples.

RP speakers will put the stress first in *a*dult, *app*licable, *con*troversy, *comm*unal, *bro*chure, *int*egral, *form*idable, *kil*ometre, *mis*chievous, *pat*ent (*pay*-tent), *pref*erable, *prim*arily, *rep*utable, *tem*porarily; but second in ba*nal*, con*trib*ute, de*mon*strable, dis*pute*, dis*trib*ute, re*search*, trans*fer*able. *Inter*esting loses the second syllable to become *intr*'sting, *com*parable to *compr*'ble. Stress on the third syllable occurs with appar*a*tus (as in *hate*), compos*ite* (as in *opp*osite), inter*ne*cine (as in *knee*).

Make sure there is not an intrusive 'r' in *drawing room* (not draw-ring), *an idea* of (not idea-r-of). Avoid the American habit of stressing -ar in *neces*sarily (not necess*ar*ily) and *tem*porarily (not tempor*ar*ily). Remember the *cog* in recognise and don't let it become *reccernise*, the short 'i' in privacy and don't let it become *eye*, and that the final 't' is sounded in restaurant. Sound the 'u' in popular, don't say *pop'lar*.

While 'h' is silent in *hour*, it is aspirated in *hotel* and so therefore takes the 'a' indefinite article (except in *The Times*, for example, which still insists on *an* hotel and other words with an unaspirated 'h' – an historic, an heroic, etc). While it is wrong to use 'n' for 'ng' in *length/strength* and so get *lenth/strenth*, the sound *lenkth/strenkth* is acceptable.

A long 'o' goes before 'll' in *poll* (vote) and before 'lt' in *revolt*, but there is a short 'o' in *resolve/dissolve/solve/golf* as in *doll*. *Either* as in *eye* or in *seize* – both are acceptable (the Queen is said to prefer *eye*). *Envelope* starts -en as in end (-on is disliked by RP speakers). *Data* has a long first 'a'.

In formal speech, say before an audience, avoid dropping the 'r' if it is closely followed by another 'r' as in *deteriorate* to get deteriate: similarly, *February* can slip to Febuary, *temporary* to tempary (but temp'rary OK), *honorary* to honary (hon'rary is preferred), *itinerary* to itinery, *library* to libr'y, *probably* to prob'ly. Avoid dropping the fourth syllable in *particularly* to get particuly but the elision of the middle syllables of adjectives of four syllables ending in -ary makes the words easier to pronounce as in milit'ry, necess'ry.

Watch out for syllable elisions in *chocolate, police, mathematics* to get the sloppy choc'lte, p'lice, math'matics. Don't let *fifth* become fith, *months* drop to 'munce', *camera* to 'camra'; make *lure* rhyme with *pure* not 'poor'. Articulate *railway*: don't let it become 'ro-way'. Don't let *conflicts* sound like 'conflix'. And don't lose the 'e' in *create* and let it sound like crate. Take care with the 'u' sound in some words: it should be *uh* in *uncle, multi, adult* not owcle, mowlti, adowlt.

Get the words right too

In speech, the rules that apply in written work can be eased a little, otherwise you could sound stilted and unnatural. Where there are uncertainties, like ending sentences with prepositions and split infinitives, forget about offending anyone. Don't worry too much about whether it is different *from* or *to*; but where *only* goes in a sentence can make a big difference to the meaning.

Never make grammatical errors like *there*'s two cars in the garage, every one of the delegates *were* present, the object of her articles *are* to inform, between you and *I* and so on, or colloquialisms like he was *sat* there. Follow the advice in earlier pages on style and construction. If you do that, you won't be far wrong when you are on your feet.

For more about speechwriting and delivery, see Chapter 18.

When speaking quickly, pronouns and auxiliary verbs easily disappear. Avoid *gonna/wanna, kinda, doncher* (don't you), *innit, wannit* (isn't it/wasn't it), 'spec/spose' (I expect/suppose). Careful speakers will retain the 't' in *facts, acts, ducts, pacts*; otherwise the listener hears fax/axe/ducks/packs. But it is silent in *often* as in *soften*. And don't forget the final 't' in *that*: it is often lost to become *tha is* for example.

American pronunciation differs markedly from the British. Some examples from the *Oxford A–Z of English Usage*: the 'r' is sounded by American speakers wherever it is written, after vowels finally and before consonants, as well as before vowels, like *burn*, *car*, *form*. The sound of *you* (as in *u*, *ew* spellings) after s, t, d, n, is replaced by the sound of *oo* as in resume (*resoom*), Tuesday (*Toosday*), due (*doo*), new (*noo*).

Americans pronounce asthma (*ass*-ma in RP) as *az*-ma; detour (*dee-* tour not *day*-tour in RP) as *de*-tour; gala (*a* as in *calm* in RP) as *gale*. They will say *trow*ma as in *cow* whereas RP speakers will say *trau*ma (*au* as in *cause*).

Some forms of pronunciation are to be especially avoided. Among these are *Arctic* (do not drop the first 'c'); *et cetera* (not *eksetera*); don't let *garage* (with stress on the first syllable) sound like *garridge*; do not drop the first 'n' in *government* or the whole second syllable; do not say *pee* for pence in formal speech; avoid making *people* sound like *peeple*; ensure *plastic* rhymes with *fantastic*; *sovereignty* is pronounced *sov*'renty, not sounding like sov-*rain*-ty; a *suit* is now pronounced with an -*oo* sound although the *you* sound is still frequently heard. *Secretary* is pronounced *sek*-re-try not *sek*-e-terry or even worse *sukk*-a-terry). *January* should sound like *Jan*-yoor-y, not Jan-yoo-ery (except in America). You take your pet to the *vet*-er-in-ary practice, not vet'nary. You buy jewel'rey not *jool-ler-y*. You look at a *pic*-ture not a *pitcher* and you make a *fort*-une, not a *forchoon*. You read a book, not a *berk*; you have a look, not a *lerk*. And it is all a matter of pronunciation, not pronounciation!

There are probably more regional forms of speech in the United Kingdom than anywhere else in the world, and it is in no sense suggested here that everyone should follow RP; adjustments have to be made as circumstances demand in various parts of the country. Just as much depends on *how* you say something as *what* you say. RP provides a useful guide.

At a glance

- The key to effective verbal communication lies in good diction.
- No one wants to hear slipshod, careless speech.
- Received Pronunciation (RP) is a useful yardstick for 'better' language.
- Placement of stress identifies RP speakers.
- In fast talking, pronouns and modal verbs are easily lost.
- Enunciate words precisely; don't drop consonants.
- Don't allow words to become slurred.
- Avoiding grammatical errors is equally important in speech.

18
Principles of presentation

Sooner or later everyone has to speak in public. PR practitioners are no exception: as organisers, they soon find themselves on stage; even the youngest recruits will be presenting to clients and customers before they know it. And there is always the staff meeting with a room-full of blank faces waiting for that important announcement, perhaps the seminar, the conference or after-dinner speech.

The ability to express yourself clearly with confidence and style is a key business skill. And the better you are, the more likely you are to land a better job or even reach the conference circuit, with attendant financial rewards.

Public speakers are made, not born. Even fast talkers with the 'gift of the gab' are not necessarily going to be good on their feet. If you can develop the skills of presentation, use body language effectively and deliver with force and aplomb, you are on the way to becoming a star on stage.

We have all suffered from after-dinner speakers too nervous to say anything but platitudes, lecturers fidgeting and waving their hands around like a windmill, technical boffins reading word-for-word from a prepared script, grim-faced production executives looking and sounding petrified, glaring at the audience, and the chairman who hisses into the mike 'Can you hear me at the back?' Avoid anything like this and at least you will have made a start.

Even if the speaker performs well, success or failure will depend on the organiser. If the mikes don't work, if the slides are upside down or if the session overruns, that is what is remembered; if the press handouts are inadequate, if anything major goes wrong, there's the possibility of lost business and, horror of horrors, a 'See me in the morning' message on your desk.

So, what makes a good speaker and organiser?

First steps for speakers

When you are invited to give a speech, there are several things you must know: the audience, title, length, timing, visual aids facilities, how the discussion will be handled, and the publicity plans. If you are advising executives on public speaking, or an event organiser, these are all crucial factors. Let's look at them.

Know your audience – and the facilities

First, find out all you can about the audience: who they are, what they do, where they come from, their average age. Establish likely attendance, whether there will be media coverage. If you are the organiser, make sure that the event is widely reported unless there are special reasons for it to be off the record. Find out if the delegates will be sympathetic or critical, the prime questions they will ask, the one you will *have* to answer.

Be prepared to involve the audience: arrange for someone to put up another flip chart and work between the two. Ascertain the name of the chairperson and who the other speakers will be, especially those just before you. And while you are at it, check the technical facilities, lighting, stage set and platform plan. Get to know the production crew. Ensure every seat allows an uninterrupted view of the stage. Check the lighting – and find out where the switches are. And make sure the doors don't squeak; take an oil can with you!

Title

Is the title you have been given right or do you want to suggest something else? Unless the talk has to follow a certain theme, you can probably agree a change with the organiser. If so, ensure that it is provocative, not a 'label' devoid of punch and verve. Keep it as short as possible. Many years ago a leading advertising agency creative director called his pleas to production executives 'Why can't I get what I want?' That title worked extremely well and was quoted for years afterwards. Make sure you have a say in the 'blurb' about the subject of your speech; provide a colour photograph of yourself.

Length and timing

Agree to speak for no longer than half an hour, with a further 10 to 15 minutes for questions. Forty minutes would be the absolute maximum, otherwise the audience starts to get fidgety. For specialist seminars 20 to 30 minutes plus a short discussion period would suit most people. The shorter it is, the better the chance of your holding audience attention.

The worst time for any speaker is the session immediately following lunch. Avoid it whatever you do. Simply refuse that slot: it is when the audience is the least receptive to any serious, in-depth presentation. The organiser will appreciate your dilemma. The best time is a morning session, but not at the very beginning because there will always be latecomers. If you are stuck with it and there is nothing else you can do, use the 'wake-'em up' tricks of a noisy tape, a snappy video or an an eye-catching slide or stage prop.

The same timing principles apply to smaller meetings and seminars. Inhouse sessions don't present such a problem: staff don't dare to nod off. No matter what kind of event, you cannot expect much response at question time if you are the last afternoon speaker. Keynote speakers usually take one of the first morning slots.

Visual aids

Slides generated by a computer program such as PowerPoint, overhead transparencies (OHPs), videos, DVDs and audio tapes all help to pep up a presentation. Don't show horizontal and vertical slides one after the other; keep to one format and include plenty of photographs or drawings. Ensure that images fill the slides and overheads as much as possible. Keep text to bullet-points and don't exceed 25 words – use fewer if possible.

Make sure you have a broadband connection so that you can quickly log on to the company website to show some particular feature of its work, personnel or premises. Consult with your IT department to see if the web pages could be projected on to a large screen rather than relying on a desk-top computer.

If there are a number of statistics, keep the slides simple with a minimum of figures. For AGMs in particular, don't have more than five or six figure-slides; any more will have nil recall. Use bold type so that text and figures can be easily read; put bar charts in strong, contrasting colours. Keep to house style throughout and repeat the company logo on everything. PowerPoint computer-generated slides from Microsoft allow maximum creative possibilities. Provide delegates with all the statistical data as a handout – but only afterwards.

Questions

Be ready for the awkward question that comes from the back. If you can't answer it straight off, there's always the 'See me afterwards' ploy. But don't use it more than once if you can help it. You can always ask 'What do you mean by that?', which can silence the questioner for good. Or you can change the question to one you can deal with. Or, as a last resort, you can refer to a book or publication, even the handout material. Run through the sort of questions you are likely to get beforehand and have your answers ready.

FIGURE 18.1 Strong design for Gold award winner Marie Curie Cancer Care in the Institute of Practitioners in Advertising's 2011 Advertising Effectiveness Awards. Agency: DLKW Lowe

Publicity

Find out the plans for publicising your speech. Important points will lead to headlines, but be on your guard against leaks. (A deliberate leak can often help to spark interest.) The organiser will give you a deadline for a summary and for the completed paper with visual aids requirements.

The summary, which should contain the salient points in not more than around 150 words, will be used for the conference or seminar programme and also for advance press releases. Provide photocopies of the slides with the text of the speech, which can be made available to the press during and after the event. Provide VNRs (video news releases) and 'B' rolls to give broadcasters footage of important segments. Ensure all information in the publicity material is accurate and does you and your subject justice. Put your speech on your website afterwards with access to charts and statistics and with a link to the press release archive.

Getting ready for the speech

You have decided on what you, your client and/or your boss want to say and have supplied a summary to the organiser. You've decided on the title, you know how long the speech will be and you have a pretty good idea of what visual aids you are going to need. Now comes the crunch. It's writing time.

Preparation

The longer you can spend on preparation the better. Unfortunately, there is not always much chance for detailed research: start to gather notes, put basic ideas together. Don't forget the internet: it could provide much additional information – but check sources. If you are writing about a familiar subject, say a company development, service or product, the information will be to hand. But if you are dealing with a fresh topic, perhaps an after-dinner speech, then it's not so easy. You'll have to devote time to digging out interesting, yet relevant, things to say.

Look for facts and figures that will in themselves tell a story. But try to restrict yourself to statistics that have direct relevance to the subject. Unless they are essential background or are needed to substantiate a financial or technical subject, don't let statistics predominate. Don't try to be funny and start off with a joke. It could fall flat. Or someone will have heard it already! But take heart from the audience that *pretends* to laugh.

Structure

Like a report or feature article, your speech should have a beginning (an introduction), a middle (the body of the talk) and an end (a conclusion). The introduction should include something about yourself, who you are, what you do, followed by a quote or attention-grabbing fact, what the talk will be about and your main message.

Build on this for the main part of the talk, with the significant points and ideas you want to put over. For the conclusion, summarise the main points and finish on a high note with a recommendation for action of some sort. If there is no action as a result of what you have said, there was not much point in saying it.

Writing the script

For your speech to impart the desired message, for it to be well received and remembered, polished writing skills are essential. Go back to the earlier chapters 5 and 8–13 in particular, for help in getting the words and style right. Now for the rest.

Brevity

Ensure that no unnecessary words creep in. This demands extreme self-discipline, but the tighter the copy the better. The script should be more like a press release than, say, a long, fully reasoned article in a learned journal. Keep to plain English (see Chapter 9) and avoid clichés and jargon (Chapter 5), also avoid pleonasms (two concepts or words containing an element of redundancy, eg frozen ice, past history).

Be factual

Use the 'you' factor. Keep to facts or else you are likely to bore the audience stiff. Concentrate on new developments, services, the advantages and benefits of what you are going to talk about. If you have a comment or personal view to express, then use the personal pronoun 'I' and not the royal 'we'. But don't overdo the 'I', otherwise you will be seen as egotistical. Sprinkle your talk liberally with 'you'; if the ratio of 'you' to 'I' is not 10 to 1 in favour of 'you', rewrite your speech.

Repeat important points

Avoid repeating a word or words in close proximity to one another. It is, however, sometimes helpful to recall a point to give it extra emphasis. The audience will understand this.

Keep to the rules of grammar

Nothing will irritate your audience more than sloppy English. But don't worry about those myths of split infinitives and ending sentences with prepositions – in fact your speech could well sound a lot better, more natural, if you are not in the straitjacket of schoolroom strictures. Don't succumb to pedantry.

Avoid foreign words and phrases. Don't try to impress with your knowledge of foreign languages or you could be seen as showing off. Stick to plain English: avoid ad hoc, quid quo pro, raison d'être, nom de plume, for example.

Be controversial

Controversy sparks interest but be careful with sharp criticism. If you must find fault with somebody or something, make sure you present your arguments succinctly and back them up with solid evidence. Unless you are careful you might have lawyers at your door!

Keep anecdotes pithy

Beware of humour, which might not be appreciated by all your audience. If you have a joke up your sleeve which might offend one person in the audience, don't tell it. Rarely is anyone other than a professional comedian good at being funny on stage!

Be active and positive

Keep to subjects you care deeply about. Use the active, 'doing' tense, not the passive: choose verbs like go, tell, make, show. Once you allow was/were/have been/being in your presentation, you're stuck in the slow lane. Use single-syllable verbs when you can: they give punch and push. Don't write 'keep you abreast of' instead put 'Tell you' (see Chapter 9).

Kill double-talk

Tautology – saying the same thing again in another way (free gift, new innovation) – offends. It's the enemy of tight, crisp delivery.

No slang, bad language

Never use bad language no matter how informal the presentation. Be careful with slang: too many geeks, spiels, luvvies, gizmos or technonerds lower the tone. Don't use abbreviations, acronyms or technical jargon that might not be understood. Catch the mood of the delegates and don't talk down to them.

Draft and redraft

Never think that the first attempt at putting the speech into final text will do. Your effort will need several drafts by the time you have cut the verbiage, deleted useless words, and cut out confusing double-negatives and meaningless abbreviations. Type it double-spaced, not in capitals. And don't forget to run it through your spellcheck, not once but twice or once again for luck. And when you do, be careful you don't introduce more errors: they can easily happen.

Getting ready

Unless you plan to memorise your speech (which seldom works), put the salient points on cards with key words and phrases clearly marked. Have the typescript at your side (in loose sheets paper-clipped together, not stapled) in case of panics. Prompt cards should be numbered and of a convenient size; postcard-size is ideal.

Text should be in fairly large type, so that it can be easily read in dark conditions. Just a few bullet-points, not all the words, otherwise you will be tempted to read them out. Visual aids should be in the right order and be sure to rehearse and re-rehearse with the production team beforehand, ending with a full run-through. Ensure the lectern is at an appropriate height; if not, ask for adjustments. Don't tap tap the mike when you are about to start – all that should have been taken care of.

When you're on stage

You've patted your pocket to make sure you have your script or notes ready. When you go to the platform or make your way to the lectern from the speakers' table, here are a few tips.

Allow plenty of time. Don't leave everything to the last minute: something is bound to go wrong or not to your liking. Arrive early. Not only will you have time to sort out any last-minute problems, it will enable you to keep stress levels down and make you feel at ease.

If you reach the platform flustered and nervous that's a signal for disaster and the audience will soon notice it. As Jo Billingham says in *Giving Presentations* (OUP), 'Remember the swan: be serene on the surface but inject energy to keep the momentum going.'

Ensure you keep to the allotted time. Don't overrun or the chairman will be forced to stop you and that's not good news for anyone. Apart from anything else, your over-long speech could mean that other speakers would have to cut down theirs.

Making the speech

Don't read it out word for word, turning the pages over one by one. That's boring. Put passion in your speech. Speak from the heart. Use those prompt cards and back up with visual aids or other props like books or objects relevant to your talk. Don't bellow into the mike. Keep your hands and arms still unless you want to point to a chart, and then preferably use an electronic pointer. Fix points in the audience and make eye contact in several places.

Always stand up when you address an audience, even at question time. The only exception is a break-out discussion session, when informality is usual. Your goal as a communicator is for people to understand and absorb your message. Pauses contribute substantially to the power of your delivery.

Silence before a particular point adds depth. Take a lesson from the way you write: punctuate the spoken word with pauses – long for a full stop, short for a comma.

If you have a standing mike, always keep it between you and the audience: if, for instance, you are looking towards the left, move slightly to the right so that the mike is directly between you and them. Otherwise, your voice might drift away. If, on the other hand, you have been given a clip-on mike, it won't matter where you are, but remember to take it off when you leave the stage.

Your body language is crucial

Getting body language right is essential for every speaker, irrespective of the kind or level of audience. Your on-stage performance will be measured by the way you present yourself, how you stand, how you look, your expression, the way you move about and make eye contact. Look happy, confident.

Posture is all-important. Stand well with feet slightly apart. A wooden, stiff speaker will put the audience off before a single word is said. If you stand like a Guardsman on Palace duty you might as well give up.

A few suggestions: don't fold your arms, don't adjust your hairdo (unless you're behind a curtain), don't fiddle with coins, don't grimace. Move about the stage, but don't overdo it otherwise it will be a distraction.

Establish a 'base' position, perhaps at the lectern or screen and return to it by taking a few short, definite steps. Use your hands occasionally to emphasise a point, perhaps to replicate a crucial element in your speech. Keep your fingers well tucked in. Thumbs sticking up in the air, a favourite trick of politicians, doesn't look in the least attractive.

Your facial expression will help to emphasise a point far better than a sharp, telling sentence. Make sure you develop regular eye contact with the audience. You need to look at different points in the group before you: look up, down and across. Fix your eyes on a particular person, but don't linger too long otherwise they will feel uncomfortable. Vary your delivery: slow down, speed up; pause for a moment or two for dramatic effect.

Getting the balance right is tricky: if you move your eyes from one group to another in rapid succession you might appear shifty; stay too long in one place and the group or individual might start to fidget. A smile works wonders but not a wide, Cheshire-cat grin: that spells insincerity. Stay in total control. Deliver your presentation as if your life, even the whole world, depends on it.

Dealing with fear

Everyone suffers to a greater or lesser extent from fear when speaking in public; however much effort you've made in getting the words right, the visuals spot on, it's of no avail if you're frozen stiff with stage fright. Take every opportunity to be on your feet. Offer to take part in the next client presentation or staff meeting: it will give you first-class practice for the real thing in a packed conference hall. Don't drink alcohol before a speech or presentation; this slows reaction at the very point when you need to be on your toes and alert.

Take some tips from Roy Topp, public speaking coach. He advises:

Breathe deeply and slowly. This controls the heart rate. Also, strange as it may seem, roll the soles of your feet from heel to toe, on the floor under the table. No one will notice and although it sounds improbable, it certainly helps. Look round the room. Concentrate on the broad picture.

Move slowly and do not let anyone rush you. When you stand up or move across the floor to approach the lectern, move easily and at leisure. This will not stop you being nervous, but it will control that anxiety and give the impression that you are in full control.

Keep your hands out of your pockets. Let them rest by your side. Keep your fingers off the lectern unless you are making a point; don't wave your arms about. Take your speech at a reasonable pace. Count slowly to three when pausing. Do not rush it. Pause, and look at your audience occasionally (you are in control). Do not talk over laughter or applause. You have earned it.

Do not be too hasty to dash away. Remember, if you have a clip mike on your dress or lapel, remove it first, otherwise you might literally bring the house down!

In conclusion

Sum up the important points of your presentation – not more than 10, as above that they'll be forgotten. Make a recommendation, or a series of them, for action to make something happen. End on a high note. Thank the audience for their attention.

At question time

Note down each question and listen to all of it. Thank the person asking it. Repeat it for the benefit of those who may not have heard it. If you get a difficult question, you can possibly refer it to another person in the audience. And there's always that get-out 'See me later' or 'I don't have the facts with me right now' – time to find a satisfactory answer after the session.

Points for organisers

The programme

A well-designed, printed programme is essential. It should give the title of every session, the speaker, with a photograph, the chairperson and a brief summary of the subject, as well as the fee, registration details and information about the organisation running the event.

It should be widely distributed to the target audiences and the press, and be accompanied by a supporting letter from the organiser. This is the main 'selling' medium for the event and it should not be skimped. The print run should allow for at least two mailings. Design should follow style for the company and the logo should appear prominently. Put the programme on the company website.

Conference papers

It is important that copies of conference papers are available not only to the press but also to delegates. However, ensure that delegates are only able to obtain copies after the speech; otherwise, they will be turning over the pages one by one and not listening or watching the screen, or – worse still – might skip the session altogether. Conference papers can be made available afterwards as a printed book – and add to the revenue.

Publicity

News releases

Restrict news releases to reporters and other editorial staff. Copies of speeches, background information, the programme and other administrative material should be available in the press office. Follow-up releases, giving important recommendations and findings, should be issued. Don't forget to provide plenty of telephones and facilities for sending and receiving emails with a broadband connection.

The press conference

If you are responsible for press conferences and briefings, take a low-profile stance and let those responsible for making announcements take the stage. Your job is to introduce the speakers, see to the administrative details and make sure the journalists have the information they need. The principles outlined in this chapter apply to press conferences and briefings in the same way as to any other presentation.

At a glance

For speakers

- Know your audience – who they are, what they do – assess available facilities.

- Allow plenty of time to sort out problems. Arrive early.

- Give your speech an attention-grabbing title. Be controversial. Use an active verb.

- Restrict length to 40 mins maximum, 20–30 mins for specialist seminars.

- Don't agree to a session immediately after lunch. Choose a morning slot.

- Prepare your speech carefully. Give it a beginning, middle and end.

- Don't forget the internet to provide information. Ask for a large on-stage screen.

- Body language is crucial in getting your message across. Rehearse, rehearse.

For organisers

- First priorities: decide on objectives and theme, visual aids, timing.

- Employ professional organiser and designer for best results.

- Look for financing possibilities through sponsorship and exhibitions.

- Estimate print costs and fees for celebrity chairperson or after-dinner speaker.

- Choice of venue is an important decision: in hotel, conference centre, abroad?

- Build in plenty of time for rehearsals when booking the venue.

- Decide on whether to make the event open to the press.

- Ensure all written material is in house style. Visual aids should carry company logo.

19
Writing for the web

Effective PR needs internet presence

Electronic communications have transformed the way we work, the way we live. An internet presence is a public relations tool second to none: at the click of a mouse we reach our audiences in an instant; we email copy to the media, send messages to clients and suppliers at no cost; we write blogs on subjects of our choice, transmit podcasts and have iPods, iPads, Androids, BlackBerrys and ereaders in our pockets. We pick up news, see advertisements, and send messages on the move. It is a communications revolution to benefit all. And it is one which changes and develops almost by the hour.

This chapter does not attempt to cover technological developments in detail: it is not the work of this book. It is the written and spoken word, how we write and present the information, that controls whether we get our messages across. No matter how useful the gadgets and gizmos, if the user fails to understand the message or perhaps even be able to read it, then time and money are wasted. That's just PR effort down the drain.

A carefully created and structured campaign could be ruined by a website that is a jumble of junky images, an email that goes adrift and lands on the wrong desk, a blog that offends, a text message that is so truncated and obscure that it is meaningless. So what are the crucial points? Here's a round-up.

Website content and design – the essentials

According to the Internet Advertising Bureau, worldwide more than two billion are now regularly online every day; that's a third of the global population. In the UK, there are over 51 million internet users – that's 82 per cent of the population. Those who aren't online tend to be in the older or lower socio-economic groups. In another few years, that figure could easily reach 30 million online homes.

Men are more likely to use the internet than women, says Nielsen netratings. Young women are the biggest online group. There are over 18 million residential broadband connections. Three-quarters of adults use the internet either on fixed receivers or mobiles. About half the adult population have a social networking profile. Usage of social networks and blogs accounts for 23 per cent of time spent on the internet in the United Kingdom, a 160 per cent increase over the last three years, according to Nielsen.

Clearly then, a company's website is a powerful public relations tool, not only for communicating directly with most consumers, but also with businesses and organisations of all sizes.

Good web writing – what it is

Journalists usually go to a company's website for first information and contacts. Therefore, it must be well-written and to the point. If that is achieved then all other users will get the benefit of seeing short sentences and paragraphs, no clichés or jargon – subjects covered in earlier chapters which all apply. Even so, web writing is not like writing a brochure or leaflet. Web users don't treat a web page like a newspaper article or book: they tend to scan it and look for the important parts, those which they want to know about.

Let's start at the beginning. Your audience is your first priority as a writer. You must first define it and take that definition as a guide for content. Is your website written in a way they will understand and appreciate? Does it give the information they need? Is it relevant? You should ensure that everything you write follows the company's house style, that it is in simple and plain language (no fancy Latin terms or foreign words).

Use the short word for the long, and go for the active tense rather than the passive. Keep to the rules of grammar, watch for spelling mistakes and don't slip into sloppy texting language whatever you do. There's no room for 'weblish' in business communications. Take a tip from the advertiser: persuade the viewer to do something, to take action of some kind, say go to a specific link, call a telephone number, send an email, perhaps contact the organisation by snail mail. Write for your audience and give them what they want. Since most visitors scan the pages, use headings and bullet points to highlight the crucial points.

Above all, ensure that there is a link to your online press office and to a press release archive with names, contact numbers and email addresses. For some, that can be an irritation and some PR practitioners prefer to use a regular email address rather than have the viewer log on to a site where enquiries have to go through a dedicated web page. See Chapter 11, Writing for the media, for more on this.

Presentation matters

Put the subject or most important point at the top of the page in the same way the print journalist does and sets it 'above the fold'. Start with a short intro to say what the page is all about. Then launch into detail but not too much of it. Most web users' attention span is short and unless you hold their interest they will give up and move to another site. Left to right and up-down eye movement should be taken into account when designing web pages or presenting information. This is the involuntary way our eyes track information.

There are several key factors here: write in short chunks, say between 8 and 10 words per line, never more than 20–30 words in all, preferably fewer. Insert a line space between each one to provide 'air' and to kill any stodgy look. Scanning readers will tend to read the first line and skip the rest. Break up your text into just a few paragraphs with each one having a central point or idea. Aim for a fact in each sentence. Cut out any waffle or needless, redundant words. And be as brief as you can.

Text design basics

Most web-page designers will specify a sans-serif typeface, for example Arial, Helvetica or Verdana for text. Serif fonts, like Times Roman or Bodoni are rarely used, except within images. Set text no smaller than 12 point, leaded one or two points. Range left to produce ragged right text, so no indents. This is far easier to read than justified text with both sides lined up. Use a light background colour with black or dark shade for text and for headings and subheadings at line-starts. Do not specify more than two or perhaps three different typefaces on one page: that can only irritate and confuse the reader.

Use bullet points, usually dots or other typographic symbols, for short one-liners of up to 10 or 12 words and to signal important items. Figures are better than letters for lists, but a bold dot will usually be sufficient. One of the best ways to secure attention is to split up text that would normally occupy a paragraph into short bullet points of just a few words.

You can cheer up the dullest page with a draw-down quote of only a few words, by inserting a picture or other illustration. Website visitors will look for the signposts that will take them to the information they want: hyperlinks will stand out in colour and underlined, but don't use bold or italics within the text. Leave typographical styles like that to headings and sub-headings. And don't underline anywhere, otherwise it will be thought to be a hyperlink.

A good heading is crucial

This subject has been covered in Chapter 7 and the principles outlined there relate also to the web page. These are worth summarising here: always use a verb and put it in the active voice otherwise it becomes bland and boring, what is called a verbless 'label' heading; be creative and think of a play on words, a double entendre or anything that will jerk the eye and encourage the reader to read on and find out more.

Make them descriptive, even funny if you like. Don't let headlines run into more than one line if you can help it, don't use capitals as they can be seen as aggressive and forbidding. The capitalised heading seems as if it is shouting at you. And that would never do.

First priority: make it readable

Readability is all-important. Consider carefully and take in all the points made in Chapter 6. Try to keep each page small enough to occupy the user's screen, and avoid the messy business of running over to another page – that is if you have held the reader's attention that far.

It helps if you vary the length of paragraphs and keep to short sentences of up to 20 words. Insert illustrations and, as previously emphasised, write in bite-sized chunks. A screen-full of text is almost impossible to read and means an instant switch to another page or more likely to a new website.

A page with white spaces – empty areas devoid of text or images – helps to make the page readable and more alive. The spaces make it easier for the reader to read and give the eyes a rest.

Don't overcrowd the screen with too much detail. It is not a good idea to have more than two or perhaps three colours on one page. Do not put text in lightish colour over another pale one: always go for contrast. Black on white works well, but is not very kind on the eye. Dark blue over a yellow, on the other hand, works well provided the yellow is not a dark shade.

Do not reverse out long runs of text using a light colour out of a dark one; you can do that in a heading but in text it sets the brain on edge. Never let type stretch right across the page: some say it would be better to put it into two columns, but even that spells too much to me. Inform, entertain, satisfy and keep it simple are key to designing a readable website page.

What makes a good website

Long before you start website writing there are some prime decisions to make. Among these are what it is for and what you want it to do for you and your company. Do you see an internet presence primarily as a selling medium, an extension of your marketing activity or as an information source? Do you want to make your website markedly different from others in the sector?

To answer such questions you should carry out in-depth market research to ensure that you will provide your target audiences with what they need and want. As a start, it would be an idea to browse through your competitors' sites and see how they do it and what 'extras' they provide, for example interactivity, podcasts, audio and video webcasts, blogs and so on.

Then you must ensure that it is easy to navigate with an option to search the site, is fully accessible to all including those with disabilities, and preferably has an online press centre with RSS (Really Simple Syndication) feeds to deliver news and features direct to the user. The home page should have a link to the online press centre which should have full contact details and contain a press release archive. See also Chapter 11.

Make provision for regular updating: an outdated site, even of just a week or so, is worse than useless. News and new developments about the company should ideally flash up on the user's screen with links for more

FIGURE 19.1 Teesside University, the winning website in the 2011 CIPR Excellence Awards. The judges saw this as an innovative alternative to a traditional way to recruit students to the university. To grow postgraduate recruitment the in-house team decided to hold a virtual open day allowing prospective students to meet and chat with academic staff online

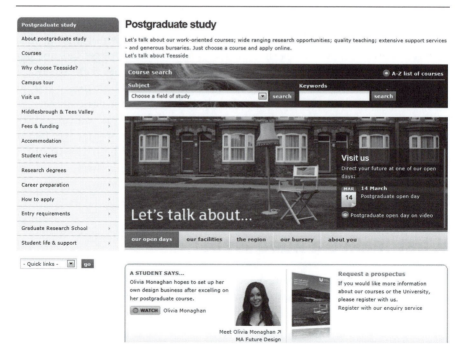

details. Include an events calendar, a site map and search facility. The home page should give the address and telephone number of the company to save journalists and others the trouble of searching through endless detail, as well as hyperlinks to the press centre and contact points.

Replays of speeches, presentations, reports and articles by key personnel to allow users to download audio files to desktop and MP3 players should be provided and be readily accessible. A virtual tour of the company and its facilities would be a novel add-on among the 'bells and whistles' of a modern website. And, of course, a webmaster to whom any comments or complaints should be addressed must be prominently displayed.

SEO (Search Engine Optimisation) should be kept in mind. Content providers and website designers should ensure that sites are organised for access by search engines. Most users don't know the particular domain name or URL of a website and tend to search a word or phrase in Google or Yahoo, or indeed any other search engine.

It is important that a website's content is optimised so that the site will be ranked high on the chosen search engine. An example would be trying to minimise the use of images (say those containing funky text) as headers instead of using normal text and adjusting the font.

Accessibility priorities

Websites now have a duty by law to be fully accessible to all visitors. Even though there has yet to be a test case, any newly-built websites must adhere to the guidelines set out by the Web Accessibility Initiative, emphasises Marie York, the CIPR's former Head of Innovation. The terms of the guidelines on navigation and quick tips to make accessible websites are given in the WAI website (**www.w3.org/WAI/quicktips/**).

A lawyer's view

Website designers must be careful not to discriminate against disabled people, says barrister Philip Circus, a partner in Lawmark (**www.lawmark.co.uk**). The Equality Act 2010 applies to any company providing goods or services to the public and forbids any discrimination on the basis of a person's disability.

The Act is usually thought of in terms of access to buildings, but as online marketing grows apace, it also covers websites. Failure to adhere to the Act is a breach of statutory duty and, he says, 'could be actionable by an aggrieved individual'. Circus adds that success in a claim would give a 'right to damages'.

Another legal point worth noting here is the need to update your electronic information. From 1 January 2007, a company's website and other electronic communications had to contain the same legally-required information as given on stationery and other hard copy documents. If the

FIGURE 19.2 Teesside University open day registration form

Teesside University

2009/10
THE AWARDS
Times Higher Education
UNIVERSITY OF THE YEAR

Postgraduate study

Register your details

Thursday 24 May

Let's talk about you

If you'd like to book a place on our postgraduate virtual open day, just fill in the form below. Some information is essential and marked with asterisks(*).

○ Back to event details

* First name:

* Surname:

* Email:

* Date of birth:
(format: 01/01/2010)

* Address 1:

Address 2:

* Town/City:

* Postcode:

* Country: Select One

business is a limited company, the company's name must be given together with its place of registration and number, and the address of its registered office. If the firm's share capital is stated, the amount must be its paid-up share capital.

'Emails are essentially business letters in electronic form and must comply. Every email should therefore contain the relevant information as standard,' says Anne Copley, Head of Legal at the British Printing Industries Federation.

New rules for cookies

New regulations for cookies – small text files that remember what sites a user has visited on the internet – came into force under Privacy and Electronic Communications Regulations in May 2011. Apart from cookies, the changes relate to the need for service providers to report personal data breaches and the powers that the Information Commissioner's Office (ICO) has to enforce the regulations.

The new regulations force website owners to obtain user consent before tracking online activity through cookies. The ICO has advised that websites should not rely on browser settings as indicating whether a user consents to having their online activity tracked. The regulations also apply to similar technologies for storing information, for example Local Shared Objects, commonly referred to as 'Flash Cookies'.

For information on the new rules go to **http://www.ico.gov.uk**, then go to the search box and key in 'cookies'. The site provides a downloadable pdf giving advice on the new cookies regulations and sets out what steps you need to take to ensure compliance.

Meeting the needs of your target audience

Be clear about the target audience. The website is a prime means of communication between the organisation and its publics and not just an information source for all and sundry. Everything you write and how it is written, the design concepts and the style of your company must come across to the user in the simplest, most concise way. In other words, it should be user-friendly, relevant and up-to-date.

The Investor Relations Society (IRS) has set out the key principles in its best practice website guidelines. Go to **http://www.irs.org.uk/resources/best-practice-guidelines** for information. The guidelines include the provision of a comprehensive site map, a search-site facility with a feedback mechanism for those having difficulty in finding what they want, and a tracking system at the top or bottom of the page to give visitors a quick reference to their current position on the site.

Other key points are that the site must be regularly updated and content reviewed at least once a month, if not weekly. Press releases should be uploaded to the website as soon as they are published. The same applies to publications such as the annual and interim reports, brochures and policy documents as well as to speeches, reports and articles by key executives.

Podcasts should be made available immediately once a presentation or speech has been delivered. The website designer should also set up an email alert system to draw attention to AGMs, conferences, exhibitions and meetings so that advance information can be requested and provided.

And of course it goes without saying that your site must be carefully monitored and the number of hits regularly recorded. The name and contact name of the webmaster must be prominently displayed, with other contact details of senior executives giving telephone/mobile numbers, as well as email and postal addresses.

A specialist PR view

'Engage, inform, entertain,' says Diana Thompson, managing director of PlusPoint PR, a specialist consultancy. 'Web design is a real art, combining both logic and creative skills. The logic ensures that the site mapping is good and users can instantly define and access information and move around the site or to links in an effortless manner.

'The creativity is required to keep the user involved and to make the content so valuable or useful that they return again and again. It is a big mistake for companies to believe their corporate or product literature can just be transferred into this medium.

'The internet is such a powerful multi-media tool and users expect both excitement and instant satisfaction. Huge text blocks are dull so should be dissected into bite-size pieces. Pages should be well illustrated with still or moving images, but bear in mind the effect your choice will have on the speed of page loading.

'Response mechanisms to involve users work well if they are effectively constructed and easy to use. Topicality is key; being out of date is a PR disaster. Users expect latest company and product data and it is also a great way to relay your latest news stories.

'And, finally, don't forget to talk to specialist agencies to ensure you are at the top of search engines such as Google and Yahoo when key words are logged in.'

A computer expert says...

Steve Sawyer, Commercial Director and web integration specialist at IRIS Software Group, says that the goal is a readable, usable site through which the visitor can interact with the organisation. Clear, consistent navigation, plenty of links to further or supporting content for the enquiring mind, and the provision for interactivity are all crucial.

'From a PR viewpoint, the designer must make provision for an online press centre with the latest press releases, easy access to archive material, the ability to download video clips and podcasts of speeches, photographs.' Above all, he says, the web offers the opportunity to engage with visitors and encourage further activity, whether that is to download materials, visit supporting sites, purchase products or services, register an interest, comment or even criticise.

Sawyer emphasises that it is important for the writer to recognise that while the organisation might have a target audience in mind, content is rarely restricted to one type of reader. 'Journalists, investors, customers, activists, detractors and stakeholders of all varieties will read the same information. Rigorous consistency of message is therefore required: you can't say one thing to one group and something else to another.'

He adds that the most effective websites build relationships with visitors, as a trusted source of information, product or service provider, or engaging in a debate.

An IT specialist observes...

Branislav Bokan, an IT specialist with Global Commodity Supplier, says that he sees a lot of 'weblish' in day-to-day communication with fellow professionals, for instance inconsistent use of capital letters, and extensive use of 'short cuts' especially when receiving messages from senior management, the most popular being 'ASAP'.

New web communication media

In recent years, says Bokan, there has been a 'significant shift' towards the new web communication media. Some people call them 'genres' which include blogs, wikis and Twitter postings. Each genre has its own 'style' of web writing and specific ways of engaging with its audiences.

Blogs

Blogs, for example, are websites that collect a series of posts to attract 'bloggers' to contribute to discussions on a particular topic. Unfortunately, quality of writing is usually poor with very few grammar and style rules applied. Even so, they attract web readers as they actively engage in information exchange.

Wikis

Defined as a website or database developed by a community of users allowing any user to add or edit content, wikis are generally used for reading or directly engaging, in contrast to blogs and tweets. 'Usually very structured websites, wikis need a specific style of writing which is more descriptive rather than engaging', he says. 'Since wikis have a very "encyclopaedic" character, web writers must ensure that information is accurately presented'.

Twitter

Twitter is popular among web readers because the posts are short and to the point. Although tweets are short blocks of text, they must be well-written to attract the reader's attention. Twitter, discussed extensively in Chapter 10, only allows 140 characters so that a statement or argument can be easily posted. To encourage interest in the content, the writing style must be engaging and messages strong. Really successful tweets are those posted by very witty writers, says Bokan.

Creative possibilities

When writing for the web, take advantage of the many creative possibilities which are not available for other forms of communication. Among the numerous website building blocks, the following could be useful for the web writer:

Hyperlinks are important as they open the door to numerous internet information pockets allowing readers to satisfy their reading curiosity or to gather data for any other purpose. But hyperlinks must be precisely presented with meaningful text.

Headings should be very meaningful as they are usually written with the larger fonts and immediately attract readers' attention. Readers' attention span is extremely short these days.

Visuals. Images and web creative devices are particularly popular but they must be presented in such a way so as to be accessible by wide reader audiences. In this age of technology, users often possess a variety of web viewers and text readers. Posting in adequate formats can therefore be quite a challenge. Adds Bokan: 'Having said that, nothing can beat the great website posted article but visuals can certainly help'.

Back to writing basics

While many people say that web is all about technology-supported postings, Bokan considers anyone genuinely interested in reading articles and web postings online still 'appreciate good writing and editing above all else'. Indeed, he says, there is 'internet speak' and jargon inevitably created from technology-influenced communication but there will always be an appreciation for the skilled writers who can clearly communicate to their audiences. 'Whether it is the story, technical article or just a tweet, the application of good rhetorical concepts and rules will help more effective communication allowing writers to build their web relationships with their readers'.

And a final word

Bokan says that website designers should make sure that navigation between pages is easy and quick, otherwise the user will soon lose interest and move on to another site. 'Keep the site simple and easy to use so that the visitor will return and recommend it to other people.'

Readers stuck for words and terms in the fields of science and technology will find the answers in the *New Oxford Dictionary for Scientific Writers and Editors*. In A–Z style, the dictionary is an invaluable guide for writers, students and professionals working with scientific material.

Best for local government communication

The North Lincolnshire Council reports in its *Style Guide* that in 2009 over 18 million pages were viewed on its website. The website is the fastest and most popular way for people to find out about the council, says Paul Harrop, the council's publications manager.

He says that every page on its site (**www.northlincs.gov.uk**) has a link on it to other pages, adding this advice: 'When inserting a hyperlink ensure that the link text describes where the person will be taken, for example the BBC website should read BBC website not **www. bbc.co.uk**.'

Accessibility is again a prime requirement. The guide advises that any images used must have an alternative text that appears when the mouse hovers over the image. This helps text-based browsers and people with visual impairments. PDF attachments should show their file size included in the web page link and when a PDF file is inserted, an explanation of the document is needed together with instructions to download an Adobe Acrobat reader.

Any language that might be objectionable to readers should be avoided, emphasises Harrop. 'For example the term "old age pensioner" or "OAP" was once considered commonplace. Today it is considered offensive.' Content of web pages, particularly email addresses and contact details, should be kept up to date and checked regularly.

Building a website

Once you have chosen and registered a domain name – through your ISP (Internet Service Provider) for example – you will have your own Uniform Resource Locator (URL). This is your website's connection to the internet and the worldwide network of computers. Start with a site plan for navigating from the entry point, the home page. Then create a site map to provide links to other pages.

PR strategy

Advice will be needed on the style of the site in much the same way as it would for a corporate brochure or house magazine. Moreover, internet strategy must fit in with the organisation's overall business plan. Making the website work for the user in the most effective and profitable way should be the prime objective. PR objectives must, therefore, be settled at the outset.

You must decide how much information should be freely available, how much should be restricted through a password and, if appropriate, how to handle payments. And you must agree policy on the provision of media information – press releases, biographies, and details about the company structure, history, staffing and contacts.

Working with the designer

Your IT specialist must not be allowed to take charge of the design. Look for a graphics designer with broad experience of setting up websites for a range of companies and products, plus a knowledge of print typography.

Ensure that the site is compatible with current browsers and with current sound and video software. Take account of any material subject to copyright and make sure that your logo and house style are followed throughout. Pay special attention to the home page: if it's a yawn, the user will give up and go elsewhere. Be wary of the design that looks pretty-pretty at first sight, but with a content so complicated that it is slow to load. That could be frustrating and a good reason to click off. And it is important to take account of accessibility: this applies particularly to users with poor eyesight.

The central object is to provide information – but not too much in one go – and with no spelling or grammatical errors. It must be updated regularly. Above all, the site must look good, sound good and read well.

Getting the pages right

The home page will set the tone. It must explain the site in a few words, preferably in bullet-point form, If there are house colours, use them; put the company logo on all pages.

Every page needs a title, and a link back to the home page. Headlines must be lively, short and pithy. Look for active, 'doing' verbs and put them in the present tense. Don't overdo the text, concentrate on graphics to tell a story in themselves; use snappy, two/three-word headings, give detail in short paragraphs of not more than two sentences. Susan Wright, a freelance journalist, says: 'Devise a menu that stays with you throughout the site so that you don't have to keep on going back to the home page. Make the type easy to read and reasonably big and don't drown the page in words.'

Keep all pages consistent in appearance: if there is a colour scheme, follow it religiously. Style sheets are available for typography, colours and for formatting different elements of the page, including background sounds, videos and graphics images.

Essentials of site typography

Website typefaces and styles are as much the 'voice' of your company as those for printwork and press advertisements. Correct choice of typestyle is crucial to the link between word and message.

There is no point in, say, an engineering company using a delicate, slender typeface when a strong, bold one would be more appropriate. There are hundreds of typefaces available from software suppliers: only your designer will know which one would work best.

Keep to the typefaces you normally use for brochures, house journals and stationery. However, since type can be manipulated electronically, departure from house style is likely. See that the designer's zeal doesn't spoil visual impact and the company's image. For this very reason, where possible give your usual designer the task of creating the website.

Aim for simplicity of layout and ease of navigation. Make the pages lively and appealing: out with the bland page, lacking strong colours. But don't use combinations that tire the eye: words reversed white out of black or red, and green on yellow are hard to read. It is better to have more pages and less text; increased links make the site easier to use. Text looks best black on white, with colours for headings. Don't set the type too small; think of the viewer with poor eyesight. But make it attractive, snappy and full of facts. Don't let it look dated: look up the new sites for ideas.

Use clear language

The language should be clear, plain and to the point. Put important conclusions and summaries at the beginning, so as to attract attention from the start. Avoid slang, but don't be afraid of humour. Make sure everything you say is believable. Keep the need to maintain brand loyalty uppermost. Keep strictly to the logo shape and colour: any departure will be immediately noticeable.

Adding pages and graphics

Put in new pages regularly: users will go for good if you don't update. Your designer will advise you on all aspects of adding pages and graphics; but if you want to have a go yourself, full information will be found in *Creating Web Pages for Dummies*. In a couple of clicks you'll have the site up and running. That's exaggerating, but you know what I mean.

Avoid that jargon

Don't use buzz words; they may not communicate the message in the way you intend. Out with the jargon; don't baffle your online users with words and phrases that are meaningless to the vast majority. Only use general expressions, not the vocabulary of the specialist. As has already been stated in Chapter 5, jargon could spoil your carefully designed site simply because it fails to communicate.

Don't put a string of initials together and expect the user to know immediately what they stand for; some, however, will be known and understood by most if not all users, like CD-RW (CD rewriter). Not everyone will know what ISDN (integrated services digital network) means. When referring to sets of initials, explain them at least once, preferably at first reference.

Publicity

Your website is an unsurpassed communication tool. A well-designed, fact-full, look-good website can be a dream come true. But it will only be so if your customers – current and potential – know about it and use it. While a search engine should lead a stranger directly to your site, aim for easy and quick access. Print the address on business cards, office stationery, press releases, all printwork including brochures, leaflets and the house magazine, and show it on TV advertisements, posters, direct-mailers and shop displays.

Give it out on radio ads. Put it on the firm's CD ROM, if there is one, on presentation slides, on company videos. Everywhere.

Count the number of site visitors regularly, and when they reach a record, say so. Mention it in interviews for the press and broadcasting media, at conferences and at seminars. Brief your staff when it is updated, and make sure the receptionist can go online and show it off to visitors.

Getting the most out of emails

Emails need as much care as any other writing. We rely on them to carry messages to clients, office colleagues, press releases, reports. Copy for digital typesetting and printwork mostly goes that way. Huge benefits have ensued: speed, ease of use, ability to attach documents and illustrations at little or no cost, plus a built-in filing system and the ability to use a range of type faces, sizes and styles.

Most of us use emails for everyday correspondence at the expense of losing the carefully crafted and typed letter on paper. Originally, it was the informality provided by the message sent at the click of a mouse that appealed. Nowadays, many commentators agree that since the email has largely replaced the typed letter, formality sets the gold standard for effective email communication in a business environment, both for form of address and content.

Formality is the better option

An email demands the same degree of care given to a posted letter or printed document. Rules of grammar, spelling and punctuation must be followed ruthlessly. Use plain English and short sentences, avoid clichés and jargon. Keep clear of text slang (u for you and thnx for thanks) unless you are emailing a friend in the office; even then it is better not to get into the habit of sloppy writing like that.

There is no room for those juvenile emoticons like :-(for sad; abbreviations (BTW/LOL followed by a line of Xs and exclamation marks) are out unless the message is to a close friend or office colleague. If they get into everyday communication with clients and contacts you are asking for trouble and likely not to be taken seriously.

For the formal emailed letter it is better to use the Dear Mr or Mrs/Miss (or first name if you usually use it) greeting with a Yours sincerely sign-off followed by name, job title with telephone and mobile contact numbers. Reserve the Hi John or the stark Hi for office colleagues, friends and for people you know well. Lucy Kellaway, the *Financial Times* columnist, also prefers the formal greeting. Examples of beginnings she likes less: Hello, Hi, Hallo, Hey, Hiya. 'Someone who begins an email "Hey There" is telling me something useful: I am not likely to get on with this person.'

Always use a descriptive heading in the subject line. If, for instance, the message is about a meeting it is better to give the date, time and subject rather than a bland, non-specific 'label' like 'Next meeting', which could mean anything. As a general rule, it is better to put any detailed information in the body of the email, not as an attachment. If you are replying to an email use the reply button rather than sending a separate message as a 'new' email.

Use of fancy typefaces and garish colours does nothing for the email except to cause annoyance to the reader. Keep to standard fonts like Verdana, Arial or Times, in 12pt or perhaps 14pt, which is easily read by most people. My own preference is for the default option which, on my computer anyway, is perfectly adequate and readable. Black on white is best: do not specify a colour either for background or typeface. Do not use capitals unless it is for a proper noun or for an initial letter. Words typed in capitals are seen as 'shouting' at the recipient.

Personal emails – keep at home

'If you enjoy receiving and sending jokes and office gossip, it's probably better to keep such messages for your personal email address at home,' says Robert Harland, former vice-president and director, International Public Affairs, the Coca-Cola Company, Atlanta. Many companies monitor employees' emails and internet usage. The implications for the employee who disregards company rules in this area are obvious.

It is important to know your company's policy regarding personal emails and internet usage. Get it in writing so as to avoid any misunderstandings. Better to be safe than sorry.

Hidden dangers lurk

As noted in Chapter 14, an email is a legal document and must be regarded as such. So check each one carefully before hitting the 'send' button. It cannot be cancelled and it could go anywhere without you knowing it. A reply is so easy to send that you might offend if it is written hastily in anger or perhaps with an ill-thought-out complaint. Your message to a client could be copied and land up in the hands of a rival company; a frivolous note might reach an employee about to be made redundant; it could be libellous or even plain wrong.

There is little you can do if something like this happens, apart perhaps from a conciliatory telephone call. But by then, it may be too late. There is little you can do except pray.

Check even the briefest email carefully before sending it into cyberspace. If it is a sensitive subject, let it sit in your 'draft' box for an hour or so, if necessary overnight. Time spent at this stage will be well worth it. For incoming mail, do not leave it in your inbox: do something with it, not later but as soon as you see it. Reply, copy or forward it. Or file it for future reference. If it's spam or you're on the receiving end of unwanted mailing lists, ask your IT specialist or internet service provider (ISP) how to prevent it.

How to control your emails

Emails can become a nightmare: researchers from Glasgow and Paisley universities found that when monitors were fitted to computers, workers were viewing emails up to 40 times an hour. About 33 per cent said they were stressed by the volume of emails and a further 28 per cent said they felt 'driven' by the pressure to respond.

Times columnist Caitlin Moran says that in a normal working day she sends about 40 emails. No doubt several hundred reach her and other journalists daily to clog their inboxes. On average let's say most senior executives can get up to 200 or even more every day, most of which can and should be handled by assistants. 'Some find themselves overwhelmed with messages and spend more time shackled to their computers answering them,' says Coca-Cola's Robert Harland. The answer, he says, is to make sure you manage them properly and don't let them rule your life.

One of the things you can do when you start your computer is to delete as many messages as you can before opening them. Easier said than done, you will say. But you will be able to recognise the ones you want by the sender's name and/or the subject line. If you are referring to the message and no follow-up or record is needed, then delete the original. If you need to keep a copy, transfer it immediately to the appropriate folder. Open a separate folder for important messages and make sure you transfer mail as soon as you've acted on it.

Other measures for email control proposed by Harland include the need to scan for new messages on a frequent basis as there might be something important or urgent that needs action. A copy of an outgoing message will be in saved in your 'sent mail' folder and so can be deleted. If you have a number of non-urgent and personal messages you don't know what to do with, put them in a separate folder and delete them when you have a spare moment.

Says Harland: 'Even the most organised person can be side-tracked when interesting messages come in. But if you follow these simple steps you'll find yourself controlling your emails instead of them controlling you.'

Organise a signature file

Every business email should carry the sender's signature detail. The signature lines can be added at no extra cost and are included automatically. Here, your full name, postal address, website URL, telephone and fax numbers should ideally be included. It will also give you the opportunity to promote a particular page or section of your website or any other PR promotion or product launch. It will be there every time until you cancel it and is tantamount to free advertising since it costs nothing.

But don't overdo it. Verbose signatures are not tolerated: the ideal is to keep the signature to no more than four lines so that they will stand out. You can put these lines in bold face or in a different font. The shorter you write, the more power you give to those few words and the more likely they are to be read.

Ezines for easy newsletters

Emailed newsletters and magazines, or ezines, mean quick and efficient communication at low cost. I gave detailed advice on how to achieve an effective emailed newsletter in an article in *Profile* magazine; it will be found in the PR Writing Masterclass archive on the CIPR website. Here are some of the main points from that article.

Ezines – an all-embracing term for emailed publications, sometimes called emags or ejournals – are produced as text-only newsletters or as HTML (Hypertext Markup Language) versions that look like a web page with colour, graphics and different typefaces and styles. They are cheap to produce once the design has been settled and cost little or nothing to send out. If you have an internet presence you cannot afford to ignore them.

They enable instant contact with clients and customers, media and opinion-formers, in fact all target audiences. You can subscribe to them (or delete them) at will. Therein lies a snag: a printed magazine is for keeps, an ezine can go at one keystroke. And readership is questionable. Many electronic newsletters are left unread when there are perhaps hundreds of messages piling up. Clean design and presentation, coupled with sparky, single-syllable words, are crucial.

Steve Sawyer, web integration specialist, notes: 'The most effective email newsletters are usually those which include a heading and single paragraph of text for each news item, followed by a link to the full story online. With carefully coded hyperlinks, this gives the benefit of also being able to log who exactly is reading what (and what isn't being read at all), as well as the ability to drive the reader to other areas of the site or elicit further engagement.'

Text-only newsletters

A few eye-catching items using plain type with bold headings in tabloid-news format are effective. Stories should be short and above all interesting and relevant. Eye-catching headlines together with short and unindented paragraphs encourage the reader to read on. Restrict the ezine newsletter to two pages if possible, and don't forget to include links to relevant website pages.

Ensure that it's easy to unsubscribe. There are thousands of newsletters to choose from and are all free. Subscribers are bound to get them automatically, but whether they're all read is doubtful. If your budget allows, it is better to have a printed version as well.

Web-based emagazines

Here is the designer's chance to use colour, graphics, pictures and fancy typefaces. Emagazines should reflect the look and 'feel' of the company website with links to specific items and information sources. Stick to 50–60 words for news stories (that's a couple of paragraphs) and two A4 pages. Don't put a hyphen between the e prefix and the key word. Keep to corporate colours so as to retain style consistency. Give a content overview at the top of the page and decide whether to direct the viewer to the website or to other information and then concentrate on it.

Not everyone can receive HTML emails (those that are web-based). Use an email program that will deliver the appropriate version or one that gives readers the ability to choose the preferred format. Your objective must be to get them read as widely as possible. Some recipients say they like short bursts of information regularly rather than a long newsletter that goes straight to the trashcan. So the usual rule for all writing applies: keep it short and readable.

Getting help

A quick Google leads you to sites and service providers for design, copywriting and mailing list management. Among them are FrontPage, Dreamweaver, Newsweaver, Bronto, Riches Communications and Bella-online. EPDigest.com provides a beginner's guide to ezine publishing.

At a glance

- Journalists first go to the firm's website for information and contacts.

- The audience is the writer's first priority: is your site relevant, informative?

- Keep a consistent style. The site is the voice of your company.

- Aim for simplicity and ease of navigation.

- Put the subject or most important point at the top of the page.

- Write in short chunks, average 8 to 10 words per line. Keep sentences to 15 to 20 words.

- Readers tend to skim copy. Put main idea in each paragraph.

- Use bullet points to signal important facts. Keep headlines short and lively.

- Clean, clear design is key to a successful site.

- Make it readable with plenty of white space.

- Ensure accessibility for all users. Upload press releases, include an archive.

- Emails demand as much care as any other writing. Formality is the better option.

- Ezines provide a convenient and cost-effective medium for newsletters.

20
Tone – the linchpin of reputation

The one essential factor in any communication is its tone, or how the message is written and perceived by the reader. The tone must be appropriate for the audience: if it offends, smacks of officialdom, sounds harsh or patronising, or is full of unwarranted jest, then you have a public relations problem.

Tone of voice is the way we speak, how we talk. It displays our attitude to other people. A smiling face, a gracious greeting instead of a glum look and coarse voice do wonders for communication. The writer should try to put into words the warmth that exudes from a person who speaks in a relaxed and friendly way. Achieving an appropriate tone that is right for every audience is the difficult part, and must be tackled. A firm's overall tone of voice in words, speech and manner is as much the image of the company as any smart logo or snappy advertising campaign.

This chapter is mostly concerned with the written word; speech is covered in Chapters 17 and 18. The tone you adopt in writing will make all the difference between success and failure, no matter whether it's an online newsletter or emagazine, corporate brochure, annual report, press release, leaflet or letter. Look now at your options and the possibilities of putting your company, your message in the best possible light, the right tone. After all, that is what public relations is all about.

Basic principles of tone in writing

What is tone in writing? The short answer is that it is the writer's attitude towards the reader and the subject of the message being delivered. The tone of an online or written message can affect the reader in the same way as tone of voice impinges on the listener's attitude and reactions to the speaker. So tone, whether in writing or speech, has a significant effect on how the message is perceived. It must therefore take a prime place in every organisation's communications strategy. But how is the writer to know the appropriate tone to adopt? That depends on the reason for writing an online or printed document, its intended audience and whether a formal or informal tone is needed.

The chosen tone must not leave the reader feeling that the writing has jarred or is in any way unsettling. No matter whether it is a letter, email, mail shot, report or document, it needs the one quality that is so often missing: charm. As Drayton Bird describes in his *How to Write Sales Letters that Sell* (Kogan Page, 2002), the ability of the writer to adapt the tone will make letters *charming* (his italics). The adequate writers, he says, write in exactly the same way, but the outstanding ones disarm the reader just as a charming individual can disarm somebody he or she is trying to influence.

Making the reader comfortable

The overall tone for the written word must make the reader comfortable and at ease with what is said. This means, in pretty well every case, using I/we rather than the third person, as in XYZ company does this or that. It also means using 'you' instead of standing back and ignoring the reader as an individual. It means using the active voice, avoiding passive verb-phrases including am, is, was, were or been. For example, it is much better to write 'I make' than 'I am making'. And once you are in the habit of using constructions with participle *-ing* or *-ed* verb endings you make the copy stodgy and unpalatable, so off-putting to the reader.

It is crucial in adopting a suitable tone of voice to steer clear of discriminatory language that can offend. That means, for a start, avoiding sexist terms and such factors as race, religion, age, sexual orientation and any kind of disability.

In business communications it is hard to adopt an all-embracing tone when there are several audiences, for example in healthcare and financial services. In both, the tone needs to be warm, friendly and caring, yet authoritative and firm when the occasion demands, whether in correspondence or printwork.

Towards a better tone

Write in a way that suggests you are helping the reader. You will need to stress the benefits of whatever product or service you are writing about, but you must avoid jargon and technical language that may not be widely understood. This is particularly important when the message is going to a variety of audiences, to shareholders, dealers and customers for instance.

FIGURE 20.1 Chatty, friendly tone for this weekly newsletter from the Advertising Association. Good title. Works well

NEWS   2/12/2011

Advertising Not Without Its Merits, Says Woman I Now Love

We have a new heroine at the home of *advertising matters* – comedian, writer, broadcaster, genius and prophet, Natalie Haynes. Natalie, who wasn't even paid or threatened by us, took to the pages of *The Independent* (it's a newspaper – like this, but not as funny) to argue that advertising might not be such a bad thing after all. In fact it turns out it's really rather good – funding kids' telly and even the Indie – as well as, we'd argue, doing all the choice, competition and cultural contribution stuff that we get excited about.

But not everyone is convinced. Over at the *Daily Mail's* Right Minds blog, Sonia Poulton takes issue with, well, almost everything to do with advertising. We'll let you make your own minds up about how coherently argued, fair-minded and well-researched her piece is but while you're doing that, why not give yourself a break from all those sexy home insurance ads that are corrupting your kids and read about a topless Lady Gaga spraying Cheerios all over her bathroom, peek under the canvas to discover the jungle couple nobody saw coming or look at the seven pictures (yep, seven) of Amy Childs going for a walk in some skintight vinyl trousers.

Unseemly stuff - particularly if you're a Cheerio.

The Wrong Prescription?

Consultants have called on the Government to introduce new curbs on alcohol advertising to protect young people, according to *The Guardian*. They warn that the country is facing an "epidemic of liver disease caused by a binge drinking culture and cheap booze."

But as is so often the case in these important debates, the evidence base and proposed solutions (ad bans first among them) do not always match up with the laudable objective of stopping dangerous drinking. The industry wants to tackle this – that's why they fund Drinkaware, don't target under 18s in ads, don't link alcohol with seduction or social success, don't place alcohol ads within 100m of schools, don't run alcohol ads in publications or around programmes of specific interest to kids, don't produce ads which link drinking with irresponsible, tough or daring behaviour, don't show alcohol being served irresponsibly in their marketing materials...you get the picture.

Lots of people have a role to play in making sure that under-18s do not drink. Parents, publicans, politicians, teachers, friends, advertisers and even sarky newsletter editors should all do their bit, but too often it seems that alcohol marketing is made to shoulder the blame for a deep-seated societal problem which seems unlikely to be ended simply by ending sports sponsorship or banning TV ads for drinks.

For some clear-headed thinking on this stuff we recommend you take a tot of Credos's recent review of the evidence around alcohol marketing's impact on consumption.

In such cases, it will probably be necessary to produce several versions of the same message. Internal budgets will usually determine whether or not this is worthwhile.

Adopt a friendly, warm style, even a chatty one provided it isn't overdone, but don't let it appear patronising. When the time comes for a negative message, use a tone that is gracious and understanding. For example, if it is necessary to tell someone their application for a loan must be rejected, don't sound officious and unhelpful. Put it so that the reader understands that your firm has its rules, and will do everything possible to help in the future. Again, if you have to write a letter to confirm someone's dismissal, write it in a considerate and caring way. You never know where that person will be employed next; he or she may be looking at *your* job application.

Don't try to bully the reader into believing something, as so many sales letters seem to these days. Don't be afraid to apologise if something goes wrong, say a delivery that went astray or failure on the part of your staff. Take the blame yourself and don't try to shift it to underlings.

It is necessary to strike a balance between a tone that is friendly but firm. There is the danger of over-informality: it kills credence, even authenticity. Write we will/would, not we'll/we'd, you are/have and not you're/you've. The shortened style is fine for ads, sales letters and mailshots, perhaps some letters, internal memos and emails, but is too sloppy for formal work.

The tone you take says something about you and what you and your company are like. Since it affects how your message is perceived, it is essential to get it right, no matter how much effort and time that might mean.

Tone for the public

Most firms dealing with the public and with many different audiences take tone seriously. A leading firm in the insurance sector has, for instance, issued its staff with a set of guidelines to give the company a distinctive tone. In correspondence and mailshots, for example, it's *you're* not you are, and using plain English with active verbs and superlatives where appropriate, but staying clear of slang words like 'fab' and 'cool'.

Rather than writing 'I'm in receipt of your letter' it's 'thanks for your letter' even though to some eyes this would appear over-informal, even slapdash. But the company's PR department says there is always room for personal expression when circumstances demand. It's all a question of combining figures and statistical information with human understanding. Everyday language is the company's watchword.

A caring tone can turn round a hostile and bitter audience. For example, the head of a city council's tax collections department at one time told bereaved families that they must pay the deceased person's remaining tax bill quoting 'chapter and verse' on how the tax must be paid without any expression of regret or sympathy. No apology was offered for making the demand in case of litigation. The council was seen as cold and uncaring, only interested in getting money out of taxpayers no matter what the circumstances. But the council's PRO says that once an apologetic acknowledgement of bereavement was given, a higher rate of tax collection resulted. 'By apologising and explaining, people paid up rather than ignoring the previous insensitive letter.' So here was a positive outcome from an improved and understanding tone.

Using a caring tone

The healthcare sector provides examples of how a friendly, yet authoritative, tone delivers a meaningful message to patients, as well as to health professionals and the wider public. For instance, a leaflet for the charity Healthy Heart UK, to raise awareness and increase understanding of the risk factors for coronary heart disease, is written in a clear, easy-to-follow style, but covering complex medical subjects. The leaflet, drafted by Ash Communications of London, explains a medical procedure in easy-to-follow steps, telling patients what they can expect from a new treatment procedure. It is printed in largish (18pt sans serif) type with a bright, cheerful cover.

Leaflets displayed in every doctor's surgery make extensive use of the personal pronoun 'you', 'we', and shortening *that is* to 'that's, *how is* to how's. Wide use of lower case for headings gives a softer, less harsh look than capitals. Such written and visual styles are the prime ingredients of a caring and positive tone, essential for effective communication to a range of audiences.

A study in 2004 by the National Consumer Council found that one in five people had trouble in understanding basic health information. 'Health literacy is essential for improving health and health services', says the NCC. Leaflets for patients should be written in plain, easy-to-understand language. Those presented in a question-and-answer format work well: for example, an NHS information pamphlet on immunisation against pneumoccoccal infection for the over-75s explains how infection is spread and what the symptoms are in an easy-read form. It is important not to downplay serious illnesses, but to give the facts without using medical terms and procedures that might not be understood.

A soft, warm tone of voice is essential for health messages. Phrases like 'you will understand/find that' are far preferable to 'you must do this or that', or 'you may feel a little uncomfortable' not 'you might/will feel pain'. Always write in a way that will leave patients feeling confident yet relaxed about any procedures they might have to undergo, and confident that the healthcare staff are there to help them at all times.

Sue Ash, managing director, Ash Communications, explains: 'The key is to pitch the message according to the audience. It is important not to be patronising, but to use straightforward language, avoiding jargon and finding a balance that will work for all levels of understanding.'

Tone in marketing communications

David Lowe, retired marketing consultant and lecturer, says that a consistent tone must be maintained in planning marketing communications, which today embrace an increasingly broad range of media. As well as the long-established mass media of TV and national press, posters, radio and cinema, there are the specialist press, direct mail and the rapidly growing fields of electronic media, email and viral advertising.

Since marketing experts are now expected to justify their decisions by quantifying results in terms of enquiries and sales, there is a growing tendency to add more measurable communications media to the mix. The target audiences will therefore receive messages in a number of different ways. 'Sometimes the tone of these messages may vary with a consequent loss of overall impact,' says Lowe. 'One of the reasons for this is that rather than one agency being responsible for everything, specialist suppliers may be used to create material for their particular media and a consistent creative strategy is not followed. For instance, the website designer may have no knowledge of how the same message will be conveyed in a direct mail campaign. They in their turn are unaware of the work the agency is producing for the trade press.'

Another factor is that audiences don't necessarily fit into neat, self-contained 'boxes'. Customers may also be shareholders, employees or live close to the factory. In each of these roles, they may need to receive different types of information. But the tone must be consistent. 'To be effective, every piece of marketing communications should have the same tone, irrespective of the medium chosen. The organisation concerned has to establish clearly what tone is appropriate for its established corporate culture and brand identity, and then ensure that this is carried through in all its communications,' says Lowe.

Developing an informal tone

Because you are writing a business letter or memo, or even a section for your company brochure or annual report, there is no need to be stiff and stodgy. Sentence structures with endless sub-clauses, perhaps running to 45 or even 60 words, fail to demonstrate anything other than the writer's ability to think up twice as many words as necessary.

The first thing to do is to use plenty of 'you' and 'your' and 'I' and 'we' pronouns. There is, however, danger in using too many 'I's, particularly for sentence starts. If you are talking about something your firm has done, or proposes to do, use 'we' and not XYZ company. But it would be egotistical to use 'I' in these circumstances, unless it is something that you have personally done or said.

The objective must be to make the communication sound natural and relaxed, but professional and authoritative at the same time. Be careful with the use of 'yourself' and 'myself', and make sure they don't sound self-effacing. Use everyday words and phrases, and don't try to be too clever by half and start talking about per annum, ad hoc and other familiar Latin terms. They don't sound friendly and can easily put off the reader who may not be as well educated as you are.

When it's time to be firm and formal

Useful tips on creating a formal tone will be found in Jo Billingham's handy book *Editing and Revising Text* in the Oxford 'One step ahead' series. The advice she gives can be summed up thus: use longer sentences than the recommended ones of 25–30 words; choose more complex words; number the points you want to make; omit softening phrases ('as you are aware' becomes 'as you know'); 'you should' becomes 'you must'.

Create a distance between writer and reader ('as you know' changes to 'readers will be aware'); long documents immediately appear more formal than short ones. And it's out with fashionable words like 'synergy' and jargon understandable to only a specialist audience. Treat the company as a single entity: XYZ company *is* not are doing something.

The best tone

The best tone is plain, unaffected, unblemished by superlatives. It neither talks down nor jazzes (nor sexes) up; it regards all readers as equal; it doesn't excuse or apologise unnecessarily; nor does it try to belittle the reader by showing how clever or sophisticated the writer is; it's not 'one-up' on the reader. It is warm and friendly if circumstances allow; it is enthusiastic about what you have to say. It is confident, yet courteous and sincere. And it demonstrates a helpful attitude coupled with an offer to overcome problems. The best tone can express disappointment but never anger.

The crux of the matter is to adapt and vary your tone according to the audience and whether the message is something you want the reader to do, or is simply for information. In a letter, for example, you would adopt a different tone to a supplier who had let you down to the one who is going to provide a special service that you desperately need.

Write with words that are similar to those you would use if you were speaking. You would write in a different way to junior members of staff instructing them to do something than you would to the managing director of a client company about a new contract. It's all a question of balance. Getting that balance right is the difficult bit.

At a glance

- How you say something is just as important as what you say.

- Tone is the writer's attitude to the reader and subject of the message.

- The tone to choose depends on the reason for writing the document, what you are trying to convey.

- Decide whether a formal or informal tone is appropriate.

- Your chosen tone must not be jarring or unsettling to the reader.

- The tone used must make the reader feel comfortable and at ease with what is said.

- Use I/we not the third person; choose the active, not passive voice.

- Steer clear of discriminatory language.

- Avoid sexist terms, and terms that distinguish race, religion, age or any disabilities.

- Stress the benefits of products and services.

- Adopt a friendly, warm style but don't be patronising.

- Over-informality kills credence and authenticity.

- Use plain English; omit jargon.

- Ensure tone is consistent across all communications and audiences.

- Keep sentences short for an informal tone, longer for formal messages.

- Don't belittle the reader by showing how clever you are.

21
Now it's annual report time

Prime PR opportunity

There can be few people in communications who are not at some time in their careers involved with their organisation's annual report. Even if it's not their direct responsibility, PR practitioners will almost certainly be tasked with producing copy for it: perhaps a section on communications strategy, details of events and other functions, maybe even a draft of the chairman's statement. In the case of trade associations, they might possibly contribute an outline of a message from the president; or if a charity then it might be an appeal by the patron for funds from supporters.

But whatever the job, it is an important one, embracing anything from content and copy to design and delivery. In many cases, the annual report serves the dual purpose of providing an account of the year's activities and financial performance and a regularly updated corporate brochure lasting the year, thus avoiding the expense of a separate, expensive publication.

The annual report is a prime communications tool. It is the voice and tone of the organisation: it enables the chairman, chief executive and directors to make policy statements, and demonstrates corporate governance credentials and responsibility for corporate social responsibility issues. In fact, it is a critical and crucial arm of corporate strategy provided it communicates effectively.

But that is where many reports fall down and waste shareholders' or members' money, while sheltering under the excuse that the annual review is something that must be done, no matter what the expense, irrespective of its value as a communication medium. To some it can be a chore, but for all a challenge to get it right.

Essential aspects

Far too many annual reports are poorly designed, badly written and fail to achieve anything but an uplift to the chairman's ego with a big picture and a self-satisfied group of directors. Look now at what the annual report must, by law, provide for a company's shareholders or an organisation's members or supporters. Even if the legal rules and regulations are seldom the direct concern of PR professionals, you should at least be aware of the main legislation affecting your organisation and its annual report.

Statutory requirements

It is a requirement of the Companies Act that every company (whether limited by shares or guarantee) is required to produce a set of accounts and put to an annual general meeting for approval by shareholders or members, with a copy to the Registrar of Companies. The directors must prepare a directors' report and, for quoted companies, a directors' remuneration report. There are severe penalties for failure to comply with the Act (the only exemption to delivering accounts applies to unlimited companies).

There are strict rules covering the content and format of the annual report and accounts to give a 'true and fair view' of the company and its financial affairs. Every member or shareholder is entitled to receive a copy of the annual report and accounts; the Articles of the company may be amended (under the Electronic Communications Order) to allow the annual report to be sent to shareholders using electronic communications. Listed companies are allowed to issue summary financial statements to shareholders, instead of the full accounts but these must be available as an option.

If the company is also a registered charity or if the organisation is a registered charity, an annual report and return should also be issued to the Charity Commission. Charities need to comply with SORP, the Statement of Recommended Practice. A number of industries are governed by separate legislation: for example banks, building societies, insurance companies and some businesses such as solicitors and accountants need to comply with the rules of their governing bodies. Trade associations are often in the form of limited companies and are governed by the Companies Act.

Operating and Financial Reviews

An Operating and Financial Review (OFR) was a requirement for all UK quoted companies for financial years from 2005. Guidance for directors has been published by the OFR Working Group.

The introduction of a mandatory OFR was a key recommendation of the Company Law Review, and endorsed in the government's White Paper *Modernising Company Law*. Full details are available on the Department of Trade and Industry website, **www.dti.gov.uk**, or by email to **ofrworkinggroup@dti.gsi.gov.uk**.

Further information

For companies: contact the Registrar, Companies House, **www.companieshouse.gov.uk**. For charities: contact the Commissioner, Charity Commission, **www.charity-commissioner.gov.uk**. See also 'Further reading' at the end of this book.

What makes a good annual report?

The prime issue here is that what is good for one organisation may not be so for another. Depending on the number printed, size and design, an annual report could cost anything from a pound or two per copy to 20 or more times that. Many reports I have seen are clearly much longer than they need to be, are over-designed and are frankly a waste of shareholders' money. (Shareholders don't pay for them directly, but they eat up profits that would otherwise be attributable to them in dividends.)

Writing in *The Scotsman*, Executive Editor Bill Jamieson says that some chairmen lavish tens of thousands of pounds and 'endless hours' of management time on the annual report, only to get no coverage whatever in the business press and at best a desultory response from shareholders. He says that 'almost all' of the dozens of reports he receives 'fail to explain clearly what the company does or makes, how it has done better or worse than last year and what the realistic outlook is for the year ahead'. His telling message for CEO and the communications team: 'I would say the bigger and more expensive the annual report, the more evident the failure.'

The chairman's statement, he says, is becoming 'formulaic': by the time it has passed through 'lawyers, spin doctors, and compliance officers he might as well have asked a machine to do the job'. It is time, he argues, that companies got a grip on annual reports and returned them to first principles: a full, clear, no-frills statement of the business and a frank assessment of current conditions.

As a first step, annual reports should be halved in size, and politically correct waffle removed; the environment would be better served by allowing the paper to 'remain on the trees'. But however well intentioned all that may be, it is easier said than done. Let's look now at the possibilities for making the annual report more readable, more creative and above all a more cost-effective communications vehicle.

An international view

Leading PR professional Toni Falconi, founding chairman of the Global Alliance for Public Relations and Communication Management, has long experience in producing annual reports for major companies. Signor Falconi, past president of the Italian Public Relations Association (FERPI), says that the issue of reporting annually is at the very core of self-expression, its ability to tell a story of a company's achievements to influential publics.

He feels it is a mistake for PR executives to be only involved in their traditional roles of responsibility for design, format, distribution and promotion. Their skills would be much better employed if they were concentrated on content, with views on financial, social and environmental issues.

Signor Falconi gives substantial support to Bill Jamieson's views. 'In general, today's reports are not very useful as they are mostly written by experts who know more about the company than appears in print. They are not written for the influential publics.' The question of language, what the report says and how it is expressed, is crucial: the PR professionals should be capable of interpreting technical and specialised jargon, including financial terms and statements, and making it readable and understandable. Otherwise, he asks, what other purpose is there for the PR person? He feels that since most PR people fail to understand properly an annual report's specialised content, they are less able to interpret it, and subsequently transmit the information in a way that satisfies neither the reader nor the company.

Returning to Jamieson's theme, he reiterates that reports should be much thinner and more readable. In-depth analysis, charts and specialised data should be left to the website for the experts to extract the information they need.

The annual report – vital communications link

The increasing level of regulation dictating what must be included in annual reports is actually causing them to communicate less effectively, according to Peter Prowse, of Waylines Consulting. 'I've been involved in analysing the communications effectiveness of annual reports since 1990,' he says. 'Every time there is a new set of regulations such as those following the Sarbanes–Oxley Act introduced in the USA in 2002, companies have to comply with yet another list of requirements.

'The result is more words and extra pages, but less useful communication. Take the HSBC annual report for 2006–2007 as an example: the Royal Mail had to limit the number of copies that postmen could carry, in order to prevent back injuries.'

The HSBC report in question runs to 454 pages. Barney Jopson, who writes about accountancy for the *Financial Times*, devoted a whole page article to the HSBC report on 13 April 2007, shortly after it was published. He wrote: 'Company executives worn down by red tape blame regulators for mandating reams of disclosure to "protect" shareholders without consulting investors about what they would like. Regulators, meanwhile, wonder just how committed companies are to telling the truth. Shareholders say both could do better.'

Europe's response to Sarbanes–Oxley is the International Financial Reporting Standards, which came into force in the European Union in 2005. It takes 133 pages of notes to explain them.

'Because they need to tick all the compliance boxes,' says Peter Prowse, 'large companies now include information about corporate and social responsibility, employment policies and directors' remuneration. The manager or director responsible for the content of the annual report goes through a checklist of things that have to be covered. The really important messages that a company should be delivering to its shareholders start to take a back seat.

'The result is a thick document that complies with all the regulations, but nobody has the time or the inclination to read it. It looks like every other big company's annual report and communicates very little about the organisation's personality: what makes it different and where it's heading.'

The chairman's statement

For most readers, the most important part of any annual report is the chairman's statement. It sets the tone and, according to shareholder research carried out by Peter Prowse, it is the one part of the report that readers will read and remember. Frequently, it's the only section to be closely examined, giving as it does an overview of the company's performance over a year and suggesting future prospects.

A well-written chairman's report will be produced with the reader in mind. Warren Buffet, the second richest man in the world and CEO of Berkshire Hathaway, achieves this by aiming his report at just two of his shareholders, Doris and Bertie, who also happen to be his sisters.

'They are a smart duo,' Warren Buffet told the *Financial Times*, for Barney Jopson's article. 'They've got practically all their money in Berkshire Hathaway, so they're interested. And they don't want to be talked down to. I pretend they've gone away for a year and want to know what's happened. They want to hear what I'm worried about and what I'm pleased about,' he says. 'Then, when I'm through, I take their names off the top of the report and put: "To the shareholders of Berkshire Hathaway".' The result is a frank and folksy report that is lapped up each year by retail investors.

Importance of good design

Most shareholders, and indeed the majority of all those who are sent annual reports, will look either for financial results and the dividend, or for photographs of people they know. Then they give up: in the bin goes the report that directors, accountants and PR people have slaved over for months. The stodgy report tightly packed with grey type unrelieved by headings and typographical tricks is the biggest turn-off of all time.

The effectiveness of a company's annual report as a means of communication to its publics depends largely on design and how the information is presented. The worst possible course is to dig out last year's copy, just change the date on the cover and print it in a different colour. Good design means high-level creative input that only comes at a price.

Something like £180 million is spent each year on printing the country's annual reports, according to annual report specialist Butler & Tanner. With an expenditure like this, much care and attention is needed on design and content.

High unit cost

A company can spend as much as a quarter of a million pounds on its annual report. A full-colour, square-backed print job on high-quality paper running to 100 or more pages for 50,000 copies could cost even more. If an optional summary report (or a corporate and social responsibility report) is produced as well, that could increase the price, since the full version will go to City analysts and institutions, to journalists and overseas investors. Depending on print run, a cost of more than £10–15 a copy would not be unusual. The annual report might turn out to be a waste of money at 75p but be good value at a fiver or more, says one former plc finance director. It all depends on its merit as a communications medium.

For trade associations and smaller companies, lower print runs can mean a far higher unit cost, particularly if expensive, quality materials are used. The relatively high cost per copy of a lavish production is often justified by using the report as a corporate brochure for the year, so saving the expense of regular updating and printing.

Influence of creativity

Today, there is scant evidence that creative design ideas necessarily reflect companies' claims for being innovative enterprises. This is borne out in surveys of Europe's top 100 companies by Peter Prowse under the title of *The Company Report Report*, which was critical of their creativity and production values: 'Quality of design is poor and at times completely lacking.'

Prowse, who now runs Waylines Consulting (**peter.prowse@waylines. co.uk**) says that in publishing those surveys, they tried to show what worked well and what didn't. It may not mean, he says, that an excellent report must necessarily cost more than a mediocre one. 'Enlightened companies realise that they are saddled with having to print a detailed document so they might just as well produce something that does the best possible job for them.' Those companies that are close to their markets tend to lead the way forward in producing cost-effective annual and interim reports.

Nowadays, of course, most sizeable companies produce their reports online through their websites, and shareholders are constantly encouraged to opt for information in digital form. The more that trend continues, the lower overall costs will turn out to be.

Electronic communications with shareholders

The Companies Act 2006, which came into force in January 2007, brings important changes to the way in which companies can utilise the internet to communicate with their shareholders. The default method of communication becomes website communication with a positive opt-in for hard copy. Now, once the right legal mechanisms are in place, the company can assume that shareholders are happy to receive information electronically unless they specifically state otherwise.

First they need to check whether their articles of association already permit them to communicate electronically with shareholders. If not, they have to pass a resolution and then write to all shareholders asking if they would prefer information in printed or electronic format. If a shareholder fails to respond within 28 days the company can assume that the shareholder agrees to have information in electronic format, that is via the company's website.

Companies trading as a regulated market are also subject to the electronic communications requirements of the FSA's Disclosure and Transparency (DTRs). See DTR 6.1.8.

The regulations apply not only to the annual and half-year reports but to all shareholder communications. The requirements of the new Act are met if a company communicates via its website; companies do not have to communicate by email.

The savings to be made from electronic communications will depend on the size of the shareholder register. For companies with a large number of private shareholders, such as the former state-owned utilities, the savings could be large. Savings for medium-sized and smaller companies will be less dramatic, and in any case many of them are deciding to continue to use print, as they believe it is the best way to communicate with their shareholders.

PR benefits from good design

A well-produced annual report can provide immense PR benefits. For the communications department it demonstrates what they and their design team can do, and it can win them an award with attendant follow-up publicity. It gets the company talked about in the trade press. Above all that, it is the voice of the company and its employees to all its audiences. This means that it must be readable, attractive to look at and a key source of information for journalists, opinion-formers and analysts. The company's reputation depends on it.

All the elements that, put together, make an annual report readable – such matters as type size, headings, use of pictures and captions – are covered in earlier chapters. The principles of good design and layout should be followed rigorously, and with a level of creativity to make it stand out from the rest. The annual report is the most important document any organisation produces; it is its flagship. As such it should get all the attention it deserves.

The Investor Relations Society produces 'Best Practice Guidelines' for printed and online annual reports which are available on their website (**www.irs.org.uk/resources/annual-reports**). Key characteristics from the guidelines include a good set of report and accounts, an opening narrative explaining significant points in the accounts, how the money is made, what worries the board, consistency and clarity and proper explanation of changes from the prior period.

Annual reports in an electronic age

Many companies, trade associations, charities and other organisations make their annual reports available online. Care must be taken to ensure that any information published in a printed report is given in the online version without any change whatsoever. While some readers prefer to read annual reports online, there are others who prefer them in a printed form. Despite the increasing popularity of online versions, communication strategies must be developed to allow all readers equal opportunity to access information, whether they read on screen or in print.

Most annual reports can be viewed on websites, and some companies ask shareholders for their email addresses so that they may request regular news and financial information. One such is the Management Consulting Group, which issues summary trading updates ahead of its interim and final results for the year, with the full updates on the 'Latest News' page of its website.

Conversely, those firms that rely on electronic technology to communicate with shareholders may fail to reach their readers as well as they could through the printed page. As the Prowse report puts it: 'What they want is something physical to hold and read.' However, the value of the printed annual report now appears to be in decline, even though there is a clear need for it among a significant number of shareholders and other recipients.

Therein lies a dilemma for chief executives and their public relations advisers: since the popularity of the online version continues to grow, a communications strategy allowing both the electronic and printed versions to benefit all readers is needed. And that, to a large extent, is in the hands of the technologist.

Investor relations in a digital age

Investor relations (IR) is no longer the distant and forgotten cousin of mainstream PR. Over the past two decades it has gradually become a crucial part of every company's communications strategy. Most, if not all, FTSE 100 companies and many others besides have an in-house IR specialist, usually contactable via the firm's website, and some also employ an IR adviser or consultant.

The IR department will, in most cases, be responsible for providing data on the company's financial performance and prospects; these are used on the website's IR pages as an information source for shareholders, the media, suppliers and other target audiences.

The Investor Relations Society's definition is the communication of information and insight between a company and the investment community. This process enables a full appreciation of the company's business activities, strategy and prospects, and allows the market to make an informed judgement about the fair value and appropriate ownership of a company.

This communication is the responsibility of investor relations practitioners, whether they work in-house or for a consultancy. Their role is to manage the flow of information between the company and those individuals and organisations (the 'buy-side') who own its shares, or who might buy them in the future.

It takes several forms. The most time-consuming, and arguably the most important, are the ongoing one-to-one meetings which take place between the company's senior management and representatives of selected investment institutions. There are also one-to-one meetings with research analysts who advise investors; they work for investment banks and other stockbrokers (the 'sell-side'), or for independent research organisations.

Group meetings may include any of these professional investors and advisers, while the annual general meeting gives private individuals who own shares the opportunity to meet the management face-to-face and ask them about the company's performance.

Much of this communication is oral but there is also a flow of written information, including company announcements, and regular statements about its progress and financial health, including half-yearly and annual reports.

The IR page or pages of a company's website play an increasingly important role in providing corporate information, often including an archive of announcements, ranging from text to video or audio versions of presentations by senior executives.

'The key to good IR, as with any form of communication, is clarity and consistency,' Michael Mitchell, general manager, the Investor Relations Society says. He adds that it is therefore vital that IR is closely integrated with a company's corporate communications. Research has shown that good IR can potentially improve share price performance, and that the lack of IR can be detrimental to valuations.

The messages a company sends to its various audiences must form part of an agreed and planned communications strategy. IR professionals have to take account of the regulatory environment in which they operate, while their corporate communications and PR colleagues need to be aware that their output can have a significant impact on investors' views. It is important to be clear about who should speak on the company's behalf to its various audiences. And as with PR, the effectiveness of IR should be measured against agreed objectives.

A two-way communication process

As well as passing information from the company to investors, IR professionals also listen to what the stock market says about the company and let its management know about the market's comments, views and overall sentiment.

There is a certain amount of coded language in IR which may be useful for the uninitiated: 'challenging market conditions' may mean things are very tough, while a company which admits to its shareholders that its 'performance has been disappointing in some areas' has probably just emerged from a particularly poor trading period. The news that a director is leaving a company suddenly 'for family reasons' or has gone on 'gardening leave' can be open to all kinds of interpretation.

There are still companies which communicate as little as possible, either because they see no point in devoting resources to IR or they regard shareholders as a distraction. The more enlightened ones, which today means most quoted companies, recognise the value of good communications with the investment community. Some go to great lengths to provide a wealth of data about the business and to encourage investors to ask for more information.

The Investor Relations Society will help

The Investor Relations Society (IRS), founded in 1980, has more than 600 members across the UK, Europe and further afield drawn from listed companies, consultancies and service providers. The majority of FTSE-100 companies, a significant proportion of FTSE-250 companies and a growing number of smaller companies are represented in the IRS.

The IRS publishes a useful set of 'best practice' guidelines and key principles of IR on its website for companies seeking to improve their online communications with investors and other target audiences. Check out the IRS website for instant information on investor relations principles and practice (**www.irs.org.uk**), and see Appendix 2 of this book.

At a glance

- The annual report must communicate effectively; too many don't.

- The provisions of the Companies Act must be followed rigorously.

- Strict rules cover the content and format of accounts.

- The report and accounts must give a 'true and fair' view of the company and its affairs.

- Regulations for Operational and Financial Reviews (OFR) applied from 2005.

- Too many reports are longer than necessary, while others are over-designed.

- The first principle is to give a full, clear, 'no-frills' statement of the business.

- PR professionals must be involved with the content from the start and be able to interpret specialised jargon.

- The chairman's statement sets the tone: it's the one part that is read and remembered.

- Some reports, written by ghostwriters, lack personality and under-estimate reader intelligence.

- An increasing number of companies offer online reports.

- Shareholders opting for electronic communications save the company print and postage costs.

- Reports can be expensive, but can be used as the corporate brochure for a year.

- Many PR benefits result from good design.

- Online versions must not differ from printed reports.

- Investor relations (IR) consultants manage the flow of information between a company and its shareholders.

- Most IR specialists are contactable on the firm's website.

22
Is it legal?

Imagine this. You are opening the morning's post and there's an envelope with 'solicitors' after a set of names. Someone wants to sell us a service of some kind? If you could be so lucky. What you read will not be a good start to the day: it says that a press release you have just issued has seriously maligned the reputation of a client's supplier, which is considering legal action and will be claiming damages.

Panic. It does not matter if a release is not published: it can still be the subject of a court action. If the damaging words are circulated to third parties, they could be defamatory even if they are not printed or broadcast in the media. And people talk in pubs and clubs. A release is out once you hit the 'send' key or once it is posted on your website. Phone calls to cancel it are a waste of time. Once it's out, it's out for good.

An action for defamation is just one of the perils any writer faces. Public relations practitioners must also be aware of legislation covering copyright, data protection, trade marks, competitions and price promotions. Besides these, there are several self-regulatory codes, mainly concerned with advertising, sales promotion and direct marketing, which must be followed. Legislation covering public relations and promotions is a complex subject, and it is not possible within the confines of this short chapter to give anything but a snapshot of the myriad laws and regulations impinging on our work. So here is a brief run-down of the main laws and rules that must be followed by PR and advertising practitioners alike.

What is libel?

Libel is the publication, in 'hard copy', of a false statement which injures the reputation of a person by its tendency to 'lower him/her in the estimation of right-thinking members of society' or causes right-thinking members of society to shun or avoid that person. It can also apply to companies and organisations, in which case it is sometimes called trade libel. It is therefore essential to look out for any passage that could be libellous and delete it, or at least rewrite so that it is no longer open to challenge.

A libellous statement is defined as one made in a permanent form, such as in written documents, pictures or drawings. Malicious statements made in radio and television broadcasts, as well as distributed emails and messages on the internet, may also constitute a defamation. If the defamatory words are simply spoken, the defamation is called slander.

Among possible defences against a claim for damages are that the statement is not published, it is not defamatory, it's true, it was made on a privileged occasion, it is fair comment on a matter of public interest, and it was authorised by the complainant (that is, consent has been given). It is also possible to make a case for unintentional defamation, where a person who publishes a libel offers to make a suitable correction and apology; if this is not accepted, it is a defence to prove that the words were published 'innocently'.

If you are being sued, you can attempt to mitigate the amount of damages that may be awarded by means of an apology, a retraction, or by showing provocation.

Who is liable?

It is not only the author or writer of the statement who might be liable: if the statement appeared in a newspaper or periodical, the proprietor, editor, vendor or anyone placing the story can be sued. If a libellous statement is broadcast, the transmitting organisation or company, and the persons making the broadcast, could be held liable. Similarly printers are responsible, jointly with the publishers and authors, for all libels published in papers printed by them.

Copyright and moral rights

As Philip Circus makes clear in his *Promotional Marketing Law: A practical guide* (Bloomsbury Professional, 2011), copyright is the right of the creator to control the reproduction of original material for as long as the material stays within copyright. It exists basically in every piece of literary, artistic, dramatic or musical work, and in sound recordings, films, television broadcasts, cable programmes and published material. An idea in itself is not copyright, and names, titles and slogans generally will not normally be subject to copyright protection (although they can be protected by trade mark registration).

The copyright belongs to the creator of the work, with the exception that in the case of work created by employees in the course of their employment, the copyright belongs to the employer unless otherwise agreed. Copyright in literary, artistic, dramatic or musical works currently lasts for the life of the author plus 70 years from the end of the calendar year in which the author dies. For computer-generated works (work such as a table that has been created by computer software) it lasts 50 years from the end of the calendar year in which the work was made.

For CIPR members, the legal helpline will advise on the basic positions on the duration and types of works attracting copyright protection. See page 235 for details of the CIPR service.

Obtaining copyright protection

Although copyright is automatically acquired immediately a work is written (or recorded in some other form such as on tape or computer disk) and there is no formal registration as such, it is advisable to establish evidence of the completion of the work, says the Society of Authors. One way of doing this is to deposit a copy of the script with a bank and get a dated receipt for it.

Moral rights of creators

The Copyright Designs and Patents Act 1988 creates two 'moral' rights, giving an author or creator of a work the right to be identified whenever that work is published, performed or broadcast, and to object to derogatory treatment of the work. The right to be identified does not apply unless it has been asserted in writing. Moral rights can, however, be waived by agreement.

Infringements

Civil remedies are available in the form of injunctions to prevent further abuse, and possible damages for past infringement by way of compensation or an account of profits. Copyright will not be infringed if it falls within exceptions provided for in the Copyright Act. The 'fair dealing exceptions' include research and private study, criticism, review and news reporting; others include use in education, libraries and archives, and the use of a typeface in the ordinary course of printing.

Applying for an injunction

If you or your organisation are the ones whose copyright is being infringed, one option is to apply for an injunction to prevent further infringement.

Nicola Solomon, Head of Publishing at Finers Stephens Innocent, writing in the *The Author* (the Society of Authors house magazine), explains that an injunction is an immediate court order preventing someone from taking certain steps, and a defendant who fails to obey it can be imprisoned for contempt of court. An injunction can be obtained in a 'matter of days or in urgent cases, a matter of hours,' she says. But since it is urgent, it can be an expensive process. 'Your solicitor will have to drop everything to learn the facts, prepare witness statements and other documents, instruct a barrister and attend the application, which may mean a long day in court.' She warns that obtaining an injunction will therefore rarely involve legal costs of less than £10,000–20,000.

The Society of Authors says that a court would only award an injunction if the infringement was 'very damaging', and another deterrent is that the plaintiff would have to give a 'cross undertaking' meaning that if it loses, it guarantees to pay any losses the other party has incurred during the time of the interim injunction. So before taking such drastic action, think carefully before committing yourself to expenditure that may not, in the end, be recoverable.

Getting permission

When quoting from copyright material, you need to obtain permission unless the copyright has expired (see above). This is normally obtained from the copyright holder or his/her agent: that is, from the creator and/or publisher. If you want to reproduce a quotation and it can be regarded as 'fair dealing' for purposes of criticism or review as defined in the Act, permission is not needed. But, says the Society of Authors in its *Quick Guide to Permissions* (available as a printed leaflet and also on the Society's website), the writer must ensure that either in the text itself or in an acknowledgement page, the title and the author of the work are given.

If you photocopy, scan or email extracts or clippings from published sources it is 'highly likely' you will need a licence, says the Copyright Licensing Agency. The CLA, which issues licences on behalf of publishers and authors, will provide standard licences that give 'blanket' permission. Go to **www.cla.co.uk** for more information.

If you take copies of newspaper articles for clients, you will need a licence from the Newspaper Licensing Agency (NLA). Working on behalf of the UK's national and regional newspapers, the NLA licenses organisations to take legal copies. Established in 1996 to manage copyright collection, the NLA authorises paper and digital copying of press cuttings in the UK press media and in international newspapers. The NLA currently licenses over 150,000 businesses and organisations and public relations agencies. Full details are on its website (**www.nla.co.uk**).

What is fair dealing?

It is not easy to say what constitutes 'fair dealing', but the CIPR legal helpline will advise on specific cases. The *Permissions* guide gives an example of the length of quotation that would fall within the context of 'criticism or review'. Some years ago the Society of Authors and the Publishers Association stated that they would usually regard as fair dealing the use of: (a) a single extract of up to 400 words or a series of extracts (of which none exceeds 300 words) to a total of 800 words from a prose work; (b) extracts to a total of 40 lines from a poem, provided that this did not exceed a quarter of the poem. The words must be quoted in the context of criticism or review.

'While this statement does not have the force of law, it carried considerable weight with a judge experienced in copyright in a leading infringement case. It does not mean, however, that a quotation for purposes of criticism or review in excess of these limits cannot rank as fair dealing in some circumstances.' The essential point to remember is that if you are quoting someone, regardless of length, you must always acknowledge the author and the source.

Data protection

In a summary guide to the Data Protection Act 1998 (available only to CIPR members on its website), it is noted that a number of new measures were introduced in this Act to protect the rights of individuals (but not companies) about whom information is held and recorded and stored manually. The original data protection legislation was limited to electronic or automated processing, but that is no longer the case.

Among the data protection principles which must be observed are that personal data must be: fairly obtained; adequate, relevant and not excessive in relation to the purpose for which it is held; accurate and up to date; not kept longer than necessary; processed in line with the data subject's rights; secure; and not transferred outside the EU without adequate protection. Under the 1998 Act, a system of 'notification' applies: if, for example, you control the processing of personal data, you must notify the Information Commissioner, saying where you obtained the data and what you intend to do with it.

Help is at hand

For PR practitioners access to a business support helpline from Croner Consulting for practical advice and guidance on running a business is available to members of the Chartered Institute of Public Relations. The free (telephone) service is run by a team of experienced, professional consultants who can assist on general legal problems as well as a range of issues from employment, health and safety to VAT and payroll. CIPR members should go to the Policy and Resources section of the website (**www.cipr.co.uk/**) for instant access.

For detailed advice on specific legal or other problems that involve inspection of paperwork or if personal consultation is required the member should consult a solicitor.

CIPR best practice guides

The CIPR has available a number of best practice guides free to members. The documents, in pdf format, cover such topics as social media, reputation and board guidance for PR consultants and board directors, work placement, and communicating with children. A guide prepared by Peter Prowse FCIPR dealing with intellectual property rights gives a general description and covers those IPRs most relevant to PR practitioners, copyright, photocopying of press cuttings for internal and client distribution under the Newspaper Licensing Agency press copy licensing service, and the CIPR Code of Conduct. Sources of information and advisory services are listed.

Data protection

There is a summary of the Data Protection Act 1998 on the policy and resources section of the CIPR website, available only to members of the Institute.

The Information Commissioner's website (**www.ico.gov.uk**) gives much useful information and there is a helpline on 01625 545745. This is a complex legal area and action should only be taken after specific advice has been sought.

Promotional marketing legal issues and problems

Much useful advice will be found in question and answer form in Philip Circus's *Promotional Marketing Law: A Practical Guide* (Bloomsbury Professional). Updated to a sixth edition, this essential reference source covers new developments in promotional marketing including the effect of the Consumer Protection from Unfair Trading Regulations 2008, which implements the EU Unfair Commercial Practices Directive; recent rulings from the European Court of Justice; latest additions to the advertising self-regulatory codes of practice which have been extended to online marketing, new laws on bribery and consumer credit advertising. It ensures the reader is aware of the potential legal pitfalls when devising and executing marketing campaigns.

Setting up your own business?

Redundancy or sheer economic difficulties may encourage PR practitioners to set up their own business. No matter how experienced he or she is in the practice of public relations, starting a business from scratch can present significant problems to those not fully versed in accountancy, contract and employment law, let alone the key skills of business planning, marketing and the essentials of profitability. Extensive advice on all aspects of owning and running a business with a creative function will be found in Alison Branagan's *The Essential Guide to Business for Artists & Designers* (A & C Black Publishers). It includes illustrated mind maps, exercises, taxes and free accountancy software for downloading.

Dealing with trade marks

This is an area where great care must be observed, particularly in articles and news releases. Apart from the need to be careful to use an initial capital letter for proprietary names in everyday use such as Sellotape, Hoover and Xerox, and observe the rules under which trade mark registration is granted under the Trade Marks Act 1994, practitioners should be aware that the 1994 Act provided increased possibilities for registration. Sounds, shapes, slogans and smells can be registered. The Register of Trade Marks is kept at the Patent Office and can be searched online.

Philip Circus points out in his book that slogans can only be registered where they can be shown to be 'distinctive'. 'Most slogans are not distinctive because they are, to coin a phrase, here today and gone tomorrow.' He considers that it would be a waste of time and money to apply for trade mark registration if it is likely that a new slogan will not be in use by the time the procedural formalities have been completed.

Again, CIPR members can get advice on trade mark use and registration by visiting the Institute's website (**www.cipr.co.uk**), which also has information on the rules covering comparative advertising and public relations material.

Competitions and promotions

If you are planning a prize competition as part of a marketing programme, it should be noted that several types of prize promotion are unlawful under the provisions of the Gambling Act 2005. Certain prize competitions would infringe civil and contractual law, some of which could give rise to criminal prosecution. It is therefore crucial for any public relations practitioner to be aware of the pitfalls that could lie ahead.

Self-regulatory codes of practice

As well as legal requirements, there is a range of self-regulatory requirements which must be observed by PR practitioners. Prime among these is the CIPR Code of Conduct, details of which are set out in the legal centre on the Institute's website. The CIPR Code of Conduct is built around three principles: integrity, competence and confidentiality.

The principle of integrity requires that members act with an 'honest and responsible regard for the public interest' and commits them to 'never knowingly misleading clients, employers, employees, colleagues and fellow members about the nature of representation or what can be competently delivered and achieved'.

The principle of competence requires members to be 'aware of the limitations of professional competence: without limiting realistic scope for development, being willing to accept or delegate only that work for which practitioners are suitably skilled and experienced' and compels them to be transparent and declare any conflicts of interest.

The final principle, that of confidentiality, reminds members to be 'careful to avoid using confidential and "insider" information to the disadvantage or prejudice of clients and employers, or to self-advantage of any kind' and prohibits 'disclosing confidential information unless specific permission has been granted or the public interest is at stake or if required by law'.

There are also relevant provisions in the British Code of Advertising, Sales Promotion and Direct Marketing. The Advertising Standards Authority took over the regulation of broadcast advertising from 1 November 2004. It is important for all public relations practitioners to acquaint themselves with all statutory and self-regulatory codes of practice and to follow them to the letter. That will go a long way towards keeping out of the sights of lawyers and regulators.

Viral marketing subject to advertising self-regulation

Promotional content on websites, social media platforms, emails and other non-broadcast marketing messages are now subject to the established advertising self-regulatory system of control. Since some of the material created by PR practitioners, both in-house and in consultancies, is within these categories, take care not to break the rules with the resultant reputation damage for your organisation or client.

Such marketing activity falls within the operation of the Code of Advertising Practice, says Philip Circus in his *Promotional Marketing Law: A practical guide*. The Code makes clear under Rule 1(a) that its provisions apply to 'advertisements in… emails, text transmissions… follow-up literature and other electronic and printed material'. Accordingly, writes Circus, virals are not excluded from the Code by having originated on a company website or forwarded by consumers.

The Institute of Promotional Marketing (**www.theipm.org.uk**) and the Direct Marketing Association (**www.dma.org.uk**) as well as the Advertising Standards Authority (**asa.org.uk**) will also provide information and guidance on viral marketing issues.

Don't forget the imprint

My collection of annual and interim reports from major companies includes 20 or so that do not give the printer's name and location – in other words their imprint. Failure to include it could mean a hefty fine: under the Printer's Imprint Act of 1961, the penalty is now up to £200 for every copy printed. Just try multiplying that with the print run and see what you get!

Although prosecutions are rare as proceedings can only be taken with the approval, and in the name of, the Attorney General or Solicitor General, or in Scotland the Law Advocate, within three calendar months after printing, its main purpose is to ensure that the person responsible for publication can be traced easily. There are exemptions for specific items such as business cards, price lists, catalogues and advertisements for goods and property for sale.

Election posters and leaflets must bear the address of the printer and publisher. Anyone contravening these provisions is liable on conviction to a maximum fine of £2,000.

Further information is available from the British Printing Industries Federation (020 7915 8300).

Further information

Additional sources of information available include: Advertising Standards Authority (**www.asa.org.uk**); Direct Marketing Association (**www.dma.org.uk**); Institute of Promotional Marketing (**www.theipm.org.uk**); the Copyright Licensing Agency (**www.cla.org.uk**); the Newspaper Licensing Agency (**www.nla. co.uk**); Ofcom (**www.ofcom.org.uk**); Office of Fair Trading (**www.oft.org.uk**); Philip Circus (**www.lawmark.co.uk/philipcircus/**); Register of Trade Marks (**www.patent.gov.uk**); Society of Authors (**www.info@societyofauthors.org**).

The CIPR provides a legal and business helpline for members. The legal service is offered by Croner Consulting (see page 235).

At a glance

- Look out for possible defamation of a person or organisation.

- If sued, try to mitigate damages with apology.

- Copyright belongs generally to the creator of a work.

- For employees, it belongs to the employer if not otherwise agreed.

- The CIPR Code of Conduct has three principles: integrity, competence, confidentiality.

- A copyright guide is available to CIPR members on its website.

- Check out the permissions guide from the Society of Authors.

- You may need a licence if you photocopy, scan or email published articles.

- Ensure you are 'notified' with the Information Commissioner.

- Make sure you comply with the data protection principles in the Data Protection Act.

- When writing about proprietary products, check whether you are using a registered trade mark, and acknowledge it if so.

- Only 'distinctive' slogans can be registered as trade marks.

- Strict rules apply for competitions and promotions.

- A failure to include an imprint notice on your publication could mean a substantial fine.

23
Keep to the codes

How to avoid brand reputation damage

Demarcation lines between the various marketing disciplines – advertising, sales promotion, competitions and PR – are blurred with the advance of new technologies, particularly with the proliferation of social media networking sites. If an advertisement or promotional campaign falls foul of the various self-regulatory controls there can be serious damage to an organisation's reputation with potential extensive financial loss. And this is where correct language is a key plank in keeping clear of bad publicity or even falling into the hands of lawyers seeking retribution on behalf of their clients.

Philip Circus, who runs the specialist legal consultancy Lawmark (**www.lawmark.co.uk/philipcircus/**) confirms this view. He says that anyone in the communications business should have a good grounding in grammar, spelling, syntax and punctuation. This is partly because effective communication requires such an ability and partly because of potential legal liability. Circus says: 'I have sat in court and watched advertising agencies who have been slovenly with the use of language try to justify the wording they have used when they meant something quite different'. He says that judges are unsympathetic to people who are supposed to be professionals in communication yet demonstrate a 'lamentable lack of expertise' at their trade.

Potential liability warning

Potential liability can be quite extensive. For example, advertisers (and by implication, PR practitioners) who don't say what they mean can easily infringe the self-regulatory codes administered by the Advertising Standards Authority. Since the ASA's remit has been extended to cover websites and social media platforms (as discussed in the previous chapter) it is fair to say that all marketing disciplines face potential liability for the incorrect use of language. 'So a PR person who drafts copy for a website can cause their client to be on the receiving end of an ASA complaint, just in the same way as someone in the advertising industry', Circus tells me.

Proper use of language, coupled with acute awareness and knowledge of the self-regulatory systems of both the Advertising Standards Authority and sanctions against print media by the Press Complaints Commission is the hallmark of the professional marketer.

Reputation damage possible

The PCC, through its Editors' Code, can call for published apology, correction and retraction, as well as publication of a PCC critical adjudication by the media to which a complaint had been addressed. If a complaint is upheld, then there could be resultant reputation damage to a company or employee covered by the adjudication. If a press release had been issued and subsequently published which was contrary to the Code, say with a misleading headline or inaccurate copy, then the originators would be subject to criticism. It should be noted that the Code should be observed rigorously not only by editorial staff but by external contributors, including non-journalists, in printed and online versions of publications.

Since public relations and advertising campaigns are frequently intertwined and interdependent, it is important that PR personnel are fully aware of how the advertising self-regulatory system operates. Here is a brief summary.

Advertising codes administered by the ASA

The Advertising Codes are written and maintained by two industry bodies, the Committee of Advertising Practice (CAP) and the Broadcast Committee of Advertising Practice (BCAP). The former is responsible for the non-broadcast Code, the latter for the broadcast Code. The Codes cover print and press ads, posters, direct mail, television and radio ads, competitions and special offers, email and text messages, internet (banners, pop-ups, virals), sponsored research, marketing communications on companies' own websites, teleshopping, cinema commercials and promotions generally.

The remit of the Advertising Standards Authority has been extended significantly to deliver more comprehensive consumer protection online. From 1 March 2011 the UK Code of Non-broadcast Advertising, Sales Promotion and Direct Marketing (the CAP Code) has applied to full marketing messages online, including the rules relating to misleading advertising, social responsibility and the protection of children. Besides advertisers' marketing messages on their own websites, the new remit covers other non-paid-for space under the advertiser's control such as the social networking sites Facebook and Twitter, as well as marketing communications on all UK websites, regardless of sector, type of businesses or size of operation.

Since many in-house public relations practitioners and PR consultancies are closely involved with these communication systems – particularly designers and writers of websites – it is crucial that there is full knowledge of the rules which apply to each of them. To help those in need of advice, both CAP and BCAP offer an extensive range of training and guidance services. These can help PR and advertising executives to ensure that ad campaigns stand out without breaking the rules, understand what is and isn't acceptable to the ASA, keep up to date with the latest developments in regulation and help avoid reputational and commercial damage.

Broad principles

The Advertising Codes contain wide-ranging rules designed to ensure that advertising does not mislead, harm or offend. Ads must also be socially responsible and prepared in line with the principles of fair competition. These broad principles apply regardless of the product being advertised.

In addition, the advertising Codes contain specific rules for certain products and marketing techniques. These include rules for alcoholic drinks, health and beauty claims, children, medicines, financial products, environmental claims, gambling, direct marketing and prize promotions. These rules add an extra layer of consumer protection on top of consumer protection law and aim to ensure that UK advertising is responsible.

The ASA administers the rules in the spirit as well as the letter, making it almost impossible for advertisers to find loopholes or 'get off on a technicality'. This common-sense approach takes into account the nature of the product being advertised, the media used, and the audience being targeted.

Full information about the Advertising Codes will be found on the website: **www.cap.org.uk/** which provides direct links to non-broadcast (CAP) and broadcast (BCAP) Codes.

ASA sanctions

An advertiser's reputation can be badly damaged if it is seen to be flouting the rules designed to protect consumers. Non-broadcast sanctions are co-ordinated through CAP whose members are trade associations representing advertisers and their agencies, and media. These sanctions consist of alerts to its members, including the media, advising them to withhold services such as access to advertising space; withdrawal of privileges such as the Royal Mail's bulk discount for direct marketing campaigns; pre-vetting of marketing material before publication for infringements of the CAP Code on grounds of taste and decency or social responsibility. CAP can ask internet search websites to remove a marketer's paid-for search advertisements when these link to a website page that hosts non-compliant marketing communications.

Marketeers may face adverse publicity if they cannot or will not amend non-compliant marketing communications on their own websites or in other non-paid-for space online under their control.

FIGURE 23.1 Press Complaints Commission home page clearly directs users to main sections with latest news headlined

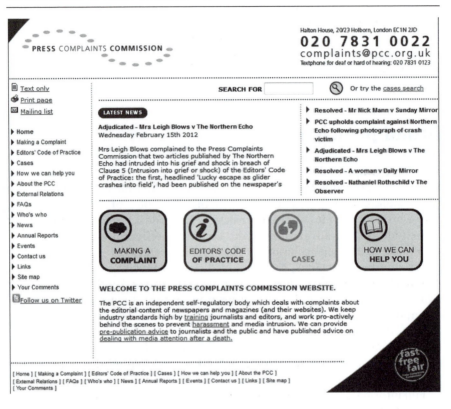

For broadcast advertisements, the responsibility to withdraw, change or reschedule a commercial lies with the broadcasters. Advertisers might face bad publicity generated by an upheld complaint to the ASA. Possibly hundreds of thousands of pounds spent on production costs and in lost revenue could result from a banned advertisement. Moreover, any advertisements that break the Codes are disqualified from industry awards thus depriving advertisers of further publicity to enhance their status.

See the ASA website (**www.asa.org.uk/**) for full details of how the self-regulatory system works and the sanctions that can be applied when the rules are flouted.

PCC Editors' Code

All members of the press have a duty to maintain the highest professional standards. The Editors' Code sets the benchmark for ethical standards, protecting both the rights of the individual and the public's right to know.

It is the cornerstone of the system of self-regulation to which the industry has made a binding commitment. There are 16 separate provisions in the Code ranging from accuracy, privacy and harassment to reporting of crime, naming of children who are victims or witnesses in cases involving sex offences, and engaging in misrepresentation and subterfuge. (There may be exceptions to those clauses if they can be demonstrated to be in the public interest.) There are also restrictions on journalists writing on financial matters.

The Code is mentioned in this chapter for the reason that a PR-generated story and subsequently published in the press might infringe the Code in some way. Full provisions of the Code are set out on the PCC website (**www.pcc.org.uk**). They should be studied carefully by all PR practitioners involved in promoting goods and services who issue press releases and contribute to the print media on marketing subjects.

Author's note

Shortly before this chapter was passed for press, the PCC announced that since the current system of self-regulation does not have sufficient powers of investigation or enforcement, the Commission should be replaced by a new, credible regulator armed with the powers needed, in other words one that has 'teeth.'

The proposal is that the new regulator should have two arms, one that deals with complaints and mediation and one that audits and, where necessary, enforces standards and compliance with the Editors' Code.

The PCC is in this transitional stage until the arrangements for the new regulator are finalised. The commission emphasises that in this period it will continue to deal with complaints under the terms of the Editors' Code and existing and new complaints will be handled by the Secretariat in the normal way.

For full details go to **www.pcc.org.uk/news/index.html?article=NzcyNA==**.

At a glance

- If an advertisement or promotional activity falls foul of self-regulatory controls your company's reputation suffers. Correct language is a key plank for keeping clear of bad publicity.

- The Advertising Standards Authority's remit now covers websites and social media platforms. All marketing disciplines face potential liability for incorrect language use.

- The Press Complaints Commission can call for published apology, correction or retraction by the media to which a complaint had been addressed. If upheld, there could be resultant reputation damage to a company or employee covered by the adjudication.

- The PCC's Editors' Code should be observed rigorously not only by editorial staff but by external contributors.

- All PR and communications teams should be fully aware of how the regulatory system works. The ASA website (**www.asa.org.uk**) gives full details of how the self-regulatory system works and the sanctions that can be applied when the rules are flouted.

- Marketeers may face adverse publicity if they cannot or will not amend non-compliant marketing communications on their own websites or another non-paid-for online space under their control.

- The Advertising Codes contain specific rules for alcoholic drinks, health and beauty, children, medicines, financial products, environmental claims, gambling, direct marketing and prize promotions.

APPENDIX 1
Confusing pairs of words

Lookalikes: differences and distinctions

Many pairs of words look and sound alike, but some are exact opposites, while others have different shades of meaning. Get them wrong and you could have a verbal disaster on your hands: at best an embarrassing telephone call to rectify what is really meant, at worst a press release or print job that has to be corrected and reissued. Here are some of them.

Adaption/adaptation: While both mean the same thing, adaptation is preferred. Adaption is eventually expected to supplant adaptation which is slowly on the way out.

Adverse/averse: Close in meaning. Adverse suggests being hostile or contrary to somebody or something, while averse means being opposed or disinclined to do something.

Adviser/advisor: Both spellings acceptable, but most style guides recommend -er. The -or variant has a pretentious, self-important ring to it.

Alternate/alternative: Alternate as a verb means interchanging one thing with another; as a noun it means things of two kinds coming one after the other. Alternative as an adjective means offering choice between two things; as a noun denotes an option to choose between two or more things.

Biennial/biannual: Biennial means once every two years, biannual twice a year or, if preferred, twice yearly. Similarly, bimonthly means every two months, not twice a month. With this pair, it is often better to write it out in full rather than risk ambiguity.

Brochure/pamphlet: A brochure is normally taken to mean a wire-stitched or square-backed, illustrated colour-printed production used for promoting an organisation's products, services or activities. There is little difference between a pamphlet, usually just a folded sheet produced in larger numbers at low cost, and a leaflet.

Complement(ary)/compliment(ary): The former means completing, supplying a deficiency, two or more things complementing each other; the latter an expression of regard or praise as in 'with compliments'.

Compose/comprise: Compose means to constitute, to form or make up a list by putting two or more things or parts together; comprise means to include or contain the items on the list.

Continual/continuous: A close pair. Continual means frequently happening and without cessation, again and again; continuous means joined together, or going on non-stop without interruption.

Counsel/council: Counsel is usually taken to mean giving advice to someone; council is a body of people or an authority.

Delusion/illusion: A delusion denotes a false idea, impression or belief as a symptom of insanity, someone who is genuinely convinced of what is not the case (*a delusion of grandeur*); an illusion denotes a false impression as to the true nature of an object, a misapprehension of a true state of affairs (*an optical illusion*).

Depreciate/deprecate: Depreciate is to make or become lower in value; deprecate means to express disapproval of something or someone.

Derisive/derisory: Derisive means mocking, scoffing; derisory equals ridiculous, laughingly inefficient.

Disinterested/uninterested: The former suggests impartial or unbiased while the latter means indifference. Most writers prefer to write 'lack of interest' rather than disinterested.

Effect/affect: Effect means to accomplish something; affect means to have an influence upon something. The difficulty is compounded by the fact that both can be used as nouns and verbs, although *affect* is more commonly used as a verb and *effect* as a noun.

Especial(ly)/special(ly): Little difference. Especial the adjective now replaced by special without much trouble; especially/specially the adverbs expected to survive in contexts where *in particular*, or *even more* is meant.

Flout/flaunt: To flout means to violate a rule, show a contemptuous disregard; to flaunt means to show off, to make an ostentatious or defiant display.

For ever/forever: For ever (two words) is for always; forever means continually.

Forgo/forego: To forgo is to abstain from or do without; to forego is to precede in place or time.

Fortuitous/fortunate: Fortuitous means by accident or chance; fortunate equals lucky.

Imply/infer: To imply is to hint or state something; to infer is to draw a conclusion from what has been implied. A useful rule to remember is that the writer or speaker *implies*, while the reader or listener *infers*.

Inapt/inept: The former means not apt or unsuitable, the latter unskilful.

Less/fewer: The distinction between these words is often lost: *less* goes with singular 'mass' nouns (population/difficulty) while *fewer* with numbers or quantities capable of being counted or listed (people/things).

Loaning/lending: The verb to loan is an Americanism gaining ground here. Mainly associated with large sums and works of art (he loaned the party a million pounds but he lent me a fiver). To lend is a verb, but loan is used principally as a noun: he is making me a loan.

Magazine/journal: Both are periodicals, but a journal is usually the more serious, professional publication, like the CIPR's magazine, *Profile*.

Masterful/masterly: Masterful means domineering, wilful; masterly means executed with superior skill.

Militate/mitigate: To militate against something is to have a significant effect against it; to mitigate is to create conditions for reducing the severity of something.

Number/amount: These two words are very close in definition, but be careful to distinguish between them: the distinction is whether they go with 'count' or 'mass' nouns, as in the *number* of releases sent out compared with the *amount* of work in writing them. As in this example, *number* is usually constructed with a plural.

Practical/practicable: Practical (suitable for use) and practicable (able to be done). What, for example, is practical is to email several news releases before the office closes, but not necessarily practicable in that there may not be the staff to do it.

Refute/deny: Both verbs dispute the truthfulness of a statement; deny says it is false, refute proves that it is.

Regretfully/regrettably: The former means an expression of regret, the latter something to be regretted, unwelcome, worthy of reproof.

Scotch/Scottish: Scotch is for whisky made in Scotland (-ey for varieties made in Ireland and the United States); Scottish for those from north of the Border.

That/which: Again close and often interchangeable pronouns. The important distinction between them is that *which* can never refer to people. That defines as in 'the PR firm that was formed', while *which* describes as in 'the PR firm, which was formed in 1990, is still operating profitably'. The careful observer will note that *which* usually follows a comma, while *that* doesn't need one before it.

Under/underneath: While there is a slim distinction between them, the simplest way to show it is to write *underneath* meaning 'directly covered by' while *under* means below or beneath. A sentence can end with *underneath* far more easily than it can with *under*.

Note: Source material for online Appendix 1 has been drawn largely from the 1994 edition of the *Oxford Dictionary of English Grammar* and from the 1974 edition of the *Concise Oxford Dictionary* by permission of the Oxford University Press.

Further examples of confusing pairs will be found in the *Oxford A–Z of English Usage.*

APPENDIX 2
Glossary and jargon buster

Information technology

ADSL: Asymmetric Digital Subscriber Line, a new modem technology, converts existing twisted-pair telephone lines into access paths for multimedia and high-speed data communications.

Bit.ly: Computer software (**www.bitly.com**) gives a unique code of characters and numbers for shortening a website address. Useful for showing a link to a video.

Bitmap: Where an item of information corresponds to one or more bits of information especially those used to control a computer screen display.

Blog: A personal website or web page giving facts and opinions, and links to other sites. Useful for issuing material to journalists.

Bluetooth: Short-range (10–100 metres) digital communication without connection by cables or wires.

Byte: Unit of measurement of digital data.

CD ROM: Stands for Compact Disc Read Only Memory.

CD RW: CD rewritable. CDs that can be recorded over and over again.

Convergence: Combining personal computers, telecommunications and television.

Domain name: Name of an internet website, or web address, the URL (uniform resource locator).

etailing: Electronic shopping or teleshopping using programmes within television schedules.

Ethernet: Name of local area network and accompanying technical specifications and products.

Flash content: Adobe Flash (formerly Macromedia Flash) is a multimedia platform used to add animation, video, and interactivity to web pages. Often used for advertisements, games and flash animations for broadcast.

Freeware: Software that can be downloaded or distributed free of charge although under copyright.

FTP: File Transfer Protocol. Means of transmitting via the internet or local area network from computer to computer.

GIF: Graphics Interchange Format.

Hashtag: Symbol (#) used on social media sites, particularly Twitter, before a word or phrase to quickly identify messages on specific subjects.

HTML: HyperText Markup Language. For creating a document on the internet.

HTTP: HyperText Transfer Protocol. Means of sending web pages across the internet.

ISP: Internet Service Provider. Examples: Freeserve, AOL.

Java: Computer language.

Listorious: An online directory of Twitter lists. Gives lists of tweeters of the subject needed by the user. Useful for identifying a target group of tweeters.

Megabyte: MB (abbr). Unit of data storage (a million bytes).

Multimedia: Combination of computerised data from, eg audio, video, text, CD ROM.

Netiquette: From internet and etiquette – a standard code: eg, no messages in capitals, users should check with FAQs before asking a question.

Newsgroup: Discussion group on the internet.

Portal: Term for a website used as a 'gateway' or starting point for those planning to enter the internet.

RAM: Random Access Memory measured in Megabytes (MB). Used to store data and details of programmes currently being run.

SEO: Search Engine Optimisation.

Server: Powerful computer storing digitised information for websites and emails.

Shareware: Software available via the internet free of charge (usually on a trial basis) or included on CD ROM disc distributed free with printed publications.

Smiley: Also called an emoticon, a contraction of emotion and icon. Smileys are read sideways: eg :-) for smiling, :-(for sad.

TweetDeck: Software (**www.tweetdeck.com**) monitors content on Twitter. Each time a tweet is published matching the known criteria, the user is immediately identified.

Twitlonger: Software (**www.twitlonger.com**) provides a line of elipsis dots (...) once the 140-character limit for Twitter has been reached.

URL: Uniform Resource Locator. The address of a website.

Voice recognition: Technology that permits copy to be voice-recognised and set in type.

WAP: Wireless Application Protocol. Connects a mobile phone to the internet. Hence WAP phones.

Whispers: Regularly updated blog from Shout! Communications on stories and events as well as Twitter feeds.

Wordpress: Website (**www.wordpress.com**) to host individual blogs.

Useful sites for unravelling web jargon

Net Lingo: **www.netlingo.com**

The ABCe site also has a jargon buster: **www.abce.org.uk**

Printing and publishing

Author's: Corrections to copy after it has been set in type; usually charged extra.

Bleed: When images, usually illustrations, extend beyond the trimmed edge of a sheet; allowance must be made for this when sizing photographs to be bled off the page.

Crosshead: Small heading placed in text, to liven the page (and fill space).

Display type: Type used for headings, in larger size than text.

Draw-down quote: Significant phrase or statement from a quote used within the page as a heading. Useful for filling space and enhancing look of the page.

Halftone: Printing term for continuous tone artwork such as a photograph; reproduces as series of dots of various sizes.

JPEG: Joint Photographic Experts Group (jpeg for short). A format for graphics computer files.

Lower case: Small characters of a typeface, abbreviated to l.c.

Makeup: Arrangement of type and illustrations on a page.

Measure: Width of typesetting, or line length, usually expressed in ems or picas (one em = 0.166044 in).

Moiré (pattern): When halftone images, usually photographs, are printed over one another, a moiré pattern can occur through different screen angles used; can occur, for example, if a newspaper photograph is screened for use in a magazine which uses paper needing a different screen angle.

OCR: Optical Character Recognition. The scanning of text for subsequent typesetting.

Overlay: Transparent covering for artwork for instructions or corrections to avoid spoiling original images.

Overset: More text set in type than is needed for a given space.

Page proof: Proof of a page for OK before printing.

PDF: Portable Document Format (usually shown as pdf).

Point (size): Printer's unit of measurement, used principally for designating type sizes. There are 12 points to a pica, approximately 72 points to the inch; 1pt = 0.013837 in or 0.351 mm.

Printer's error: Mistake by the printer. Should not be charged to the customer.

Progressives: Progressive proofs, sometimes called progs, made from separate plates in colour work, showing the sequence of printing and the result after the application of each colour.

Ragged left: In typesetting, where the left-hand edge is ragged and the right-hand edge is aligned.

Ragged right: Reverse of ragged left: here the type is aligned on the left.

Ream: Five hundred sheets of paper. Paper for short-run work is normally bought by the ream.

Register: When two or more printing images are printed in exact alignment with one another they are said to be in register.

ROP: Run of Paper. Material printed in a magazine or newspaper as part of the main text.

Running head: A title repeated at the top of each page of a magazine or book.

Serif: Short lines at the ends of main letter characters in some typefaces. Typefaces without them are sans serif types.

Set-off: This occurs when the ink of a printed sheet rubs off and marks the next sheet.

Showthrough: Where the printing on one side of the sheet shows through to the other side.

Sidebar: Panel of text, usually in colour or white reversed out of black, alongside feature article giving supporting detail or illustrations.

Small caps: Small capital letters, about the same size as lower case characters.

Stock: Another word for paper or printing material. Also called substrate.

Subhead: Inferior to main headline.

Transpose: When a letter, word or line is exchanged in position for another.

Trapping: Where a wet ink film is printed over a previously printed ink, or where dry ink is used over a wet ink. When the colour is held then trapping has occurred.

Web press: Printing press which prints on reels of paper, as used in long-run newspaper and magazine printing.

Investor relations

All-Share Index: The FTSE All-Share Index consists of the FTSE-100, FTSE-250 and FTSE Small Cap Indices. The companies it comprises account for over 98 per cent of the UK's total market capitalisation.

Authorised share capital: The amount of capital a company can raise in shares at any given time.

Bear market: The description given to the market when share prices overall are going down.

Bed and breakfast: A term used when a share is sold on one day and bought back the next.

Bull market: The situation when there is optimism that share prices will rise and continue rising. People are sometimes said to be 'bullish' about a continuing upward trend in prices.

Debenture: A fixed-rate bond stock secured against a company's assets.

EBITDA: This stands for: earnings before interest, tax, depreciation and amortisation. EBITDA is one of a number of ways of measuring a company's profits.

FTSE-100 Index: Based on the share prices of the UK's biggest 100 listed companies, measured by market capitalisation. Membership of the index is reviewed every three months. This index is often used as a barometer of the stock market as a whole, and some investments are linked directly to it.

Gearing: A measure of a company's debt: definitions vary, but typically it is the ratio of a company's loan capital (its debts) to the value of the ordinary shares (its equity).

Gilts: Fixed rate stocks issued by the UK government.

Hedge fund: An investment fund which uses derivatives and other types of investment as well as conventional equities. Some also invest in currencies.

Investment trust: A means of investing in a range of companies. Movements in an investment trust's share price usually reflect the fortunes of the companies in which it has invested. Normally considered safer than an investment in a single listed company.

Market capitalisation: The value of a company's equity at any given moment; it is arrived at by multiplying the number of shares in issue by the current share price.

P/E Ratio: The price ('P') of a company's share divided by the profit (or earnings, 'E') attributed to one share over a 12-month period. The profit for each share is calculated by dividing the company's total profit by the number of shares in issue. The P/E ratio is one of the measures used by analysts to assess a company's financial state.

Preference share: A share which entitles the holder to a fixed dividend. Payment of the dividend takes priority over dividends paid to the holders of ordinary shares.

Rights issue: When a company wants to raise additional funds it may offer existing shareholders the first opportunity to invest in more shares. The number they are offered is based on the size of their existing holding. Shareholders are usually offered these additional shares at a discount to the market price.

Scrip issue: New shares which a company gives free of charge to existing shareholders.

Short: Going short is a term used to describe the action of someone who anticipates a fall in a share price and expects to make a quick profit. They can effectively 'sell' shares which they do not actually own yet, hoping to buy shares more cheaply later to fulfil the sale.

Yield: The financial return a shareholder can expect based on the current price of a share, taking gross interest and dividend into account.

Acknowledgements. The author wishes to thank Richard Bowler of Langbourn Communications for his help in preparing this short glossary of terms, and to acknowledge Rosemary Burr's *The Share Book* (Roster's, London) for some of the references.

APPENDIX 3
When you're lost for words

Overcoming writer's block

You can't get going, your insertion point keeps blinking. If you've typed a few words, they're rubbish and you delete them. The screen's blank again, the trash can is full, the waste bin is brimming with scraps. You've got word freeze. You're brain dead. What do you do?

Several things. First, don't panic. Walk around the office, talk to colleagues, have a drink (but no alcohol), snatch today's paper. Grab your firm's annual report, check your firm's website for news stories, and look for salient points. Study recent correspondence or papers on the subject. Anything to get going.

For the moment, forget the computer keyboard: just jot down in bullet-point form, as two to three-word headings, the essential thoughts and ideas you want to get over. Concentrate on facts and figures, the human angle. Put your thoughts in logical sequence. If it's a release or article, think up some possible quotes that can be cleared later. You are halfway to your first draft.

Now switch on your computer and click on 'new document'. Even if you can't get everything organised the way you want, just get typing. Start with something easy, say the main facts you want to communicate. After that, subsidiary points will follow naturally. If you're still unhappy with your efforts, read out what you have got to a colleague. It may mean a rewrite, but you're getting there, albeit slowly. Now's the time to get the grammar and style right. Get rid of clichés and verbiage. Polish again. You're on the way.

And what should you never do if the words won't come? If there's a chance of doing something else, don't take it. If all else fails, dictate your thoughts into a tape recorder. Play back and see what they sound like. That might help, but you're probably back to square one.

Controlling your nerves on stage

An outline of measures to combat nerves at the microphone is given by speaking coach Roy Topp in Chapter 18. Here are some additional points for dealing with stress on stage, given by Sarah Dickinson in her *Effective Presentation* (Orion Business Books). Release tension with exercises to relax the body and to develop the voice. 'Practise your text ... tape yourself speaking at [a slow] pace. You may be surprised at how some of it sounds perfectly normal.' It is important, she emphasises, to realise that what is eaten and drunk before a performance will dramatically affect how the speaker feels. And the better he or she feels, the better the presentation.

Useful tips on presentations will be found in John Seely's *Oxford Guide to Effective Writing and Speaking* (OUP).

Your nerves will be controlled much more easily if you are relaxed, confident that the technical arrangements for visual aids, microphone and sound checks have been made, that you have a copy of your speech in your pocket and that any props are easy to reach. You should know who's in the audience and that the press handouts are ready. And of course you have rehearsed and rehearsed. You can't have enough of that.

Then it's all up to you.

FURTHER READING

Aitchison, James (1994) *Cassell's Guide to Written English*, Cassell, London.

Allen, Robert (2004) *Pocket Fowler's Modern English Usage*, Oxford University Press, Oxford.

Amis, Kingsley (1998) *The King's English, A Guide to Modern Usage*, HarperCollins, London.

Ayto, John (2003) *Oxford Dictionary of Rhyming Slang*, Oxford University Press, New York.

Bird, Drayton (2002) *How to Write Sales Letters that Sell*, Kogan Page, London.

Branagan, Alison (2011) *The Essential Guide to Business for Artists & Designers*, A & C Black, London.

Burchfield, RW (2004) *Fowler's Modern English Usage*, Oxford University Press, Oxford.

Butterfield, Jeremy (ed) (2007) *Oxford A–Z of English Usage*, Oxford University Press, Oxford.

Butterfield, Jeremy (2008) *Damp Squid*, Oxford University Press, Oxford.

Circus, Philip (2011) *Promotional Marketing Law: A practical guide*, Bloomsbury Professional, Haywards Heath.

Cresswell, Julia (2003) *A Dictionary of Clichés*, Penguin, London.

Crone, Tom (2005) *Law and the Media*, Focal Press, London.

Crystal, David (2001) *Language and the Internet*, Cambridge University Press, Cambridge.

Crystal, David (2011) *Internet Linguistics*, Routledge, London and New York.

Cutts, Martin (1995) *The Plain English Guide*, Oxford University Press, Oxford.

Cutts, Martin (2007) *Oxford Guide to Plain English*, Oxford University Press, Oxford.

Davies, Gillian (2011) *Copyright Law for Writers, Editors and Publishers*, A & C Black, London.

Dent, Susie (2003–7) *The Language Report*, Annual update, Oxford University Press, Oxford.

Dunay, Paul and Krueger, Richard (2011) *Facebook Marketing for Dummies*, Wiley Publishing Inc, Hoboken, New Jersey.

Economist Style Guide (2010) *The Economist*, London.

Evans, Harold (2000) *Essential English for Journalists, Editors and Writers*, revised by Crawford Gillan, Pimlico Random House, London.

Fitton, Laura, Gruen, Michael, E and Poston, Leslie (2009) *Twitter for Dummies*, Wiley Publishing, New Jersey.

Gowers, Sir Ernest (1987) *The Complete Plain Words*, Penguin, London.

Marsh, David and Hodson, Amelia (2011) *The Guardian Style Book*, Guardian Newspapers, London.

Metcay, Allan (2010) *OK*, Oxford University Press, Oxford.

Montague-Smith, Patrick (2006) *Debrett's Correct Form*, Debrett's, London.

Olausson, Lena and Sangster, Catherine (2006) *Oxford BBC Guide to Pronunciation*, Oxford University Press, Oxford.

Ogilvy, David (2004) *Confessions of an Advertising Man*, Southbank Publishing, London.

Partridge, Eric (1973) (ed Janet Whitcut 1999) *Usage and Abusage*, Penguin, London.

Partridge, Eric (1978) *A Dictionary of Clichés*, Routledge, London.

Phillips, David and Young, Philip (2009) *Online Public Relations*, Kogan Page, London.

Ritter, M (2005) *New Hart's Rules*, adapted from the *Oxford Guide to Style* by R M Ritter, Oxford University Press, Oxford.

Ritter, R M (ed) (2003) *Oxford Style Manual*, Oxford University Press, Oxford.

Ritter, R M (ed) (2005) *New Oxford Dictionary for Writers and Editors*, Oxford University Press, Oxford.

Robertson, Geoffrey (2002) *Media Law*, Penguin Books, London.

Seely, John (2005) *Oxford Guide to Effective Writing and Speaking*, Oxford University Press, Oxford.

Seely, John (2009) *Oxford A–Z of Grammar and Punctuation*, Oxford University Press, Oxford.

Smith, Bud E and Bebak, Arthur (2006) *Creating Web Pages for Dummies*, Wiley, Sussex.

Society of Authors Quick Guide to Permissions, Society of Authors, London [online] http://www.societyofauthors.net/publications/ index.html (accessed 9 November 2004)

Strunk, William and White, E B (1999) *The Elements of Style*, Allyn and Bacon, Old Tappan, NJ.

The Times Style and Usage Guide (2003) HarperCollins, London.

Truss, Lynne (2007) *Eats, Shoots and Leaves*, Profile Books, London.

Waterhouse, Keith (1993) *Waterhouse on Newspaper Style*, Penguin, London.

Yang, Jonathan (2006) *The Rough Guide to Blogging*, Rough Guides Ltd, London.

Note: There are very many books and guides available on style, including several published by newspapers for their own staff, for the reader to consult. The titles in this bibliography, and others mentioned and acknowledged, form a selection recommended by the author to be of special interest and use in day-to-day writing and editing.

INDEX